NO PASSPORT

A Discovery of Canada

Eugène Cloutier

OXFORD
UNIVERSITY PRESS

OXFORD
UNIVERSITY PRESS

8 Sampson Mews, Suite 204, Don Mills, Ontario M3C 0H5
www.oupcanada.com

Oxford University Press is a department of the University of Oxford.
It furthers the University's objective of excellence in research, scholarship,
and education by publishing worldwide in

Oxford   New York

Auckland   Cape Town   Dar es Salaam   Hong Kong   Karachi
Kuala Lumpur   Madrid   Melbourne   Mexico City   Nairobi
New Delhi   Shanghai   Taipei   Toronto

With offices in

Argentina   Austria   Brazil   Chile   Czech Republic   France   Greece
Guatemala   Hungary   Italy   Japan   Poland   Portugal   Singapore
South Korea   Switzerland   Thailand   Turkey   Ukraine   Vietnam

Oxford is a trade mark of Oxford University Press
in the UK and in certain other countries

Published in Canada by Oxford University Press

Library and Archives Canada Cataloguing in Publication

Cloutier, Eugène, 1921-1975
No passport : a discovery of Canada / Eugène Cloutier ; translated by
Joyce Marshall.

(The Wynford Project)
Translation of: Le Canada sans passeport.
ISBN 978-0-19-543458-3

1. Cloutier, Eugène, 1921-1975--Travel--Canada. 2. Canada--Description
and travel. I. Marshall, Joyce, 1913-2005. II. Title. III. Series: Wynford Project

FC75.C5713 2009   917.104'643   C2009-906030-2

Drawings by Bob Hohnstock

Cover image: Archives of Ontario. C 330-4. John Macfie.

Oxford University Press is committed to our environment. This book is printed on Forest Stewardship
Council certified paper, harvested from a responsibly managed forest.

Printed and bound in Canada.

1 2 3 4 – 14 13 12 11

Introduction to the
Wynford Edition

It was during the mid-1960s that most English-speaking Canadians finally realized that all was not quite business-as-usual in Quebec. The election of Pierre Trudeau and the October Crisis of 1970 were yet to come, but even as the country celebrated its centennial in 1967, Quebecers' unhappiness with their place in Confederation—and, for that matter, their place in the political hierarchy of their own province—was coming to a boil.

Responses to the situation were many and various. Some of them—the policy of official bilingualism, for instance—remain with us to this day. Others have faded. Among the latter I would number the self-conscious effort by mainstream English Canadian publishers to translate and promote the work of French Canadians.

That's not to say, of course, that such translations don't continue to appear and win readers. (And the same process occurs in the other direction, from English to French.) But publishing such translations no longer seems to be regarded as a vital contribution to national understanding—perhaps even survival—as was the case in the '60s. In Canadian publishing, the two solitudes are perhaps more solitary than ever.

Matters were somewhat different in 1966, when the Canadian branch of Oxford University Press commissioned an English translation of Quebec novelist and journalist Eugène Cloutier's travel book *Le Canada sans passeport*. Heading Oxford's Canadian office in those days was Ivon Owen, who had a considerable interest in Canadian literature in French as well as in English. Owen was not only a skilled editor but a gifted translator, and, among other projects, prepared for publication by Oxford English editions of two of Trudeau's books, *Two Innocents in Red China* (1968), written with Jacques Hébert, and *Approaches to Politics* (1970), both of which remain in print today.

Quebec publisher Pierre Tisseyre first approached Owen in 1965 about the possibility of an English translation of Eugène Cloutier's novel *Crosière*. Though Oxford under Owen and editor William Toye was a major force in the 1960s in the burgeoning field of Canadian literature, novels fell outside its remit. But Owen had through a mutual acquaintance heard that Cloutier was working on a nonfiction book about Canada, and asked to see it. When the manuscript finally arrived, it met with approval from Owen, Toye, and outside reader Joyce Marshall, who declared in her report that 'I have never read a Canadian travel book that was written out of such honest pleasure and delight.'

In due course Marshall was engaged to translate Cloutier's original manuscript, which ran to 300,000 words and (after some pruning) was published in French in two volumes. Toye applied to the Canada Council for a grant to underwrite the translation. His letter of application is as good a précis of the book's merits as one is likely to find: 'Mr. Cloutier's book is the work of a perceptive, well-travelled observer, whose sympathetic and unexpected reactions to the whole of Canada . . . should be of the greatest interest to English readers. It is an unpretentious work, shunning stereotyped information and data about industry and commerce to concentrate on people, his contacts with them, and his very personal impressions of places. These are often memorable and are conveyed with the charm and elegance we associate with French writing. . . . It is quite unlike any other travel book on Canada.'

Won over by Toye—and perhaps desirous in the centennial year of adding another plank to the bridge between the two solitudes—the Council issued a $2000 grant for the translation: a not inconsiderable vote of confidence, given that this was the equivalent of $13,000 in today's currency.

The outcome was not only a translation but an abridgement of Cloutier's original work, which *The Globe and Mail's* 'Quebec Books' column had described as 'humorous and acute' but also 'too long' and 'too tightly packed.' As Marshall herself pointed out in her translator's note, she tried to maintain the relaxed feel of the original while cutting out large chunks of historical background that English Canadian readers might feel to be superfluous.

She was successful: *The New York Times* remarked favourably on Cloutier's 'rambling, unhurried account of his wanderings' and praised his open-mindedness and fairness. *The Times* also found evidence in the book for many of the clichés that still define Canada to Americans: 'The impression [Cloutier] gives is one of an immense civility, extending coast to coast,' and Canada as described in *No Passport* is a land of 'great challenge and opportunity.' In its review, *Canadian Literature* played the two solitudes card, declaring the book 'eye-opening . . . for Canadians of both heritages, showing the Anglophones how they seem—faults and virtues—to a man of that other Canada of Quebec, and revealing to separatist Francophones— and one hopes at least some will read it—the community they will lose if once they sever the hope of building a diverse and unified land.'

Although Cloutier first came to prominence as a novelist during the

1950s, it was travel writing that filled the latter years of his life, and the French and English versions of *No Passport* were but the beginning of a series of travelogues that included accounts of his journeys to Sweden, California, Japan, Romania, Yugoslavia, and Chile. None of the later books were ever translated into English, which is a shame: Cloutier possessed an eye for the revealing detail and an ear for the telling phrase, both of which qualities are golden in a travel writer.

Certainly those characteristics are evident in *No Passport*, which forty years later represents a journey not only through space but through time. For the English Canada through which Cloutier travelled is in some ways as foreign to twenty-first century anglophones as it was to a Quebecer of the mid-1960s. His 'Verdict on our Highway Restaurants' (page 159) is a timely reminder that the age before there was a Tim Hortons on one corner and a McDonald's on the other was not quite the paradise of locally grown cuisine we like to remember. And anyone who has visited Niagara Falls lately will find Cloutier's observation that 'the region was destined for a great industrial boom' ironic in hindsight; for by now, of course, industry has not only arrived but long since decamped to other parts of the world.

Mainly, though, it is Cloutier's intimate and sometimes surprising portraits of people and places that make *No Passport* still worth reading—whether his depiction of the enigmatic Captain MacLeod (page 20), the disconcerting statement that 'Whitehorse is Tahiti' (page 56), or this first impression of the capital of Newfoundland: 'It might be Naples; it is only St. John's' (page 124). The Canada of Cloutier's wanderings is today lost beyond recall: but we can still revisit it through the eyes of this perceptive yet amiable guide.

David Stover
2010

David Stover is president of the Canadian branch of Oxford University Press and an author whose books include *Beyond a World Divided: Human Values in the Brain-Mind Science of Roger Sperry* (1991).

Translator's Note

Eugène Cloutier's *Le Canada sans passeport* as I saw it first was a manuscript of nearly fourteen hundred pages—a detailed and discursive record of a six-months' journey across Canada, with abundant historical and background material. M. Cloutier later cut this manuscript to about 800 pages, for the two-volume edition of the work published by Éditions HMH in 1967. Working independently from the same manuscript, he and I have not always made the same selections, and so now we have two books, one in French and one in English, which to some extent complement one another.

In making my own choice of material for translation—about a quarter of the original manuscript—I have tried as much as possible to keep the leisurely quality that was so charming a feature of the original. I have eliminated all the history and made my culling from those pages that seemed to me most personal and individual. Much that was of great interest has had to go. I have not tried slavishly to offer what I considered the 'most typical' scenes, but where, for instance, the original account described visits to almost all the Canadian universities, I have kept only one or two; I have also let a small number of investigations of ethnic groups speak for the large number M. Cloutier included, and a scattering of references to legislatures exemplify his descriptions of almost every one of them. I have, in short, endeavoured to provide sufficient variety of experiences and encounters to indicate the even greater variety of the original. I have at no time added anything. The experiences, the responses, and the conclusions are all M. Cloutier's: only the selection is my own.

Joyce Marshall
1967

CONTENTS

British Columbia

VANCOUVER THE BEAUTIFUL I have always felt a secret attraction towards British Columbia. Ever since my childhood the name of Vancouver or Victoria has evoked for me festivals of mountains, flowers, the ocean and the sun. But it all seemed so very far away. And I was not mistaken. It took a powerful DC-8 six hours to transport me there from Montreal. Are there very many countries one can fly above for so long at an average of six hundred miles an hour? We say that Canada is big, immense; it is immeasurable. Flying above it like that, I had the feeling that it was covered with forests and lakes. Only rarely did I observe the presence of men.

Vancouver makes one think first of San Francisco. It certainly has a bridge that suggests the Golden Gate, but the city has its own pattern, and this is too elusive to be captured at a single glance. San Francisco delivers itself in its entirety to the visitor's glance, whether he comes from the land or from the sea. One must discover Vancouver, rearrange pictures of the city, and fit them into one another as in a Chinese puzzle.

At first sight you would think this forest of Douglas firs marks the end of the city. It is the celebrated Stanley Park and it doesn't mark the end of anything at all. It juts resolutely into the bay like an eagle's beak and if you go right around it you will come back almost to your point of departure, which is only a few minutes from the centre of the city. A moment ago you were on Granville Street, one of the principal business streets . . . and then you are suddenly in a little resort centre — English Bay, Crystal Pool, Stanley Beach — with beaches, hotels with sunbathing terraces, walks along the seashore. You look around for the casino, there is none. In another direction, and this time in the continuation of Granville Street, you find yourself unexpectedly on the wharves of the Canadian Pacific — a name you will find almost to the point of obsession in all the cities of the West. From there turn your head to the left or the right; you will have an apocalyptic vision of the harbour. Ahead of you is Grouse, a superb mountain.

Sea and mountain. Here is a very fortunate city. It could aspire only to beauty. The third Canadian city in order of size, Vancouver seems to me by far the most beautiful of all our cities. But this is not really its fault. It was born so. If we forget the configurations of the ocean and the majesty of its mountains, its streets and buildings and the atmosphere that reigns among them could well remind us of a rather unkempt American city. But it would be cheating to forget them, for above all Vancouver is sea and mountain.

TALKATIVE STREETS The street is always full of instruction. Its rhythms are better able to reveal the soul of a city than the most informed conversations. It was in the street, for example, that I learned that Vancouver has developed certain complexes about Montreal.

'We haven't got buildings of forty-two storeys like you,' I was told.

This notion seems a little odd. But it is very deep-rooted. And in all the large cities I walked in, people always hastened to show me first the buildings whose storeys could be counted with pride. They were sometimes horrible, but they had twenty, thirty, or forty storeys. Skyscrapers are in some irreversible way the sign of progress. I shall always remember the little provincial town where my companion made a detour so I could admire a building twelve storeys high, the highest building within a radius of four hundred miles. This was in a corner of the country where there wasn't a single town for four hundred miles. It was touching.

I began, then, by admiring one of Vancouver's skyscrapers, the picture of which appears on all the tourist folders — the Hydro Building. I did not count the storeys, and I apologize. But it is a well-proportioned structure, and is transformed at night into a luminous cube. It was very often useful to me when the time came to find my way back to my hotel, whose haughty neighbour it was.

So I walked for several hours on Granville Street and its little cross-streets, and then I went along Hastings Street, which continues to offer big stores, banks, offices, shops, and commercial houses, first as elegant as Granville but finally shading off a little, until at Main Street it becomes much like our St Lawrence. Here and there along the sidewalks were solidly fixed stone benches where weary pedestrians could catch their breath. The cenotaph square was crowded with faces tanned by the winds of the high seas or work in the forests. Men were sitting all over the stone ramps or even on the edge of the sidewalk, taking a breath of fresh air between two glasses of beer. For that is a characteristic of Vancouver; despite heavy traffic, its air seems fresh. I doubt that it is, and it surely is not during the great heat of the summer, when gasoline vapours are held down against the earth by a sort of fog, rather as in Los Angeles, but the sea and the mountain seem to rid the air of this refuse most of the time. In any case it was as good to breathe that day as it is in the Laurentians.

I was very surprised to see the number of cars that filled the pavement wherever I looked. To cross the street, not only in Vancouver but in all the cities of the Canadian West, is a difficult and very frustrating experience. At each important intersection the signal is given to pedestrians for only a few seconds. You have waited docilely, like everyone around you, for the appearance of the WALK signal, sometimes for a minute and a half. WALK lights up only to change at once into a blinking red WAIT. Out of pure reflex, you continue on your way. You arouse glances of sympathetic curiosity: old hands at the game do not do this. Not only the streets, but the daily lives of our western neighbours are full of interdictions — slightly vicious rules, notably in everything to do with the consumption of alcoholic beverages. In one sense, and to sensual spirits, these interdictions might smack of perversion. Accepted in the right way, they add to the pleasure of drinking.

The street sometimes instructs rather brutally. This crowd, for instance, does not know how to walk and is badly dressed. The faces are diverse and very interesting. But why should one be astonished that they are diverse? Vancouver includes about sixty ethnic groups. Some of them we know. Here and there is golden hair around alabaster faces — this is England. But this afternoon's crowd is dominated by faces of American pink — these are the pablum babies. I have seen these faces in Tokyo and in Paris. It is a handsome breed and is found almost everywhere.

May had just begun and I could already see the first Bermuda shorts, those shorts prolonged to the knees made fashionable by modest America, which were partly to spoil my trip. It was a warm day, and the young men were walking about in shirt-sleeves and ties while the girls had inaugurated their bermudas. It was a distressing sight. But let us not hold this against Vancouver. Good taste has deserted all our cities, at least during the day. With night it makes a timid reappearance.

I went back to my hotel, one of the most renowned in the city for the excellence of its food, and here I had my first dinner since my departure from Montreal. It was a painful experience and filled me once again with secret anguish. Fortunately, for good or ill, generalizations are always false. If one is able to keep one's sense of adventure within prudent limits and gives up any hope of gastronomical pleasure once for all, one can survive a stay of several weeks in the Canadian West.

THE MILLIONAIRES West Vancouver is built on the side of a
mountain, facing the bay, Stanley Park, and the city. Some of
the most beautiful properties in Canada are distributed here as
across a park. All are adorned with rock gardens, which I never
suspected could be so elaborate. Several hundred feet are sometimes cultivated in this way, in terraces up to the house, on
either side of a monumental stairway. The rock garden is clearly
of Japanese inspiration, but it did not keep its native sobriety
when it crossed the Pacific. Instead, it is quite submerged by
brilliantly coloured flowers, squeezed between the rocks, with
here and there, like a leitmotif, the mauve vibrations of forget-
me-nots. I do not like these orgies of colour, but I must suffer
from some mysterious deviation, for everyone here goes into
ecstasies before these displays and, among these fine people,
there are some that have educated tastes and have traversed our
little planet several times.

In West Vancouver, which perhaps possesses more millionaires to the square mile than any other Canadian city, I had the
good fortune to set foot in a house worth a hundred and sixty
thousand dollars, a rock garden worth thirty-five thousand
dollars, and a basement worth twenty thousand dollars. To my
great surprise I was at once catapulted into the basement, before
I had had time to admire the great fireplace in the living room
and the paintings of a collection that appeared to be of the highest interest. This has become a rite in America and I have observed it more than once; the proprietor of a house, however
beautiful it may be, always has a basement to show you, the
plans of which he has drawn up and which he has most often
built himself, at least in part. This has never shocked me. It is
normal and rather touching to be attached like this to the things
of one's own invention. And I am willing to inspect all the
basements of this earth to see once more for a moment that
glow of pride in the eyes of my host. These little details keep
us human, despite the hold of technology over our daily lives.
I am willing to continue to spend as much time inspecting all
the basements of the earth, but not in Vancouver . . . not in

West Vancouver. As I crossed the living room and dining room I had had time to observe one of the most beautiful prospects one could imagine, and yet here I was between four walls of pale and pleasant wood, with windows inaccessible to my eyes, even if I stood on tiptoe.

One might claim that in all these hundred-and-sixty-thousand-dollar houses that abound in this ultra-residential district of Vancouver, most evenings among intimates are spent in the basement near a bar, a bridge table, or a TV set. But this would be dishonest. I have had enough encounters there to know that West Vancouver includes a great number of civilized people who are able to appreciate the splendours of their landscape and the pleasure of conversation prolonged among friends, over a fine meal. But the others, and there are others, ought to be stripped of their useless goods and sent to live in a neighbourhood entirely and exclusively made of basements.

THE JAPANESE AFFAIR   During the war it was natural, after the savage attack against Pearl Harbor, that Vancouver should become the headquarters for all our armed forces of the Pacific region. The numerous Japanese that had lived there peacefully for several generations know something about this. It mattered little that they were almost all Canadian citizens. By government decison they were withdrawn into the interior. Several of them were to all intents and purposes dispossessed of their goods; others had to sacrifice them at ridiculously low prices. It is a painful story, totally unjust to the Japanese Canadians, who today are scattered through the harsher regions of British Columbia, even as far as the south of Alberta. Canada cannot sleep quietly as long as it has not repaired the wrongs it has done them.

A few Japanese have returned to Vancouver where they were born. They no longer speak their language but live like all perfectly assimilated immigrants. But you will not see them in their city. They have found openings in industrial fishing and also in independent fishing where they have more opportunity to give free rein to their ingenuity. The latter live near Stevestone, a curious dependency of Vancouver that is half residential, half farmland, and is situated below sea-level. Deep, very wide ditches are needed to drain off the water that impregnates the soil. There, in a retired corner, work a great many of the Japanese who returned after their deportation into the interior. They form a quiet little colony. They have preserved no bitterness. They simply went back to work without dreaming of their former prosperity. It is a fascinating picture just to watch them. They have nothing about them of the Japanese as I knew them in Japan, nothing in their behaviour, their clothes, their language, or even their features . . . and yet I should have known them by the first look. It must be the soul of their country that gives them so much silent courage, the soul they have preserved in the deepest part of themselves, with an infinite modesty.

Stevestone is indissociable in my mind from an incident that troubled me about the rest of my stay in western Canada. Suddenly I felt crushed by the need to carry the entire weight of the province of Quebec on my shoulders. And as one of my friends said, 'When you think of all our iron mines . . . ' Well, yes, it was not to me that one of my companions suddenly began to speak, but to the entire province through my modest person.

Without warning, and with a passion I am still not able to forget, 'See those Japanese,' he said. 'They are perfectly assimilated.'

And he looked at me balefully. Only a moment ago, I had been treated with all the consideration due to writers that have strayed from the beaten tracks. Now I was a dangerous instigator of trouble, a sort of peasant dressed in Sunday clothes, an outsider speaking some species of ancient patois, who had grown up under the protective shadow of the parish priest.

For this is rather the picture my questioners had of all Quebec. Were they an exception? I thought so that day, for I am of a generous nature. But after all my experiences in the Canadian West, I am no longer so sure. It will take us some years to change the picture that is held of Quebec. It is regarded as a poor and illiterate province, completely dominated by a retrograde clergy, etc. etc. True, in almost all milieus I found English Canadians who were perfectly well disposed towards Quebec, but few seemed to me to have even an approximate idea of the profound transformation of our society and its rapid evolution in the last ten or so years.

And they continued, 'In British Columbia we have no minority problem. Everyone speaks English.' And they enlarged upon the point, 'Look at the United States. Did the Estonians want to teach their language in Chicago? They all learned English.' And they concluded firmly, 'There is no future for Quebec if they don't learn English.'

Passion arouses passion as friendship attracts friendship. Standing on the rocks of Stevestone, facing the modest fishing equipment of the Japanese, we discussed the matter for a long time. I remember concluding my exposition with a ringing 'If you wish to understand, you must learn.'

I have heard on the radio and read in the newspapers extraordinarily unfair accounts of Quebec. But I remember certain articles and certain interviews about the Canadian West that ignored the particular sort of friendliness that surrounded me at that moment — a rather conspiratorial friendliness which I recognized and whose limits I accept. And the passion also, which had been offered to me as a gift — a passion that lies on the threshold of a greater knowledge, of which it is, as it were, the first manifestation.

All Canada seems to me to be in a state of shock. Events in Quebec are only the precursory signs. Quebec's crisis is a crisis of maturity. Canada is on the point of knowing its own. It will not be essentially different. Canada will choose to define itself against the United States. The process has already begun. Political independence is an illusion in a country economically possessed by a neighbouring country. For the moment Canada is only a notion, and that very vague, of what it might hope to become some day. It is a mosaic of different ethnic groups that are eager to identify themselves in terms of the mother country. Only the two great peoples that have built the foundations of this future great country can claim before history the right to complete their work.

In this perspective Quebec seems to be a stroke of good fortune for Canada, its originality. The rest of the country offers a mere copy of our great neighbours. And despite the splendours of its situation, I do not see, in its streets, in its buildings, in its people and its institutions, what distinguishes Vancouver from an American west-coast city. But that is still only an impression, which I shall set myself to combat. For if at the present stage Quebec seems to me a stroke of good fortune for Canada, I should be delighted to discover some originality in English Canada — which would be a stroke of good fortune for Quebec.

FRENCH SOCIETIES   I investigated the French districts of Vancouver and the little settlement of Maillardville in the immediate neighbourhood. And henceforth I shall always feel a certain uneasiness in the face of all that is written and said in Quebec about these French minorities of western Canada, which to us are only far-off abstractions. Our pity for these minorities seems to me as offensive as our indifference, our lassitude, or our ignorance.

Some of us speak of them much as did Voltaire of the 'few arpents of snow'. Whatever position we adopt towards this agonizing problem, the disconcerting thing is always the lightness of the tone. The 'French fact' in Vancouver, as in all British Columbia, as in Alberta, in Saskatchewan, or in Manitoba, is a moment of our history, the same moment we experienced in Quebec right after the conquest. It is a grave, serious, and important fact, and our own conscience is very far from clear. There is no need to be dramatic. Yet I saw the actual sufferings and hopes that we ourselves knew from day to day, not so long ago. I heard the same reproaches we ourselves used to address to France, also yesterday. And I sensed, above all, the same stubbornness we possessed.

In the absolute, it would have been more normal for Quebec to begin to learn English the day after the conquest. We did not do so. And yet we are a little startled by the determination of these francophone minorities to preserve, sometimes in shreds, all they have been able to retain of their culture, their language, and their faith. It is utter nonsense, which cannot bear analysis. But history is made of such nonsense.

THE PARISH OF ST-SACRAMENT   The street was wide, pleasant, edged with trees. I might have been on the main street of a suburban village. We were in the heart of the Vancouver parish of St-Sacrament, to which six thousand French Canadians belong. The church is tiny, simple, poor, and very touching. I was lucky. There was some animation there. People were going in and out. Cars were coming and going. Perhaps there was an evening service, or confession. I took the opportunity to introduce myself to some of these French Canadians. Their welcome was open and casual.

I was, of course, quickly struck by a French that bore the marks of isolation. The young people are luckier, since they get an hour and a half instruction in French a day. It's little, but in time . . . They have the habit there of saying 'les canadiens' to designate the French Canadians. One wonders what the others are. There was a great deal of spontaneous talk about the Laurendeau-Dunton commission. For several of them, it was the moment of truth. They fancy that . . . But of course they realize that bilingualism is not for tomorrow.

How many of you are there? I asked. Sixty thousand in all British Columbia. Sixty thousand that really speak French? No, of course not. Sixty thousand that have French names; only two-thirds of them have kept their language. We are told that your children are all anglicized, that they are perfectly assimilated. Your prime minister has said so.

'Did the prime minister tell you that a number of English families have enrolled their children in our French schools? Has the prime minister been in our houses? At my house the children speak French, otherwise they don't get any dessert.' It was a man still young who made that reply, in a quiet voice. His phrasing was perfect; only his accent showed the daily efforts that must be made here to give the French language some colour of its origin.

But I was already late. Father Bélanger would be growing impatient. One frequently finds priests at the head of the French groups of the West, priests of the same slightly mad breed that enabled Quebec to remain French against all logic. We forget to thank them today, and in the West people also find it quite natural that men should devote their entire lives to sustaining a culture that to them seems inseparable from their ministry. Everyone in the French milieus there knows Father Bélanger. He lives in a little presbytery, one of the most modest houses on the street. He received me in a bare room that could scarcely have contained three persons. He gave me the solitary armchair and sat on a straight chair where I could scarcely have remained for ten minutes. As we came in, I had noticed at the end of the corridor what seemed to be at once kitchen and dining room.

It was in this austere setting, which would have been unbearable to anyone who suffered from claustrophobia, that we had the most spirited, the warmest, and the most unashamedly lively conversation of my stay in Vancouver.

FATHER BÉLANGER'S ITINERARY   Father Bélanger was born of a family of farmers at Rivière-du-Loup. I would have laid a bet on it. Only a farmer's son could have kept till a ripe age that frankness of gesture and that sparkle in the eyes. He went to school at Sainte-Anne-de-la-Pocatière . . . and perhaps was heading towards agronomy, when suddenly in 1918 he entered the Fathers of St-Sacrament. After two years' ministry, the Fathers of St-Sacrament sent him on mission to the parish of Notre-Dame in Chicago. He remained there from 1925 to 1946, breaking himself in on the various problems of those little islands of French Canadians — problems which demand more generosity than science and more moral and intellectual expenditure than learned theories. Father Bélanger was in his element; it is clear that he prefers fighting with realities to playing with ideas. He was well prepared to assume the new responsibilities that were given him, the establishment of a mission among French Canadians in Vancouver. So in 1946 he arrived, with what apprehension one can imagine.

He said his first Mass at the Cathedral and was surprised to discover that his server had a French name. A surprise that led to another. He spoke a word of appreciation for the skill of his server, which was answered only by a pair of lost eyes raised towards him and the reply, 'What's that?' The young man had nothing French about him but his name and knew not a single word of the language of Molière.

It was a bad beginning, but Father Bélanger found on the spot reasons for hope — notably the Sisters of the Good Shepherd of Anger, who were already engaged with great success in the rehabilitation of young girls. In the Sisters he found valuable collaborators. He began by renting a little hall, the news spread, and the phenomenon of sedimentation began. At first people came from a distance to be present at Father Bélanger's Masses, to hear him preach in French, and to confess, and then they began to settle around the little hall. Today the parish of St-Sacrament is largely inhabited by French Canadians.

It has its professional men, three doctors and a lawyer, a few businessmen, and, of course, a predominance of skilled and unskilled workmen. The skilled workmen earn an average of a hundred dollars a week, and a number of them own their own homes. The church is modest but it belongs to them. An annual subscription raises about ten thousand dollars, which is almost enough to balance the budget of the parish.

One of the most active couples in the French milieu is Blair Neatby, an English Canadian professor at the University of British Columbia, and his French Canadian wife whom we have had several occasions to see on our television screens and whose lucidity never fails. Her position is clear and perfectly healthy. She admits that the English Canadians around her are among the most sensitive to Quebec affairs, but she frequently points out to them that they might well begin to discover the French Canadians living among them of whom they know nothing.

AN IMAGE OF VANCOUVER My lunch with three mannequins. The tables were so close that I might have entered into conversation with those three admirable girls without needing to raise my voice. But apparently they considered it a grave sin even to look at a man, and I could observe them at leisure without the risk of meeting any of those pairs of lovely eyes. The movies have been here. Almost feature for feature the trio was composed of Elizabeth Taylor, Brigitte Bardot, and Audrey Hepburn. They spoke little, they smiled not at all. Average age — twenty-two or -three. I was fascinated to discover so much gravity in persons so young. The futility of their remarks caused me no surprise and is not the property of a city or a country. But the gravity — truly, I have rarely observed it elsewhere in circumstances of this sort.

I had many things to think about and should have prepared my program for the afternoon, but the proximity of this garden of Allah forced me to a certain voyeurism. How, for instance, could I not succumb to the temptation of noting their menus? The dishes passed under my nose one by one. I didn't need even to raise my eyes from the newspaper I was pretending to read. Brigitte Bardot was partaking of a pastry covered with a mountain of ice cream, Audrey Hepburn of tomato juice and coffee, Elizabeth Taylor of toast and coffee. It was lunch, the meal that would have to keep them alive till evening. Their bills were fifty, thirty-five, and twenty-five cents.

I myself was suffering a hunger that must have seemed somewhat Falstaffian in the face of this spectacular sobriety. As the restaurant specializes in fish and seafood, I composed a menu for myself comprising various delicacies fit to occupy an honest man. There would have been no harm in this if the waitress had

My lunch with three mannequins.

not been a hysteric. She took care to repeat in stentorian tones everything that I ordered with studied discretion. This took on a certain tinge of provocation in the eyes of my lovely neighbours. Roles were exchanged. Now I was the centre of attraction. Every swallow I made was discreetly watched. Especially at the moment when the white wine I had ordered was brought to me. The waitress had warned me, and the entire neighbourhood, that the restaurant had nothing but Canadian wine. I had trembled a little. And now here was this half-bottle, completely submerged in a champagne bucket that could have held a magnum of that precious nectar. But God was watching over my health. Surprise, miracle — I would have liked to kiss everyone. The half-bottle that had been suggested to me as some Canadian wine or other was an authentic vintage '55 from the Eschenauer vineyards of Bordeaux.

At the end of the meal I asked the waitress if they served espresso coffee. Her reply: 'No, it's Dickenson.'

SPRING   As soon as you leave the Vancouver Island ferry, you are well aware that an entrancing experience has just begun. You have leaped a fortnight in time. The vegetation here is ahead of Vancouver's, which had a considerable advance on ours. It is not enough to say that Vancouver Island is a garden; it is an explosion of verdure and flowers. The road that took me to Victoria might have been the central avenue of a public park.

I entered the city by Government Street, the first road built west of the Rockies. It is a strange and curious street that has its moment of grandeur and style only to end up two miles later, after crossing the city from north to south, in poverty and factories. It is laden with history, if one is willing to give this word its North American sense. Some of the houses that line it were built at the beginning of the century. At the corner of Simcoe lived Emily Carr, a painter unknown in her lifetime of whom death has made a legend. We soon reach the parliament buildings, whose wide lawns join with those of the Empress Hotel to enclose the little inner port.

The parliament is a massive structure, capable of enduring for centuries against hurricanes. It gives an impression of power and majesty all day but is transformed at night into a sort of palace of wonders. Thousands of shining bulbs meticulously outline its contours and the lines of its structure. So much sobriety by daylight and so much levity at night — one does not expect this of a British institution.

The Empress Hotel, where I had reserved my room, is an enormous object, surrounded with lawns and flowers — part French château, part English manor-house. But one has seen nothing till one has wandered from one immense hall to another immense hall. Where could they have dug up those unbelievably high-backed armchairs that adorn the corridors of the ground floor? In what attic? Perhaps that of Buckingham Palace. They are a strange sight, this collection from another age, but what age precisely? They seem to have been conceived to hold old wrinkled queens or the witches of Salem. Most of them are covered with tapestries, whose colours have been washed away by time. But I see the attachment felt for these armchairs, for a good half-dozen of them have been newly repaired. I dreamed for a long time in these corridors, wandering about in a Kafka setting.

A flash caught my attention. Night had fallen: the giant sequoia in parliament square had just been lit up. It is the biggest Christmas tree in the world.

Later I fell into conversation with an old gentleman who had just come to settle in the city. He had decided to spend his retirement at Victoria some day and still had not managed to convince himself that his dream was now a reality. He was a man of modest circumstances who had taken advantage of one of Victoria's innumerable low-cost housing schemes. He kept looking at his watch; soon there would be no more buses to take him back to his little bungalow in the suburbs. He had no car.

As he left, he turned to give me a farewell wave of the hand. He still wore the same glowing smile. On his whole person he bore the marks of years of exhausting work. He had travelled from one lumberyard to another in the interior of British Columbia. But each day, no doubt, a single ambition had supported him — to live the last years of his life in Victoria. Till now I had believed that this ambition was only within the reach of English millionaires. He would know the same sun, would breathe the same flowers, enjoy the same mild dry winters, the same rainy but perfumed summers. It was a long time since I had seen a smile of this quality. I had never seen it, in any case, on the lips of a millionaire. It sang of a personal victory, tinged also with social conquest. Retirement in Victoria is no longer the exclusive privilege of the great of this world.

SUNDAY IN VICTORIA   Even the birds were silent. Over the whole city there hung a torpor as of the day after a cataclysm. A sailor passed whistling in the street; he could not know it was Sunday in Victoria. In the lobby of my hotel, people were consulting the list of churches and services pinned up in more convenient places than the programs of cinemas and concerts. And this was quite natural, for today the cinemas would have closed their doors, like the restaurants, the stores, the groceries, the cafés, the bars, and even most of the service stations. Oh, I know. Most of the cities of the Canadian West, and even of Ontario, try more or less each Sunday to achieve this nothingness, but none of them manage it with the same fine simplicity as Victoria. This little city, this great capital, does not don its Sunday silence like an adornment. It strips itself, frankly and totally, and yields up its most secret beauties. Would you have even the desire or the time, for instance, on any other day but Sunday to make the tour of the private gardens, as you are invited to do at certain seasons of the year? Of course not, but it is an entertainment quite in harmony with the silence, the peace, the giddy solitude of Sunday. I visited these private gardens. I found the same rockeries as in the residential sections of Vancouver, but here the flowers almost cover the stones, and I was happy. They had burst out of their prison. They had won.

MOTHER'S DAY   It is the Château of Versailles in its Court of Miracles version. I am speaking of the dining room of the Empress Hotel at Victoria. Perhaps not on every day of the year, but this particular Sunday, the evening of Mother's Day, there was an atmosphere of Ali Baba's cave, or perhaps the Black Mass. One expected to see a procession of witches emerge, bearing candelabra. Walls and ceilings are of dark wood, peculiarly sculptured into lace. From all sides the anxious faces of old women regarded us from frames that seemed to have fixed them to the walls for eternity; these were the wives of all the Canadian governors general. It was a haunting sight, and you tried in vain to look away from it. But to see what? The movement to and fro of waitresses, the youngest of whom must be forty-five and the oldest of whom could be your grandmother. These elderly ladies were charming, constantly smiling, and moved from table to table as best they could. But when they disappeared towards the kitchen, you obscurely suspected that you would never see them again.

This was a dinner of a certain poetry, and I was in the centre of at least a hundred and fifty tables occupied by as many local families. At each of these tables was a triumphant mother, justly proud of her brood. The menu was elaborate, the cooking careful, and the prices competitive. It is in the old and picturesque railway hotels that one can obtain the most decent meals across Canada. They have their traditions, and the standards have been established for a very long time by experienced travellers. But I could not distract myself from the odd decorations and the atmosphere of this immense hall. I was telling myself that we lacked only a great organ to confirm our sentiment that we were sharing the last meal of the Christians in the catacombs. Well, I heard the great organ. I thought I was dreaming. And then I saw, very far away at the end of the room, a minuscule person seated at a giant keyboard. For an hour we were to be treated to her repertoire, from 'Tico-Tico' to *South Pacific*. Then she rose and, without waiting for an applause that was slow in coming, she gave a little bow to a room that was not looking at her and retired in rather ill humour with a great rustle of skirts.

She returned a little later, in a new panelled dress, no doubt drawn from the same attic. This time she had a look of peaceful resignation on her features. Great artists are always alone. She began to play for herself, giving up the Tico-Tico style, effects, and skilful combinations of keys. I saw it myself — an entire room fall silent to listen to a simple refrain. But in it there was sensitivity, an accent, an accord. Grandpapa, who was in the room, managed to release a thunder of applause. Our artist had an agitated moment. I saw her later bearing her triumph from one table to another. I do not believe the greatest virtuosi have ever known such perfect moments of glory.

NANAIMO   I was in the region of Nanaimo, driving without destination towards the interior, when I found myself almost without warning in a forest of giant Douglas firs. You feel a violent dizziness. You have not known such excitement since the day of your first walk in a forest. To experience it again at an adult age introduces some profound reconciliation in your being. It is to this emotion perhaps that I owe the gentle sense of complicity with which the little port of Nanaimo inspired me. For, in the final analysis, it is only a little town — very well situated, it is true, but I have seen many times elsewhere the same openings onto the sea, the same charming streets zigzagging down to the harbour. I have seen bastions more moving than the poor little Nanaimo bastion that carries on its own the entire historical pretensions of the locality. I was told about a coal mine, about Indians, about the Hudson's Bay Company, but I was told such things everywhere and would continue to be told them all across western Canada. I was told stories about fishing, lumbering, yachting, golf, when I had already heard more such stories than I could remember. I was taken to the business streets and shown stores, restaurants, modern hotels, and the ultra-modern hospital. I was exhausted. I was taken last of all to see the tennis courts.

And yet I was happy in that town. I believe that it is with a new town much as it is with people. Certain moments are more propitious. There is a climate, an instant to seize.

The road from Nanaimo to Campbell River, ninety-five miles to the north, is one of the most beautiful you could dream of. 'One of the most beautiful' is the expression that suits it best, despite the attrition of the words, for it is neither picturesque nor imposing, it is quite simply beautiful as so many coastal roads claim to be and so few are. Here, nature is still supreme and nothing you see on the ground can distract you from a glorious and permanent confrontation with the splendours of the Strait of Georgia.

PORTRAIT OF CAPTAIN MACLEOD   Less than sixty miles inland from Vancouver there is a pearl, an oasis, a port of call of peace and beauty — Harrison Hot Springs. Oases of this sort, it is true, are less prepared to provide free watering for camels than to sell you one. You will see more motels than private houses, more souvenir shops than corner groceries, more restaurants and bars than churches, and the great hotel of the place is the centre of attention, dignity, and respect. But why complain, since no one can ever manage to spoil the wild aspect of the lake, and the great hotel itself is one of its principal ornaments? You reach it as if in a park, at the end of a magnificent drive along the water.

When I think back to Harrison, one image comes back to me with great clarity — the silhouette of Captain James MacLeod. I am seated at a table, drinking coffee, and he is there, standing in front of me like some huge wild animal.

I asked him questions, and he did not reply. Propped against an invisible hammock, he smoked his pipe, and his eyes were lost in contemplation of the lake. They were fixed on a point that might be the island in the middle of the lake, or perhaps the mountain, chain of mountains rather, that enclosed the scene. The lake must be forty miles around but it seems tiny. This is a matter of perspective. Today it was calm — you could float upon it on a toothpick — but sometimes it unleashes its fury, and it swallows its victims every year. Last year there were two — young people caught by a storm.

Before the development of the network of roads of the region, the lake had ferries. It was on one of these that Captain MacLeod was finally ruined. But this I learned only after an incalculable number of questions, apparently of not the slightest interest to Captain MacLeod. How old could he be? Sixty . . . seventy . . . eighty? One can never be quite sure with these people out of the general run, whose last words will be heard for a mile around and whose expiring sigh will knock over the bedside lamp. Ideas of this sort passed through my mind, while he continued to smoke his pipe, two paces away from me. Why was he so close, if he was not interested in my conversation — or rather my monologue? It occurred to me that he might be deaf and I determinedly raised my voice. He gave me an amused look and sat down at my table. He could do this without asking leave, for he was the proprietor of this little café, one of the best-situated on the street.

Seated now, he continued to keep silent, and his head remained resolutely turned towards the lake. I no longer knew what attitude to take, to tell the truth. Should I continue to speak into the void like an imbecile, or would I be better advised to withdraw in my turn into silence? There was no one but us two in the place. It was still very early, and the sun was struggling over the mountain, like a balloon in difficulty. Through the clouds it reminded me of a heavy moon that had mistaken the continent. Without another word I drank my last drop of coffee and prepared to ask for my check. Captain MacLeod began to give dull grunts, interspersed with spells of silence. He had not said a word, his eyes had not left the lake, and he continued to draw with religious application on his pipe, but it was clear that he would soon begin to speak. I made myself very small so as not to hinder the mechanism. And suddenly a tremendous voice, which seemed to come from the depths of the Grand Canyon, announced that 'it's going to rain again and the lake will let loose.'

The words and the style were Shakespearian. A few minutes later the wind began to blow and the crystalline surface of the lake broke up in all directions. Only a sea captain could have caught so sudden a change in the wind. The rain would not fall for an hour but the clouds were already gathering and it was clear that the sun had lost the game. The captain's victory humanized him a little. He is renowned in Harrison Springs for his knowledge of weather lore. And you need a good deal of skill and science not to be wrong several times a day in this region where the sun plays an incessant game of hide and seek with the clouds. And I understood his silence, which he could now relinquish. All this time he had been following this weather crisis with the attentiveness of a stalking hunter. He had hung upon the slightest yielding of the sun, unmasked the intentions of the wind in the leaves, could foresee the evolution of the first little clouds. He had been at the theatre and I had disturbed him. Or perhaps he had obscurely acquired the conviction that he was the author of this serial show and must watch over it till the curtain fell.

Captain James MacLeod had now returned to his post behind the counter and his hands rested on the taps at each side of the percolator, as if on the wheel of a ship. And he was off with his little restaurant across the lake. He would be able to master the storm and bring me safe to port.

I remember only snatches of our conversation. He was clearly not of the species of whom I could ask, 'How many years have you been here?' or 'What brought you to this region?' Now that he had begun to speak, at least at intervals, I quickly understood that I should have to proceed by a method I had had occasion to perfect in Japan. I began with a statement, as for example, 'Harrison Springs is obviously a delightful place in more ways than one — a sort of paradise.' I was immediately corrected by a powerful voice, which left no room for discussion, 'It's a horrible place. Just come here in winter and you'll see what I mean.'

In Japan I used this method to respect the modesty of the Japanese, who are averse to direct questions — or questions of any sort. Dialogue, at least that which I had most often with the Japanese, even if they were my friends, was made up largely of arrangements of statements — a discreet and subtly shaded arrangement that was full of charm. With Captain MacLeod this method enabled me to turn his inordinate spirit of contradiction in whatever way suited me. If I had said, for instance, 'It seems clear by your accent that you were born and brought up in Ireland,' he would have been profoundly silent. Instead I said, 'You're obviously from the region.' He became almost angry and began to tell me the story of his life. There was no complacency in it. He named off the principal signposts, in the manner of *Who's Who*. Born in Ireland, farm family, arrived in America — I shall never know in what corner of America or at what age — served in the American navy, took part in the war against Japan, was assigned after the war to the merchant marine, came here to take command of a ferry. He stopped. He looked back at that time. For him it was the beginning of his downfall. I would learn nothing more certain about Captain MacLeod. Only that his martyrdom had begun sixteen years ago and that he would endure it stoically until his death. He, Captain MacLeod, in command of a ferry on a lake, when he had braved the high seas, ploughed all the oceans of the earth, survived the perils of war. One could indeed understand why he was not very chatty about the period of his life that had begun here.

A truck driver made a noisy entrance and ordered toast and coffee. MacLeod did not look at him. Perhaps he did not even see him. An aged trembling woman came in and went towards the table at which the truck driver had just taken his place. Captain James MacLeod had once more retired into his interior universe. He was over there in the middle of the lake, struggling alone before God against a violent storm.

PRELUDE TO THE GRAND SYMPHONY   As you approach Kamloops, the Trans-Canada Highway announces what it is soon to become — one of the most spectacular arteries in the world. One forgets the vital role it plays at the heart of the Canadian economy; it seems to have been constructed solely for the pleasure of the traveller. Mountains, lakes, and valleys have been distributed by an architect with delusions of grandeur; even at seventy or eighty miles an hour one seems to be strolling.

MEMORIES OF REVELSTOKE   I had decided to stop at Revelstoke, chiefly to make the highly recommended climb of Mount Revelstoke. It is a classified site, a national park since 1914. The road would take us to an altitude of six thousand five hundred feet by the itinerary that has gained the reputation of being one of the most picturesque in Canada. I skirted the Columbia River for a while between the Selkirk and Monashee mountain ranges. These were not the Rockies yet but they were grandiose already. I am tired of using this word, for one must eke out one's vocabulary when one is only a few miles away from the Banff National Park. But what can we do? The grandeur of the scenes will anaesthetize our eyes long before it does the words we use to describe them. The repeated shocks of splendour will finally blend into a continual aggression against our nervous systems and we will enter a new dimension of unawareness and detachment. Between the Okanagan and Mount Revelstoke I should have taken a bath of banality for several days, in some desert. But Canada is a violent country. It had decided to deliver all its mountain splendours to me at a single cast only to withdraw them brutally at the threshold of the prairies. This is how I explain my secret indifference when I asked the road to Mount Revelstoke, as soon as I entered the little town.

I was told, as if I were a Martian, 'But it's closed.'

'For several days?'

'For more than a year.'

'So I can't climb to the top of Mount Revelstoke?'

'You'd better take a helicopter.' And the huge woman walked away with a smile of incomprehension.

So I took a room for the night at an excellent Revelstoke hotel. There is not a single place in Canada where one cannot find

decent, or even very pleasant, accommodation, since our standards are almost identical with those of the United States. To
consider motels alone, tiny hamlets are equipped with real hotel
villages, which can answer the entire range of tourist demands.
The quality of the cooking does not always equal the material
equipment, but I do not believe that this is a characteristic exclusive to us.

I was frankly happy to have no one to see here and nothing
definite to do, to be able to choose between idling, reading, walking, or sleep. Night does not really fall upon this little town, it
settles upon it. It rests like a veil upon the mountains around.
Oh, I know. Night cannot have such lightness every evening, but
may I be permitted to believe that it has? My memories of Revelstoke are inseparable from this transparent night. I saw it announce itself from afar, float a moment over the town and drift
down upon it, but I was also to see it dissolve in a white light,
coming suddenly from the four corners of the horizon like a cinema effect. It was exciting, but my eyelids were heavy and I was
close to distress. A wretched sportsmen's conference had chosen
this very night to hold its annual festivities in all the neighbouring rooms.

I had read and put a little order in my notes and was about
to sleep the sleep of the just when the noise began in the next-
door room. I could hear the conversations distinctly and they
were not without a certain humour. I soon joined in the sonorous
laughter, despite my confusion at finding myself involved in this
joyous party from my bed, through a wall and in the dark. And
now other voices, coming from another direction, probably the
room across from mine, burst out after a series of slamming
doors. I felt that I had set up my bed in the middle of a railway
station. I was wrong. I was in the centre of a fair, for there were
new voices right at my ear. One might believe that the third
wall had disappeared and half a dozen people had come to give
me a surprise party. I cursed the architects of this superb hotel.
They had built everything well, except the walls.

I dressed and went back down to the lobby. I walked for almost an hour, then returned. It was after midnight. The bar was closed and there was no longer anyone in the room except the night receptionist and an old gentleman talking politely together. I approached and told them my troubles. Before I had finished, the receptionist leaped upon the telephone and engaged in conversation with the kitchen. She was a plump young person and not hard on the eyes. She explained that she knew the very thing: there was nothing better than hot milk. It would be right up. She put down the phone. . . . But I could drink gallons of hot milk and still not sleep in such a din. Now it was the old man's turn to pick up the phone. He knew a good place. For what? For whisky, after hours. This was my first surprise. Here was a very small town, which had its scarcely concealed bootleggers. He did not understand why I refused his suggestion, but he had dozens of others that could help an honest man while away the hours pleasantly till dawn when he could rest. For one need have no illusions, the parties in the rooms would last till dawn. They took place only once a year, so you understand . . .

I was past understanding anything. I was resigned. I returned to the calm, cool night. I walked till I almost collapsed with tiredness. But in a sense tiredness supports you. When I returned it was perhaps three o'clock and I felt in better form than ever. I had no trace of sleepiness left and could have leaped into my car and set out at once for Banff. But one should always distrust this second wind. I know that very well, for this was not the first sleepless night of my life. The old man was still there, and the receptionist awaited me with bad news, at least from her point of view. She knew two clandestine gambling houses, but one was closed now and the other had moved away. I was now completely reconciled to my insomnia. It might have taken me days of inquiry to track down information of this sort. A little way out of town there was a house where . . . well, you can guess. If I had been in Montreal, in Toronto, in Vancouver . . . but Revelstoke, a town of not even four thousand inhabitants. A town whose uneventful sleep I know, a town on which night settles like a diaphanous veil, a little mountain village, discreet and tranquil, so tranquil, so calm, so tranquil, so calm . . .

UNFORGETTABLE VISIONS OF BEAUTY Neither man nor animal nor bird had yet been born. On a little planet, lost in infinite space, a springtime of earth was beginning. The sea of ice climbed to the north, descended towards the south, while the fire withdrew into the centre of the planet. But the earth's crust was thin, it cracked all over under the weight of melting ice. Soon there were left only some little pieces drifting upon an immense expanse of water. Very much later, when had come trees, birds, animals, and then man, someone got the idea of giving names to these loose fragments of land.

I was driving at that moment on one of them, and I could see that it still bore the marks of its tormented birth. If we smoothed out the crust of the earth, if we were able to make its wrinkles and hollows disappear as we do with a cloth, we might perhaps be able to join America to Asia again and Europe to America. But the cloth has split, the pieces have shrivelled. I always feel when I start out along a mountain road that I am on the site of a cataclysm, and it is of little importance whether this cataclysm took place yesterday or millions of years ago. The wounds of the earth still gape and the beauties I admire are living sores. So there is always pity mixed with my admiration — pity for the small things that we are, for the microscopic dust that is the earth, pity for this apocalypse of genesis that had not disturbed the order of the universe — an apocalypse, yes, the agony of a neutron.

It was cold, though it was the end of May. But even so I lowered the roof of my convertible so I should not miss any of this part of the Trans-Canada Highway that goes from Revelstoke to Golden. I was obliged to cover my head and shoulders with everything woollen I could find in my valises. It must have been a curious picture and yet I felt as if I were riding in a skidoo in my shirt-sleeves. But I had no regrets, I felt invaded already by the euphoria of an alpinist.

The road offered so few difficulties that I finally forgot it. It was not I that advanced but peaks ten thousand feet high that danced a fairy ballet around me. Black backs curved at right angles under crests of everlasting whiteness. A wholly new vegetation rose from the earth, quivering on either side of the road. From time to time I thought I must be driving over broken glass: it was a cascade falling vertically in the hollow of a rock. I was happy. I was not really disturbing any of this wild and grandiose life. I was only a vague scorpion on a giant's boot.

The culminating point of this part of the road is, of course, Rogers Pass. You must have risen a few thousand feet without being too much aware of it, for suddenly you are in discreet familiarity with the snowy summits that seemed anxious to disappear into the scenery not so long ago. You are no longer a little scorpion on a giant's boot, you have become the giant himself, and your confrontation takes place at eye level. I got out of the car. I should have liked to walk for a long time, but despite break-throughs of sun that seemed to want to endure, the high-altitude winds had won. No woollen garments could offer the slightest protection. I put up the hood of the car, turned on the heat, and swore to come back again in July or August.

There is a certain place on Rogers Pass where the view of Mount Sir Donald, the Bonney Glacier, the Avalanche Glacier, and Mount Rogers form the most exalting but at the same time most harmonious panorama. When you got your first painting-book it was thus that you beheld in your imagination the mountains you could not manage to draw. Later, you saw a great many adventure films that sometimes gave you glimpses of mountain landscape that had been revealed to you first in your childhood dreams. Then you travelled over the world, and everywhere the mountains offered hints of your first ecstasies, particularly in the Alps . . . perhaps also in the Atlas of Morocco . . . but it was never exactly right. But one day you find yourself quite naturally following the interior roads of your dreams. You recognize the surroundings. You know that just there, at the end of a little promontory where the road widens to permit you to stop, the scenery will burst, there will be an explosion, and your eye will be able to embrace in a single instant's dizzying excitement the gigantic waves of earth as they rise to assault the sky. You have fixed this instant in a corner of your imagination and you will find it unchanged, as it will be for eternity. There where the earth becomes fire . . . flames become ice . . . vibrations, rhythms, ecstasy. You are the sole living creature in the midst of a living death . . . in the midst of an eternal moment of this living death of the earth.

I travelled through my country in a friendly spirit, with the intention of concealing none of my impressions, favourable or not, so I am under obligation not to hide that my journey through the Rockies surpassed by far all I had experienced during the other mountain journeys of my life. For me it was a revelation, brutal to a degree. I had been flung into another dimension. I was to feel during the rest of my stay in the Rockies a curious insensitivity towards the beauty that surrounded me, some of which might compete in grandeur with my vision today. But it was never quite the same impression. It seems that one can share only once in this rapture of the earth in flight towards the sky.

While I continued my journey from Golden towards Banff, I tried to understand the reasons for my ecstasy. Perhaps I was mentally 'conditioned' . . . predisposed in some way by the splendours I had been promised. But I remembered that such predispositions often work in the opposite direction. The promised marvels do not come up to those you have imagined. Or perhaps I had been psychically 'conditioned'. I had slept less than three hours. And everyone knows that lack of sleep makes your sensory perceptions very much sharper than ordinarily and, even if you have to call upon your nervous reserves, you will live your sensations to their finest ramifications. Under such conditions it might well be that my eye had deceived me and that that place of savage splendour lacked the mysterious harmony with which I had endowed it. I wished to have a clean conscience about it. So now that I no longer felt intoxicated, I turned and went back several dozen miles to the top of Mount Rogers. There was no change. I was seized by the same vertigo at once painful and marvellous. Again I saw the waves of land, fixed in a minute of eternity, just when they were about to invade the sky.

It was perhaps pure madness after all. Unless it was a perfect coincidence between reality and a childhood dream.

Alberta

BANFF, OR ENCHANTMENT   I spent the night at Banff, where I had the privilege of having my dinner with a black bear. We were separated from one another only by the large window of the dining room of the Timberline Hotel. I can still see him. He was as interested in my menu as I could possibly be in his.

I saw him drink his daily milk in a Coca-Cola bottle and then apply himself to some chicken carcasses. He is a familiar of the establishment and — against the instructions of the management, the municipality, and the government — the waiters stealthily leave him various little dainties that he comes to sup upon each evening. But this was the first time he had come right into the dining room, or almost so. This is what the European mountains lack — the presence of wild life.

A little later I raised my eyes from my newspaper for a moment and saw a magnificent moose in the middle of a clearing, a few hundred feet from the terrace of my room. He stayed there for half an hour, and for half an hour my eyes never left him. A moose is not something one sees every day. I had not seen one except in the movies until now. What a magnificent beast. And what a sense of power in even its slightest movement.

A young Frenchman told me about his life in Banff, in the very heart of this extraordinary wild-nature reserve. I rather suspect that he had fled a very complicated family situation. For several years he lived for brief periods in various countries of the world and he had expected his itinerary to take him on to Asia, until, several centuries after Jacques Cartier, he discovered Canada. He wished to hear of nothing more. He had found paradise. He is a devotee of camping, fishing, and hunting. He has lived in Banff for only a year and he knows all the fauna of the park; he knows where the Rocky Mountain sheep are to be found, where I should go to see wild goats, herds of deer, foxes, bears, and moose. His dog has become friendly with a coyote, a sort of jackal. He explained the customs of the magpie, who was foraging for food outside the window, and whom we soon saw flying away in a great black and white cloud — superb birds whom the poets have greatly slandered. In short he knew everything.

I, who had just come from British Columbia, could tell him absolutely nothing of the marvels of the province, which he seems to have travelled far and wide. He is a specialist in curious things. He told me about the famous cable car, for instance, in the Boston Bar region, where at the time of the Gold Rush a stage-coach and its oxen were carried across the river just by the action of a winch. The cable exists still, and the basket too, and one can put a Cadillac in it, but the winch has been replaced by a motor. In a way the conversation of this young French adventurer was very vexing. I had seen so many things in British Columbia, and yet in his eyes I had missed all that was most interesting. He was at his best when he talked about animals. I could have listened to him for hours. And to see the enthusiasm of a foreigner for the splendours of my country awakened some depth of chauvinism in me that I had believed vanished forever.

Banff was as I had imagined it, or rather as I had dreamed it. I had believed the films had tricked me, had conspired to show me only untouched landscapes. Banff, known to the entire world, and for so many years — it seemed unlikely not to find a sort of monstrous fair, a giant tourist trap. But it is not . . . and that is a great joy. The most secret of little villages, between two loops of rivers, well hidden in forests of conifers, a narrow valley, or rather corridor — it is hard to understand how Banff can be at once the highest-ranking tourist centre of Canada and so well protected against the invasion of bad taste.

Tonight there was unaccustomed bustle — the annual opening of the Banff Springs Hotel. At the station, dozens of handsome gentlemen and pretty ladies were waiting on the platform for the arrival of the train from Calgary, while an uninterrupted fleet of big cars and taxis took the road to the airport. Night had not yet fallen when the lights of the main street went on. The town was eager to show the visitor its evening dress.

Borne along by the current, I first visited the Banff Springs Hotel where the Rotary Club had reserved all available rooms for the opening week. It is a sort of Château Frontenanc, stone and brick, towers and copper roof. Solidly anchored at the foot of Sulphur Mountain, it dominates the valleys of the Spray and Bow Rivers. I was told that it is in the Scottish baronial style but I would call it rather the CPR style, a baroque style, but corresponding, it seems to me, with the concept of beauty our pioneers must have had.

Connoisseurs of sunsets should not leave Banff without going to the top of Mount Norquay at the end of a day, preferably the end of a day that has been lightly cloudy. One can go by car, by cable car, or on foot. I am not a frantic lover of sunsets and yet I went, for what reason I do not know. Perhaps I had a presentiment that this evening the sun had decided to set in blood and light with unwonted considerateness. It would be more discreet than usual and I might have judged as well that it would usually leave the starring part to the clouds, hastening behind Sulphur Mountain in several minutes the better to enlighten them from the prompter's box. This evening I saw the sun roll gently into an opaque cloud, penetrate it, and at last make it burst like a red balloon. I saw the cloud draw together, prepare a calculated vengeance and, just when it was about to manage to form a screen, change into golden dust.

Below, in the valley, life went on unchanged in the little mountain town but I knew that all along the river the deer, sheep, and wild goats had stopped for a moment to watch this struggle between a thin cloud and the setting sun. They had guessed. A cloud of this quality would not willingly admit defeat. It would call its allies to its aid, spending the entire night gathering them together if need be. Next morning rain would fall in torrents, and the sun would spend the day in defeat. I would have known that evening if I had spoken the language of sheep, deer, and wild goats. But instead I returned to my hotel, announcing to anyone who would listen that after such a sunset I was sure the fine weather had settled in for centuries.

AND SUDDENLY THE PRAIRIE The Rockies had disappeared. The road was straight as an arrow, lightly stretched upon a semi-desert immensity. I could not accustom myself to this image. Since my departure from Victoria and across British Columbia the mountains had been with me everywhere. Now they appeared only in my rearview mirror, and already so far away — a small luminous lace, a shudder of earth. Before me, as far as my eye could see, the line of the horizon was cut by a few zones of shadow. It had been traced by a clumsy child. He had been trying to draw the silhouette of a modern city but he'd run out of ink. Only the bases of the buildings he had dreamed of were there. And the sheet was full of spots. But even so it was a strange sensation to watch the approach of a city like this without losing sight of it for an instant. It is rare that a hill, a wood, or a river doesn't get in the way. I felt that I was crossing the approaches to the Sahara.

A CITY OF ABUNDANT LIFE At the entrance to the city, in an angle of the road, a map for the motorist shows the layout of the principal streets and points out how he can avoid the centre of the city if he intends to continue by the Trans-Canada High-way. It is a happy practice and should be introduced into Europe. But in the case of Calgary, you would need a map to lose your way. It is a longitudinal city, whose plan is only disturbed by the slightly whimsical crossing of the Bow River. Roads cut avenues at right angles. I was to find almost the same design in all the cities of the West. A thing that struck me from this moment was the importance accorded pedestrians. I had not yet entered the city limits when a large panel warned me of the pedestrian's absolute priority at intersections. But this was not sufficient. Almost everywhere in the centre of the city I was to see im-mense cotton streamers at crossings stretching from one side of the street to the other. I first thought these were announcements of an international fair, a boxing match, a regatta, or even the Stampede, though I was a month too early for the celebrated annual rodeo. I was simply being reminded that here the pedes-trian is king. He is so rare in Calgary that they want to preserve him at all costs. According to statistics, Calgary has the largest number of cars 'per capita' of any city in America except Los Angeles.

Calgary is above all a small modern expanding city. Through it pass the millions of dollars of the important petroleum and natural gas industries, and it is here that the big companies have installed their business offices. The administrative buildings are the only structures in the city that rise towards the sky. Every-thing else sprawls along the surface. As you drive towards the south, you are surprised to see on a telephone pole, in the midst of open fields a quarter of an hour after you have left the last dwellings, a plaque on which is inscribed '106th Street'. They have thought big here. Plans have been drawn up for the years to come; it is expected that the population will increase at the same rate as in past years. And this rate is prodigious: 506 in-habitants in 1884, 43,000 in 1911, 168,000 in 1955, 277,000 in 1963.

I spent the first evening with old friends. The man is fifty but doesn't look forty. He is a dynamo and never still. He always has a telephone call to make. He belongs to that race of young bosses of local manufacture, destined vaguely to liberal careers, whom the discovery of oil thrust into the business world. They were the sons of middle-class families, able to study at Edmonton or Toronto at their choice. They are not numerous, and for this reason there are still too many Americans on the executives of the big companies. A lack of local managerial personnel is a very Canadian malaise. His wife is still young, sparkling with intelligence, and with a charming smile.

Both are very much alive, and I suddenly realized that I had not met a very great number of people who were really alive since the beginning of my trip through western Canada. Oh, there must be innumerable people everywhere that don't just wait for death while playing bridge and drinking whisky. I say only that you do not meet them by the dozen. All of us in America live more or less under the threat of some sort of disaster. Our most marvellous projects are carried out like vacation homework. Our laughter contains more nervousness than joy. We have forgotten how to talk to no purpose. We never eat without counting the calories. We will finally make chocolate without sugar. Taken in a certain way, life very quickly becomes a Chinese torture. Some of Chekhov's characters count the days, hours, and minutes that separate them from the death they long for, in their fine houses, a glass of vodka in their hands.

My first great joy in Calgary was to begin my stay in the company of two human beings who had the same little light in their eyes, who were making plans to spend a month on their ranch, not for reasons of social standing or any such preoccupations, but because they passionately loved ranch life, dreamed of it for months in advance, and each year got a sort of second wind there. If this thoroughly alive couple had been an exception, I should have passed them by without these various allusions. But scattered throughout Calgary I encountered human beings for whom life seemed a fascinating adventure, a challenge made to man's measure, an experience full of the unforeseen. But let us not give way to euphoria. The city has its agonies, its inner struggles, and just to be fully alive creates an infinity of little daily problems. I wish only to account for a general atmosphere, which I felt without the least difficulty in the course of my comings and goings.

A SORT OF CRUCIBLE Calgary is an amalgam of a number of ethnic groups, which are perhaps more assimilated here than elsewhere. The fruit of prosperity perhaps, and of common efforts towards the realization of great common projects. At any rate, it is an easily verifiable impression. I was no more able in Calgary than in other cities to prevent those I spoke to from openly bringing up the platitudes about Quebec, the problems of Quebec, separatism, the demonstrations, the bombs. But strange as this may seem, there were no more Rockies as a screen. In all the milieus I entered, and they were very diverse, passion was lacking in our conversations. My questioners were badly informed, but they were aware of it. The difference is considerable. And we could at last talk to some purpose.

Artificial or not, a certain unity of aspiration seems to reign in this city. Americans — they are very numerous and powerfully installed in high finance — Germans, Ukrainians, Italians, and the various other nationalities, including six thousand French Canadians, deliver the same speech, curiously impregnated with chauvinism. A child asked me if Paris were really more beautiful than Calgary. A university student spoke to me of the generosity of the city's millionaires — there are about a thousand of them — in the tone the young painters of the Middle Ages might have used of the Medici. One would have thought they had covered the city with museums and art galleries; questioned, he proved to be thinking particularly of MacMahon, who had underwritten the construction of a football stadium.

THE VALLEY OF THE DINOSAURS With a companion, the son of a professor, I followed the Trans-Canada Highway towards the east and then went north to Drumheller, which is considered the capital of the Badlands. Drumheller is a vision of hell . . . or perhaps of the void . . . a vision that plunges us into another element. Not a tree. A village at the end of the world, in the centre of a completely denuded region.

Perhaps this sombre little town will some day become an important centre for blasé tourists who wish to enjoy a lunar holiday. For the whole valley is made of rocks, some of them more than three hundred million years old. You have only to drive a short way out, in whichever direction you wish, to walk upon the fossils of crustaceans deposited in the stony bed of the inland sea. As far as you can see, and all around you, there are stones, strata of stone, canyons of stone, precipices of stone. All life was arrested here millions of years ago. If the Hilton chain ever discovers this place, it will build a great palace, which it will call 'Suicide Hotel'. As neighbour it will have 'Dinosaurs Hotel' or 'Motel Dimetrodon'.

I was beginning to forget that it was to see where paleontologists had discovered their enormous specimens of prehistoric animals that I had come to the valley of Drumheller. And I would continue to forget it for several hours more, since the pleasant pharmacist who had taken it upon himself to show us the region first obliged us to make a complete tour of the oil and gas wells. Drumheller, which once lived on its reserves of coal, has obtained its revenge. The commercial value of its coal diminished and it discovered an oil of exceptional quality.

I was still waiting for my dinosaurs, but I felt in no way frustrated. The more I drove about this valley, the more permeated with its atmosphere I felt. A while before I had told myself that one would have to be misanthropic, hopeless, and intellectually perverted to be willing to live in such a place. I studied the pharmacist stealthily and I could not understand his calm or discover the significance of his smile. He seemed to find this landscape just like any other, with its own beauty and ugliness, quite commonplace, as if I might find its like almost everywhere in the world. I wanted to say to him: No, not at all, you're in a sort of trap, you've been hideously deceived, there are places where the stone has vanished into the entrails of the earth, there are towns where trees grow, fields where there are vegetables and fruit, meadows where birds sing, lakes where fish play, rivers that are alive. He talked to me at length about oil, about the defunct coal. He showed me little stations, now disused, that had had their time of glory, abandoned houses, deserted streets . . . but the dinosaurs, sir — do you think if I scratched the earth a bit, as you did, there'd be the slightest chance of my also finding a dinosaur in my garden?

But I had to go on waiting, for unlikely as it is the chief tourist attraction of the place seems to be the so-called 'biggest little church in the world'. It is also said that it can seat a hundred thousand people, six at a time. It was only a little white speck at the foot of a rocky promontory. We visited it. It was indeed tiny, prettily enough shaped to make a pleasant ornament in a child's garden. It is of recent construction. It appears that tourists are very happy about their visits here and that it could be considered a brilliant idea. Ordinarily I am a good audience and I have laughed at light comedies that seemingly bored my distinguished colleagues. But when it came to 'the biggest little church' . . . and this wasn't all. We had to go in and take a seat . . . one of the six seats. Your eye is suddenly caught by a sort of luminous jukebox, similar in all respects to those that adorn most of our restaurants. Another brilliant idea — you need only deposit a twenty-five cent piece to hear the hymn of your choice. I could not tell you the extent of the repertoire, but all the principal denominations are represented. I also learned that marriages are solemnized here from time to time and that the validity of the ceremonies is recognized.

AT LAST THE DINOSAURS At last I saw the place where the most important dinosaur fossils were obtained — a veritable quarry where teams of specialists continue their search. The richest layers are not necessarily the deepest. Prehistoric discoveries are not exclusive to us, and a map showed me a significant number of places in North America that are well provided with beds of fossils of all sorts. But the best known are not situated, as is Drumheller, close to main highways. It is this characteristic that gives it most interest for the future. Who would refuse to go fifty or so miles north of the Trans-Canada Highway to meet our spectacular predecessors, who died prematurely ninety million years ago?

I felt a certain panic when I went into the tiny Drumheller museum and was greeted by a gigantic Edmontosaurus. He fills the whole room and if he were able to return to life for a brief second he could shatter the walls and ceilings with a single shake of his head. This skeleton, which does not lack a single articulation, was preserved in stone for seventy-five million years.

An amiable elderly lady told me the history of this monster and its fellows. For her it all took place yesterday. Man had not yet made his appearance on the earth, but it is clear that in her eyes we are but dim parasites in the great adventure of the earth — accidents, tiny pimples. Real history for this lady is just the part that covers the fifteen hundred million years before the appearance of man. She drew me fascinating pictures of things I had had much trouble memorizing when I was at school. Now it was all so clear.

Thanks to her explanations and the graphs she took from her drawer, I saw the first living cell become transformed into a multitude of invertebrates during the Cambrian period, then to fish, amphibia, and reptiles along the paleozoic ladder that stopped abruptly after about two hundred million years. Then the dinosaurs began to appear on earth, whose reign was to last for a hundred and twenty million years. Those that were found in the Drumheller region, and notably this Edmontosaurus (for whom I was beginning to feel a certain sympathy), died when the enormous mammals — who were to degenerate to the birth of man — began to spread into the four corners of the earth in search of fresh grass. Their great originality was to radically change the methods of reproduction then in use, and man owes it to their initiative of seventy million years ago that he does not have the painful and ridiculous obligation today of building a

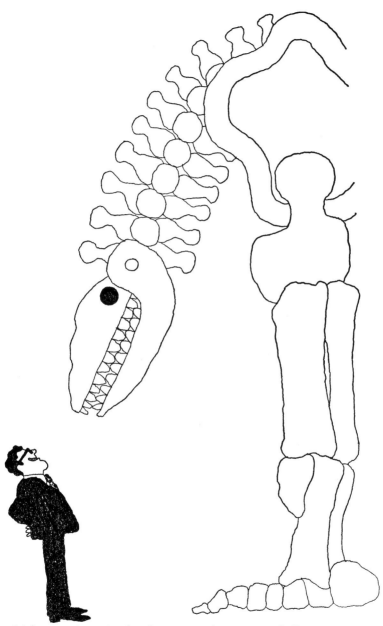

I felt a certain panic when I went into the tiny Drumheller museum and was greeted by a gigantic Edmontosaurus.

nest and incubating eggs. I raised my head at right angles; seen thus, on a slant, I could believe that the monster's jaw had moved a shade. He was undoubtedly smiling. These remarks had nothing to do with him. In his time, they knew how to extract tons of flesh and bone from a single little egg.

UNFORGETTABLE DAY AT HIGH RIVER   Even the smallest town in Alberta has its rodeo, so that you could make them the attraction of your vacation Sundays by simply travelling over a radius of a few hundred miles. The Calgary Stampede is by far the most important, but chance dictated that I should be present at the one old connoisseurs consider the most authentic and the most interesting. This is the stampede held at High River, about forty miles south of Calgary, on the road that leads to the U.S. border. Its chief point of interest lies in the fact that only young people of less than sixteen are eligible to enter the various competitions. The event takes place each year at the end of May and is directed to the local population.

With joy mixed with apprehension, I disguised myself for the occasion as a real cowboy. They have an expression in those parts to describe city-dwellers who amuse themselves playing 'western'. They are called 'dudes'. But had I any choice? My host had seen to all the details of my uniform himself. I quickly understood that at the High River rodeo it was better to be a 'dude' than a traveller in a business suit. Between two absurdities you must choose the lesser, and for me this was guarantee enough of the authenticity of the show.

The day began at ten o'clock in the morning in a shady garden. I was in the midst of a group of old farmers of the district discussing the thousand and one problems of cattle-raising, the quality of the stock, and the difficulties and dangers of the late spring. It had been awaited for long weeks and suddenly the grass grew at accelerated speed. I learned that bovines have all characteristics but continence. Already there had been several accidents reported in the region. Two cows had eaten so much that they had just given up the ghost. I felt myself somewhat of a barbarian to take this lightly. Each time it is a small tragedy. It is no good keeping thousands of heads of cattle; two cows represent a net loss of four hundred dollars. And these are always the two beasts to which one is particularly attached.

We were talking together when I heard the voice of my host, an old man, whose good face baked by the sun and the wind I shall always remember, 'Well, Gene, do you care for a rapid one before the parade?'

I wondered what could be the meaning of this sybilline expression, 'rapid one', at ten o'clock in the morning. His wife, assisted by a young girl, was already bringing glasses, bottles, and ice cubes. They immediately withdrew. The group had been increasing for several minutes. There were now about fifteen of us, men on one side of the garden, women on the other. I was introduced collectively as 'Gene, a French Canadian writer from Montreal'. For a moment everyone surrounded me and asked me amiable questions. They were a little timid, and so likable. They were all related and had come from a distance of a hundred miles around, to be present as a family at this annual event. I might have disturbed their habits, but in a very few minutes I felt myself essential to the equilibrium of the group.

The simplicity with which I was drawn in is a quality of rural milieus. Yet this family is composed of city-dwellers. It is clear that they were all well educated, that most of them have travelled a great deal, and that the men have fairly important careers in commerce or industry. One of them directs a sales and import company in the Coleman region. There were also a teacher, a banker, and a journalist. Two of the young girls teach in Calgary. But it was the ancestral chromosomes that triumphed today. My host alone, so deeply rooted in the soil of High River, was enough to create the atmosphere. The women in their light dresses and the men in their western uniforms had renounced their city personalities; we were all, for the day, old ranchers anxious to watch the young people handle the cattle. We would find out if the line is assured. And, talking about them and their future, we light-heartedly drank two, and then three, 'rapid ones'. On days of celebration one takes one's liquor neat on the ranch and, as I accompanied the group to the main street down which the opening parade would pass, I had every reason to believe that we weak city-dwellers possessed incredible reserves. It seemed to me that I had found my childhood legs again. I could have gone to the parade at a run. But I was careful not to, for it might have been thought . . . and besides, I was shown how to walk western-style. One plunges one's hands in the 'revolver-pockets', which are cut at a diagonal on each side of the thighs, and advances the leg while describing a quarter circle, which should recall the shape of the horse from which one has just dismounted. A 'dude' does not succeed at the first attempt. I went my way to the parade on the back of an enormous invisible horse.

The parade was unusual. In the first place it seemed that everyone in the village was in it. There were more people in the street than on the sidewalks. In its dress attire the brass band drew up in two ranks, drew out its notes, drew out its pace to make itself more important. A whole series of vintage cars from the remarkable collection of the Calgary Club banged cheerfully along without taking too much trouble to explain their participation in the event. Then came several floats, whose subjects referred to almost everything except rodeos, ranches, or cattle. There was even one, pleasantly conceived, on which one saw film censorship being cut in two by public opinion. This was a thrust against the incidents that had marked the appearance of *Tom Jones* in the West.

At last, four abreast, came the young boys and girls who would take part in the events of this important day. They were all in the saddle, but on young animals. This afternoon they would ride two-year-old bulls. The young faces, I saw, were anguished, serious, grave. Their eyes did not participate in their smiles. This time it was solemn and for keeps. I have seen this expression only in the eyes of matadors, when they seek the *muleta* for the final phase of the *corrida*.

Back in the garden, before charcoal fires where an unlikely number of beef fillets were grilling, while my host offered a few more 'rapid ones' to the reassembled group, I was still obsessed by the expression I had seen in the eyes of sixteen-year-old boys. This was not Spain. What I had believed to be the fear of the matador was only the hysterical anxiety of the child to prove himself in public. These young people would only perform this afternoon the exercises they had been practising for years on their fathers' ranches. For the sons of stock-breeders, all free days are rodeo days. I got back my serenity. And I finally accepted two or three more 'rapid ones' before lunch, with a courage equal to theirs. To each his little rodeo.

The events were to last from one until six o'clock. Some fifty young people in all would participate in thirty-two different events. It is enough to say that, despite the length of the display, the variety and number of the events would give it pace and rhythm.

I was seated beside the judges, on a little wooden platform, which overhung the entrances and exits of the horses and wild steers. The platform was jarred constantly by the movements of the animals enclosed in the passage that would soon give them access to the track. On several occasions we had the feeling that the whole structure was about to splinter and that we would be hurled upon the course with our notebooks. We did not need to read our programs to be convinced that these beasts were wild. As well, I was able to see how hard it was for the frail adolescents to mount in the precise second that preceded their appearance in the arena.

The crowd was seated in several rows . . . there were about ten thousand people. The first events threw clouds of dust upon them, which seemed not to bother them in the least. The sun was blazing, the sky cloudless, but the wind rose, throwing screens of dust in several directions, which put none of the spectators to flight. It was obvious that nothing could stop the show, and I was told that it had continued the first year in spite of a storm that would have discouraged spectators a little less broken in upon the various challenges of western life. This crowd was still close to the pioneers. I was to see on several other occasions that a certain stoicism is natural to them. And it is difficult to imagine such competitions, in which only young people under the age of sixteen participate, taking place in any other part of the country. The parents themselves must have learned to dominate the animals completely in order to permit their children to face them so calmly.

So I saw almost all the classic rodeo events, the greater part of which are very spectacular. The young riders had to remain till the whistle blew on the back of a horse or wild steer that had never been approached by man. The judging dealt not only with the length of this acrobatic prowess, but with style, with the difficulties offered by each beast, and with the technique and skill of the young horseman. Immediately before it entered the ring, just passing a cord or a girth around the belly of the beast was enough to make it completely mad. It sometimes achieved enormous leaps, and the contestant was inevitably flung into the dust. These falls are not without danger, and I remember the little girl of fourteen, for a moment unconscious, whom stretcher-bearers hastened to aid in the middle of the ring. She quickly came to, refused the stretcher, and stood up, her legs buckling. She was carried off by two men, struggling fiercely, with a cry of marvellous pride: 'Leave me alone, I'm not a baby, I know how to walk.' I have heard the same protestations some-where in Spain, in a tiny village, on the day of an impromptu novillada in the village square. Everything here reminded me of that universe of pride into which one is sometimes plunged without warning in Spain — a pride that might well be a dimension of dignity. And I was happy, very happy, to find its face here, in a tiny corner of my immense country.

In this age of the cinema I am not going to describe thirty-two different events in minute detail. I shall simply recall two — one of them truly graceful. Imagine dozens and dozens of foals, accustomed to the broad spaces of the ranches, thrust pell-mell into the relatively confined enclosure of the ring. At the same moment boys and girls, none of them more than ten years old, set out in pursuit of them. The test consisted in their catching one in a lasso, mastering it, and leading it back to the starting line. Only two succeeded, but the attention was drawn everywhere at once, and the victories were less amusing than the fruitless attempts. The event is absolutely without danger and the spectators can follow the performance of the animals and the children in an atmosphere of entire security. The second, the last, is the staple of all rodeos, including the celebrated Calgary Stampede — the chuckwagon race. The wagons were reduced here to the height of adolescents and three pairs of very young horses were hitched to each of the six vehicles on the track. The race was a mile. We followed the clouds of dust with rising interest. One could close one's eyes and still be informed about the progress of the two favourites by the waves of applause and the shouts of their supporters. At the end of the event, the victor made a circle of the ring and I saw the young girls run out, wishing to be the first to kiss him. He had now halted his wagon and stood in the entrance passage, letting a weary smile float out over the crowd of his admirers. He was not sixteen years old. But at this moment he had attained the splendour of a dream that had just been born: perhaps some day he would be one of the stars of the Calgary Stampede.

Sun, wind, and dust — our throats were dry. I was offered a number of 'rapid ones' and I was astonished to be still alive after a day already well laden with 'rapid ones'. But it was a festival day and, on festival days at High River, one must be able to drink often and neat if one does not wish to sully forever the already tottering reputation of city-dwellers. Everyone was waiting to see me suddenly crumple. What god protected me? I kept command of my sailboat. I shall not say that it did not jerk now and then, but I had the pride of sailing on this agitated sea with the sureness of an old sea captain.

CLOSED TO CITY-DWELLERS If one is a real lover of the prairies, as we imagine them, one must leave the road for a little, at Foremost, almost midway between the border of Montana and the town of Medicine Hat. Here is the Texas tradition. Ranchers tour their domains, high in the air, in their own aircraft. These farms have their own grain elevators, of a capacity of thirty-eight thousand bushels. Mechanical seeders cover strips fifty-eight feet wide, and all the equipment used here has been built for a race of giants. Not far from the farmhouses you can see landing fields. These are sometimes covered on Sundays with the private planes of neighbours come to have a friendly drink. The lightest of these aircraft will have cost twenty thousand dollars. Everything else is in keeping. And this also is an image of Canada.

I remembered the little vegetable garden of my childhood. My mother had managed to fertilize a corner of the inner court that had escaped being covered with asphalt. She was so patient about it that she might have been growing vegetables in the cellar. So for several weeks each summer we had fresh lettuce and tomatoes still warm from the sun. All this was the result of a miserable rectangle, great effort, and maternal science. And yet the results were so bountiful that I used to imagine that all the vegetables in our markets came from such tiny gardens. Later I realized that this poor little garden had always uncon-sciously served me as a standard in my appreciation of the rich-ness of a farm. Need I specify that these enormous expanses caused my measuring instrument to break and that henceforth nothing remained to me but a little green dust and a tender nostalgia?

IDLING IN EDMONTON Edmonton is a pretty city — pretty in the absolute, because harmonious. A city can be attractive without resembling Paris, Rome, or San Francisco. The streets and ave-nues are distributed fairly equally on both sides of the North Saskatchewan River, a sinuous river, a sort of green serpent that glides throughout the interior of the city. Never set about follow-ing its course; you will turn back again in your steps. Bridges have been built across it but there are not enough of them. As the river divides the city fairly equally into a northern section and a southern section and you will rarely have the privilege of living on the same side as your work, the principal arteries are literally blocked at the closing of plants and offices.

I very much like the way the banks of the river have been left in their natural state, even in the heart of Edmonton. Every time I got off the elevator on the fourteenth floor in that enormous and pleasant structure that is the Macdonald Hotel, a window outlined a romantic landscape, a corner of French countryside, between an array of new apartment buildings. River, poplars, and aspens — I could even see a little footpath that lovers must take in the evenings. Yet we were right in the centre of town and I had only to cross the hall to be caught up in the joyous stir of Jasper Avenue.

I did not find in Edmonton's commercial streets the slightly artificial atmosphere shared by several of the other cities of western Canada. The big stores were there, sure of themselves, as were the banks, cinemas, and restaurants. In the middle of a rectangle of pleasant but dilapidated old buildings, which are soon to be torn down for the establishment of a civic centre of the Place Ville-Marie family, is the new, gleaming city hall, of an architectural concept that will soon have spread everywhere, like that of airports.

FEMININE CIRCLES   An image I associate with Edmonton, though it belongs actually to the daily existence of several cities of the West, is women's groups. Don't misunderstand. The city has a respectable number of social, cultural and charitable movements, directed by young, and less young, women, as do all cities of the British tradition, whether in Canada, Singapore, Australia, or Ceylon. But it is not of these pious movements that I am thinking. I can still see those restaurant tables invaded by clusters of blonde heads and smiles of all ages. Everywhere I went, there they were. They frolicked, they were gay. Man had become such a tiresome animal that not a single representative of the species was admitted to these segregated lovefeasts.

Where did they come from? I was given a thousand answers. Sometimes it was a bridge club, celebrating a victory of its members. Sometimes the youngest of the group was leaving on a journey. Sometimes it was the end of the school year, sometimes . . . it was nothing at all, they simply wished to have tea together every Wednesday, or Thursday, or Friday. I used to count heads; there would be ten, twelve, or fourteen. They occupied the centre of the restaurant or tea-shop. Tables had been drawn together, chairs pulled close — you would have thought they were a table of conspirators. And there was something liberated, something joyously masterful in their eyes. I felt that these Edmonton women were giving the impression in this way that they were living a great adventure of emancipation. The suffragettes of the last century must have resembled them. Now that others had succeeded in winning social, political, and economic equality for them, they intended perhaps to assert their independence of man. It was an image at once charming and pathetic. I should be more inclined to believe that they were trying to while away their boredom. In our modern society man is so attracted by advancement that our women must also launch themselves on the labour market if they are not to perish of solitude and loneliness. The multiplication of women's groups in our cities is a symptom. These informal groups that are being formed with an accelerating rhythm confirm the malaise. Man is already absent from the daily life of our women. He is in process of deserting their minds, and hearts. A sociologist might believe that men and women — and the phenomenon is not to be observed only in America — have begun to travel along parallel ways. It is still possible to build bridges at all points of their journey. But the more the roads part, the more costly and artificial bridges become. Perhaps the generations of the future will be the products of electronic brains.

PORTRAIT OF MR KOWTON   During the last war, Edmonton was an important centre for our armed services. There are still signs of this today, notably the multiplicity of airports. As well as the international airport, a marvel of modern architecture, and that of the private flying clubs, there is of course the industrial airport, almost in the city, a few minutes from downtown. It was in that direction I was driving in the car of Mr Kowton, the executive secretary of the Edmonton Area Industrial Development Association.

Kowton had the personality of those young businessmen who abound in Hollywood movies. They are young and peaceful lions. Their teeth are long but not very sharp. They concentrate for a moment to give you an outline of the news you have read in your daily paper. Their aggressiveness is smiling. It is exerted upon no one but is only a glorious affirmation of their dominance over life. They are handsome to look at. Even when they are confronted with the worst difficulties, you will see them wearing their cocktail smiles, well adjusted, as if television cameras had been hidden here and there in the walls of the room. But at this moment Mr Kowton was anxious. He was not sure that he wasn't losing some precious time. A writer? But what would he be able to tell? And just where did he come from? And for whom exactly was he gathering his information? He knew I had visited the French-speaking parts of the city, and that some friends had acted as my guides. Had they been able to show me the real beauties of the city, enable me to guess its exceptional resources, convince me of its unforeseeable future? A population of four thousand in 1901, of more than three hundred and twenty thousand in 1966. If my researches were really serious, why had I conducted them until now with amateurs? It was his particular mission to instruct journalists or curious writers. He had at his disposal all the figures, all the graphs, all the means. And he was well able to prove this to me this morning, since he was putting a helicopter at my disposal.

Yes indeed, we were going to fly over Edmonton and its surroundings, we were going to go as far as Duke and see the big refineries and factories. Mr Kowton was smiling but I still felt that he was anxious. He was in the habit of piloting groups of businessmen interested in the industrial and commercial possibilities of the region from the viewpoint of definite projects, sometimes distant but still definite. They had an industry to launch or a sales office to set up. They had questions one could always answer. Where would they find the personnel? In what section would they build the new factory? How much would the taxes be? Would not heating be a negligible factor in a province in which reserves of oil and natural gas abound? In what atmosphere would negotiations with the unions be conducted? But with writers, one never knows in advance. They ask utterly useless questions. They confuse plants for synthetic products with refineries. They scarcely look at the brand-new skyscraper apartment buildings that are beginning to proliferate on the shores of the North Saskatchewan, dominating a rural landscape that is only a few minutes by foot from the centre of the city. Rather than asking you for figures and graphs, they want to know whether the association for the industrial development of Edmonton is an original formula and you are forced to reply that it is not. It is embarrassing. They insist, they claim they are encountering this type of organization for the first time, at least in western Canada. You are obliged to admit that it was invented in the United States, where it was quickly found to be a working instrument of rare effectiveness. The expenses are assumed jointly by the municipalities and the enterprises. Mr Kowton was still smiling but he was more and more tempted to believe that the president of the Chamber of Commerce had put the helicopter at our disposal to no verifiable purpose. And in a sense he was right. Writers will never be in a position to appreciate in its totality the economic explosion that Alberta knows at the present moment. When I took my seat in the helicopter, even though my companion swore he would furnish me with all the explanations necessary in the air, I had the vague feeling that I was joining in a hunting expedition from which I would return empty-handed. Such game is for specialists.

However, I managed to get an impression, to fix certain images, and to retain certain figures. I shall simply toss them out in the order in which they are written in my notes. I saw the Technological Institute, whose installations were even more important than I had believed when I visited it on foot. Without transition I learned that Edmonton is in the second rank, immediately after Toronto, in the slaughtering of cattle. We went down almost to the level of the telephone wires to make a voyeur visit at the establishment of an oil company whose construction cost amounted to ninety-five million dollars. I also saw where the pipelines set out for Vancouver and for Sarnia, Ontario. One can count four hundred factories within the city limits. The volume of their production climbed from a hundred and nineteen millions in 1950 to four hundred and twenty millions last year. There would be excellent opportunities in the conversion industries from oil and natural gas, the two most important industries in the province. This particular point was insisted upon with such persuasive force that I regretted not having a few millions in my pocket. I was missing a good stroke of business, and I felt a bit abashed at having to confess that I was absolutely not in the position to seize such a rare opportunity.

Mr Kowton was no longer in the least anxious. His sense of humour had freed him from his first apprehensions. I must have communicated a little of my own euphoria to him, for I felt truly fortunate to be travelling above a great city on a day tinged only with joyous clouds. The engine wasn't too noisy and we could exchange confidences as long as we were willing to shout them a few inches from one another's ear-drums. All this was amusing, a little bizarre, and would find its place in a Chaplin film. I sensed that my companion was on the same pitch. He had forgotten his great books and his heavy responsibilities. I asked to see the university campus if it weren't too difficult. A sign to the pilot and we made a half-turn. A little outside the city, we dived to a few hundred feet from the ground. He showed me the new house he was having built, which dominated the whole region from a plateau. We saw that the workmen were conscientiously at work and I joined him in making friendly signs to his wife, who was returning along a still unsurfaced road with a spaniel . . . unless . . . the pilot went into a diving half-turn, it was indeed a spaniel. It was all most unreal, and fascinating.

Edmonton has no suburbs, which is the privilege of youthful cities. It cuts off abruptly into a bed of greenery. Public parks line the North Saskatchewan almost the length of its urban journey; now it coils across farms in complete freedom. The farms themselves are cut off at right angles, and their various buildings are set about an inner court, no doubt for protection against the rigours of our winters. On certain days in January the wind must blow from a great distance. From Calgary we constantly see the foothills of the Rockies. We are very far from them here. And although the city's altitude is something like two thousand feet, we could believe ourselves in the centre of the great western prairies. But if the prairies we have imagined always wore the face of the outskirts of Edmonton, they would be an image of paradise. I saw at every instant the farm where I could live. It recalled the gentleness, the peace, and also the richness of the English countryside — richness of trees, of colours, and of the buildings themselves. The born city-dweller can never be seduced by the beauties of country life unless no image of desolation or decrepitude is mingled with it. And unless isolation is not confused with solitude.

I was to have the occasion to meet some of these farmers. They have found the equilibrium for which we are all more or less seeking: they live their city lives while remaining in constant dialogue with mother nature. But I am letting myself be carried away. Let us return to useful work. The president of the Chamber of Commerce would not be pleased to learn that I had not taken any serious note aboard his helicopter. Let us show him: Alberta has been able to keep the second place in Canada in mineral production. As I write these lines, 11,426 oil wells are in production, 1,438 wells of natural gas, assuring a total production of almost seven hundred millions. Edmonton alone last year had a total cattle sale of 108 millions, its curing houses had a business figure of 132 millions, its wheat and cereal harvest was to the order of six million acres, and for those that would push intellectual curiosity to the point of perversion, let us add that the Holsteins of the Edmonton region alone poured into the economy all they were able to offer, which represented on the local market twelve millions in milk, butter, and cheese.

The helicopter had settled on the tarmac, but the engine was left running. They were no doubt about to set out again with another personage, who I hope was this time more important. Mr Kowton belongs to an air-borne organization that will never pay its expenses with vague writers.

Yukon Territory

TAHITI, YES INDEED   I am about to utter an enormity, and I am well aware of it: Whitehorse is Tahiti. I had this impression from the moment I arrived, I kept it all through my stay, and now when I come to think back after several weeks, Whitehorse is even more linked with Tahiti in my memory. Why should this be? Whitehorse is verifiably the opposite of Tahiti. I should not think that so close to the Arctic we are in danger of finding the marvellous climate of the south-sea paradises, eternal summer, palms, an easy life, vahines, great beaches of white sand, the sea, the lagoons, singing and dancing, and the most beautiful and indolent indigenous people of the world.

From the air Whitehorse is drawn cleanly upon a base of conifers, within an amphitheatre of very high mountains. When our DC-4 entered a diving turn in search of the runway, I felt for a moment sad at heart: to fly for hours and hours above an inviolate natural landscape to see this, a sort of large village, the sketch of a town, an abandoned barn, a corner grocery. I felt that I had been the victim of misrepresentations.

The aircraft settled, I entered the modest airport, and all at once I felt myself captured by an ambiance, a rhythm, which I had already known elsewhere but could not identify. Dozens of smiling faces awaited the travellers. Joyous remarks were exchanged with the newcomers, though none of the people waiting had come to meet them. They had come to talk. The airport is a salon where one talks. People come like this for each arrival of the planes from Edmonton or Vancouver. The aircraft had time to turn around and fly off towards Fairbanks while conversations were still continuing in little groups.

The airport is a place, a clubhouse, an autonomous entity. I was to understand later that it filled another function. The only proprietor of the single club in Whitehorse goes there each day to appraise the cargo and gives his card to those he thinks worthy to eat with him. For his club isn't open to everyone. You must have the key. Just for looking like a good customer, you receive the key, and the proprietor's card with it. But all this happens by stages. You will not be subjected at any moment to the slightest pressure. Several notables of the town go every day to meet the plane, first to converse with colleagues, then to ascertain the quality of the new arrivals, finally to help them. Several came spontaneously to me and questioned me out of simple curiosity.

My story quickly caught the attention of a little group. I was perhaps the first French Canadian writer ever to stray in that direction. I was studied from all sides with sympathetic interest. And from one group to another I fell upon the manager of the CBC station at Whitehorse. We immediately exchanged professional remarks. He had in fact been delegated to welcome me and to facilitate my first contacts with the town. When we left the little airport together, I looked at my watch. An hour had passed since I had landed. All this time had been devoted to the discovery of an exceptional mentality, an engaging charm, a solitude inhabited by men, a corner of earth where everything fades away before sentiment, fancy, smiles, the simple pleasure of talking together and dreaming a little. And at last I could identify my profound impression. It had been just like this when I arrived at Tahiti. Palms and sand and sea are perhaps merely accidents. The last paradises may owe their fascination to the human presence that permeates them.

PERHAPS RATHER A STEAMSHIP AT ANCHOR   I am going to utter another enormity. Whitehorse is not Tahiti, it is a cruise-ship — a ship of about ten classes. The first deck is inhabited by government officials. They are numerous. They form a society that is rather closed but of a certain quality. And for them the cruise will last only two or three years, so they don't get too accustomed to it. And what might be a nightmare for permanent residents becomes a source of entertainment to them. The first deck group also includes important personages like my first cicerone, the likable Hans Konow. If you believe that the CBC representative at Whitehorse could pass unnoticed . . . each time we walked in the town, he was the target of enthusiastic or reproving comments on the whole broadcast schedule of the English network. Someone would say, for instance, 'Your football game was terrific,' or 'Try to give us some livelier music. Your last concert was deadly.' So here he was carrying the entire CBC on his shoulders. Fortunately television is not his province. I arrived in the middle of a civil war about the movies presented over the closed circuit — a cheerful civil war, like all the little Whitehorse wars, which are settled finally over a bottle of whisky. The subscribers of this private company have to pay a hundred and twenty-five dollars for the station, thirty-five dollars to have the set installed, and fifteen dollars a month. In the whole town there are only about five hundred subscribers. But these subscribers form a society apart, united by the same grievances. They are shown only old movies, for which there is no market anywhere else. And I heard for the first time that phrase that was to return like a leitmotif: 'Anything is good enough for Whitehorse. In television as in food, we have to take what they give us.' Truly this town is dependent upon the outside for almost all the daily necessities. And the outside is several hundred miles away. One finally forgets the outside. Whitehorse is a cruise-ship, provisioned at sea. It never needs to return to port. One forgets that there are seaports at the end of the expanses that separate Whitehorse from all civilization. The news from Edmonton or Fairbanks comes to us as if filtered, with the same exotic accent as does the news of Montreal, Paris, or New York.

A cruise-ship on which all the passengers of the same class have free access to the various cabins. At certain hours of the day one can imagine that the little town has been transformed into an immense bar. You can enter a house and find a group gathered together for cocktails. But you don't even have to take the trouble. You will be seen from the window and invited to join the happy assembly. How many times, at the risk of my appointments, I was obliged to make such absolutely unforeseen stops on my program. Besides, it is ridiculous to make a program at Whitehorse. You will never be in a position to keep to it. During my whole stay at Whitehorse, I never once succeeded in meeting the people that were waiting for me at the moment we had fixed. Something always happened.

On the second-class deck you will meet the officials responsible for the maintenance of the famous Alaska Highway.

In third class are the characters, the originals, those that have fled here from complicated family situations. This is the class I prefer. And chance willed that I should know it rather well. It is full of slightly mad, intensely likable beings. Their intimate dramas carry them. They will never know mediocrity. Their marginal existence shelters them from routine and servitude. They have placed themselves in the category of the exceptional and they will never be able to escape it. It is at once a prison and a garden of wonders.

The fourth class is made up of a white proletariat. The town depends almost entirely upon the Edmonton region for food. It must be transported in refrigerated trucks over more than a thousand miles of roads that are sandy in summer and very dangerous in winter. These risks in transport are reckoned in figures. As always, it is the consumer who pays.

The fifth, sixth, and seventh classes of the ship would be occupied by the Indians of the region. In spite of all the government aid they receive, they remain on various levels of wretchedness and squalor.

The other classes are the squatters, most of them also Indians though there are a few whites among them. These are human rags. They came here in pursuit of the old dream of the Gold Rush. From failure to failure they tumbled to the bottom of the well they themselves had dug. But they represent only part of the leavings of a great and engaging adventure. They have given up, but the greater part manage to eke out a living. In the Yukon there are still almost two hundred isolated prospectors, we will have occasion to talk with the most picturesque of them. Meanwhile, the squatters have settled on municipal land and spent the winter — the mercury sometimes goes down here to 60 below zero — in cabins in which you would not leave your dog.

Yes, indeed. Whitehorse resembles a cruise-ship in a haunting way. It is clear that the upper classes are ignorant of everything that takes place in the hold.

THE MIDNIGHT SUN   It was only June. I waited for the night and the night did not come. Half the sky seemed to wish to grow dim but the other half remained as luminous as at four o'clock in the afternoon. We had just entered the summer cycle. So what does the sun do? I had learned once, but one always connects these notions with legend as long as they do not become incarnate. This evening it became incarnate for the first time. In a little town, surrounded by high mountains, miles and miles from all civilization, the sun went down as far as the line of the horizon on the other side of the mountain and refused to go any farther. As in Trenet's song, he sat in his armchair of clouds and after studying for some hours what nights are made of, he decided they were not worth prolonging indefinitely and began to climb up and up. This day would last for several months.

KINGDOM OF THE EXCEPTIONAL   Among the obsessed people that
these remote towns always manage to gather together, you will,
of course, find a number of bad eggs, who have been banished
from the city of their birth. But there are also simple victims
of life, often pure and disarmingly innocent.

There was a woman, trembling, of exquisite sensibility, who
lived her personal tragedy with infinite modesty. I shall never
know anything about her except that she has suffered atrocious-
ly. She is like a wounded doe. She performs a humble job, but
like a somnambulist. Her spirits wander in some other dimension. She does her work to the satisfaction of her employers,
but no one speaks to her any more; it is not worth the trouble
since she does not reply to the questions asked of her. Her only
remaining tie with material existence is her brand-new car. On
certain evenings she goes out and drives for hours along the
Alaska highway. At first people used to be anxious about her.
Now everyone knows she will return during the night. And they
believe that in her own way she is happy.

A REAL SEEKER FOR GOLD   And there was also the seeker for gold
in the tradition of those who shared in the great rush to the
Klondike. He seized me by the shoulders one evening after
dinner and begged me to extend my stay by a week. In a week
he would finally make his strike. In prospectors' slang this means
fortune, the vein, the nuggets, the shining metal at the bottom
of the trench, mixed with the sand and stone. His eyes beheld
the treasure. I asked him how long he had been searching. For
twenty-two years, he informed me. I looked at him attentively.
He must be about seventy-five. His face was wrinkled and bony,
his body ravaged. I got to know him well. He was a native of
Alberta, he owns a claim that is regularly registered — and he
has been digging about in it for twenty-two years.

Until he found his vocation as a prospector, he had wandered
from one job to another, without ever finding the way of life
that suited him. The Yukon suited him. It is the land of hope.
The expression is his own. For he spoke French, spoke it rather

well, but you would think I had brought him a revelation. He called everyone to witness the fine speech of France and made me do my little turn before the belated customers in the restaurant, several of whom surrounded us with sympathy. I felt like a little boy who had been asked to speak a piece. But he was so happy that I couldn't escape.

Later I saw where he lived. A modest room, in a comfortable enough house. But he lives there only at intervals. His real domain is the wooden cabin he built with his own hands on his claim. He sets out from town on foot and always manages to get a lift from a truck on the Alaska Highway. Only once did he have to walk with his knapsack the twenty miles that separate him from his kingdom. He needs to spend only a few dollars a week to keep himself alive, but where could he have been getting even this for twenty-two years? He had some savings at the beginning, and later his stubbornness must have moved some of his family. This at least was what I understood, for his nephew in Calgary wrote to him often. And furthermore he had just applied to the government for a grant. He was confident. His file was certainly remarkable. It was easy for him to demonstrate his good faith and also his unshakable confidence, after twenty-two years' systematic prospecting. The population of the Yukon is still so scanty that it hasn't its own government. The territory is administered by a federal commission. But I did not know that the commission was encouraging individual prospecting in a substantial way. I read for example in the Whitehorse newspaper under a two-column headline: 'The program of assistance to prospectors for the year 1964-65 is now in operation. It is addressed to all prospectors over the age of twenty-one, who can show their aptitude and the necessary means to carry out the work.'

Grants are nine hundred dollars a season, two-thirds as an advance and the final third sixty days later upon the proof of work accomplished. It was one of these grants that my seventy-five-year-old prospector had just applied for. His sole fear was that it might come too late, for it was now, or perhaps last month, that it would have been of most use to him. In a week he might be a millionaire. The Yukon, land of hope, as he expressed it himself. It would have been a happy expression on the lips of a young stallion of twenty-one; it came rather pathetically from an old man. Yet I could not quite consider him a victim. He knows how to live, eat, and dress, and how to behave in public. He has read, travelled, and reflected. He knows so many things that he perhaps knows how to provide a basis for the most dizzying hopes.

IN A PURE STATE   Whitehorse is to me a collection of personalities. Whenever I try to describe it physically it escapes me, it dissolves into a look, behind a smile; it borrows a face, mannerisms, a bearing. I have written many pages about Whitehorse and have said nothing about its museum — yet I spent long hours there; it is tiny but full of valuable documentation — nothing about its churches — ten in all, ten for a population of a few hundred people; the Catholics are very proud of the Cathedral of the Sacred Heart — nothing about the brand-new hotels, new streets, new houses, its residential neighbourhoods that have just risen from the ground, its huge municipal campgrounds, its swimming pools, its beaches, its lakes where you can catch trout as long as your arm, nothing about the Bamboo Club where Indians and high government officials mingle together to hear excellent jazz, nothing or very little about the Club 202, a key-club frequented by lovers of good food and good wine, the only decent restaurant in Whitehorse, run by a Netherlander of cheerful disposition, a collector of bearskins and hunting guns. But one cannot fool with one's memories. One city comes back to you in the form of a street, a moment, an encounter; another fixes itself in a face. Whitehorse has enclosed its essential truth in the beings that inhabit it and we should seek it vainly elsewhere. In spite of the beauty of its situation and the charms of its comfortable existence outside the limits of civilization, the traveller could overlook all these without needing to offer explanations. Men and women live there in an unreality that determines their behaviour. But is it really un-reality? It was in Whitehorse that I was able to measure the artificial character of our cities. Freed of a certain number of our conventions and driven to that fellow-feeling born of isolation, the people there live an existence truer than ours, and simpler too, that protects the sentimental values of which we have lost even the memory. Friendliness truly exists here, not the friendli-ness of Mr Carnegie, but real friendliness, that of adolescents. And love . . . I could tell a thousand stories of love that would tear this record apart. Not sophisticated anecdotes, more or less related to our marriage fair, but love in its most intense and most tragic dimensions. Whitehorse is essentially a human city and to catch a few palpitations of its soul, one must be able to question faces.

His name is Mr Wednesday. He is a young Indian. After quite a good education, he is employed by the government. His work consists of registering claims throughout the Yukon and sub-mitting the applications to the experts. For one has the right to a maximum of eight claims within an area of ten square miles. A claim measures 1500 feet by 1500 and one has to pay ten dollars a year to keep the right to prospect. Inspectors pass by in the course of the year to value the work done. If it is discovered that you have folded your arms, they might decide to cancel your rights. There are still about two hundred independent pros-pectors in the Yukon, some of whom still use the old techniques of the gold-seekers. Others have modern equipment and oversee their claims by helicopter. The soil of the Yukon still contains tons and tons of gold, but the time is over when you could just scrape the sands of its rivers to make a fortune in a few months. Today you have to work hard. Some workings are very pros-perous and make net profits of several thousands of dollars a year, without destroying the hope — common to all seekers for gold — of some day finding a vein large enough to unleash a new gold rush.

Mr Wednesday considers it very likely that the adventurers will eventually take the road to the Yukon again. Every day he registers new applications for claims and he has met several old prospectors who live retired on their property with very significant caches that they will not always be able to hide from the curiosity of reporters. One certainty was given to me by this sympathetic Wednesday — that most of today's gold-seekers make a profit; one can still find gold in the Yukon even if one isn't a mining company.

To learn all this I had to inform Mr Wednesday that I was an Indian myself. It was a sudden inspiration. And then there's no certainty it isn't the truth. My ancestor Zacharie, God love his soul, was a man who knew how to fill his leisure time. He began his career by acknowledging twenty-one children. And besides he lived at Ancienne Lorette. And besides, above all, a learned botanist-geographer claims that eighty per cent of French Canadians must have Indian blood in their veins and that this should be a matter of national pride. Be that as it may, in order to thaw out a Mr Wednesday who stubbornly insisted on considering me a superior being simply because of the colour of my skin, I presented myself with Huron descent. And surprise — and pleasant to boot — he found this Huron ancestry quite apparent. I even had the eyes and the forehead of his uncle, Black Crow. In short, I learned that even for an educated young Indian, brilliant, armed with an excellent job, and of very attractive appearance, life in the bosom of our society weighed rather heavily.

ACROSS THE YUKON It is not so simple to travel across the Yukon. Carcross is on one side, Mayo in the opposite direction, and Dawson is to the north, right at the mouth of the Klondike River. When it is not the tourist season you must get about by your own means. I was lucky enough to meet an American, newly come from Alaska, who invited me to accompany him on a trip he was making for an important company selling farm and business machines.

With him I drove about sixty miles along the Alaska Highway for the first time. It is very well constructed. It stretches across an overwhelming landscape built on a giant scale, which re-called my first trip across the Rockies. Snowy peaks rose here across curtains of mountains of four to six thousand feet.

The Canadian portion of the road is not surfaced. No one here seems to suffer from this. They have got used to the dust. In midsummer one drives with all the windows shut as pro-tection against the stones flung up at times by buses and trucks and breathes the dusty air of the air-conditioner. In winter, well, one never ventures out except in a caravan. In temperatures of sixty below zero the best cars can break down, and this would be certain death for travellers caught in the middle of this icy desert. I was not enjoying driving today in the suffocating heat with all the windows shut. And the continuous crackling of gravel against the car had a nightmare quality. When we picked up speed, the noise exploded like a stick of dynamite. My com-panion must have been a stock-car buff. He seemed close to intoxication. And he pressed the accelerator at the very moment I was about to beg him to slow down a little. But at eighty miles an hour the air rushed into the air-conditioner with such pres-sure that the atmosphere suddenly became fit to breathe. Even if our machine was floating upon exploding firecrackers, I made my decision and concentrated my attention upon the real beau-ties of the landscape.

Not a soul was alive. And suddenly Carcross appeared, right out of the photograph album of a prospector. Especially the little station. And the wooden hotel, just as in a Western movie. An outlet of Bennett Lake comes right into the little town. To cross it, we had to use the railway bridge, driving right along the tracks.

While my companion attended to his affairs, I walked about, then visited the paddle-wheel, *Tou-Shai*, which seemed to be awaiting travellers on its ramp. It was of course in drydock. For a moment visitors had forsaken it and I had to climb a rope ladder, then use the unusual staircase provided by the immense paddle-wheel to reach the main deck. The inside was completely empty of its furniture. I was able to imagine the atmosphere of a cabin only on the last deck. Here everything was still in place and the picture was very curious on board this phantom vessel. Double bunks, an armchair with a carved back, a mirror framed like the portraits of our grandfathers, and in a corner, on a low table, a pottery carafe and wash-basin. All the decks are trimmed with wooden lace.

I wandered for a long time in those empty rooms, which still seemed permeated with the slightly mad dreams of the travellers of the first half century. The trip up the Yukon was full of delirious joy. After incredible expeditions, one was finally approaching the goal. The return-trip was most often tinged with the disappointment, bitterness, and despair that still haunted the decks and the cabins.

ALL THAT REMAINS OF A GREAT EPIC   Dawson is the most frequently filmed city in the Yukon, not only in dramatic films, but for its own sake in half a dozen widely shown documentaries. Dawson, the poor little phantom city, the prisoner of its past. It reminded me of a lonely old man with his photograph albums. If you took his albums away from him, he would die. If you are not interested in the photographs in those albums, he is miserable.

Dawson is first of all a site. The little town sprawls along the banks of the Yukon, between screens of high mountains. But these mountains do not want us to cry out in admiration. They are as discreet as possible, round their backs, retire, and intertwine; they are themselves spectators. They have decided to leave the starring role to the main street of Dawson, as it was at the beginning of the century. You no longer have to make any effort of the imagination. The gold-seekers have gone, but their city remains and seems to hope for their eventual return. You need only look at the centre door of the Aurora Hotel — it is wide open. On the wooden sidewalk two old men sit smoking their pipes — 'Just as in those times.'

The little town through which I walked was only a vague marshy tract in 1896. Two years later, fifty thousand seekers for gold were camped here. They quickly built themselves shelters in a carnival atmosphere. I saw an announcement on a photo of 1898: 'Help wanted. Miners 15 dollars a day. Woodcutters, cooks, millers, name your own price.' Dawson, a slightly mad human dream, a living legend. We can only capture a fragment of its truth. As they rummage in their memories, each one finds only a few formless nuggets. Dawson deserves better than this. It is the golden sand, but it is also the river-bed, it is the river, and it is the host of men and women that it saw enclosed in their dreams, consuming themselves alive, sometimes with a smile.

LEAVING WHITEHORSE   It was very disappointing not to be able to find any acceptable way of going from Whitehorse to Yellowknife in the Northwest Territories. A few weeks later a bus would have taken me there, if I made frequent changes and were not too offended by an ultra-fantastic route, rather as if a Montrealer were to go to Quebec by way of Lake St John. In the final account, I would have to charter an aircraft and a pilot or go back to Edmonton and fly to the Northwest Territories with a rival company. Here it was a rather commonplace practice to charter an aircraft. The cost would vary between two and five hundred dollars, according to the type of plane, for only a few hours.

I will not say that there are as many aircraft for rent as there are cars, but year in and year out they are unrivalled for certain prospecting, fishing, or hunting expeditions. And I know a mine owner who rents an aircraft and a pilot for all his journeys about the Yukon with the same simplicity as we take a taxi in our cities. You call him and he says, 'Don't move. I'll be there in a few minutes,' as if he happened to be down at the corner. He is in fact several hours' drive away, but only twenty minutes by plane. I know very few people who are able to ignore so openly the contingencies arising from this domination of man over the machine. I for my part did not have to consult my bank manager to know my annual budget forbade any such elegant improvisation.

And I set out for Edmonton, telling myself that our great and unmeasured country would be less so perhaps on the day when all our cities were linked at once by train, road, and aircraft. Is this a dream? Not in the least. The way we still have to go in this direction is less than the distance already covered. I had just circulated quite easily in the Yukon, although the smallest journey would have represented a real expedition twenty-five years ago. Everywhere I found hotels, restaurants, and decent accommodation, often comparable to those of our most populous centres. The bulk of the structure is in place, we have only to tinker with it a little.

Some friends had come to say good-bye to me at the Whitehorse airport. They put so much warmth into it that this time I had no more doubts, it was Tahiti. There were misty eyes in this little farewell gathering. I looked about and saw that all the departing groups were similarly moved. And this was not the least charm of this little town, lost within its amphitheatre of mountains, those mountains planted miles and miles from all civilization.

Saskatchewan

THE FRANCOPHONE A GEOGRAPHICAL REALITY Between Edmonton and Saskatoon I could have stopped at any instant among French Canadians, stayed in little French Canadian hotels, eaten in French Canadian restaurants, entrusted my car to French Canadian garages, bought wheat, vegetables, wood, and coal from French Canadians. Outside Quebec our minorities are not a phenomenon of great weight in the ethnic design, but it was becoming more and more evident to me that French Canada is a geographic reality. Anyone who applied himself to it could travel from Vancouver to Halifax without leaving French Canadian milieus. Is this aspect of the phenomenon known? For me it was a revelation. And it is of the first importance. If you say that Saskatchewan has about sixty thousand French Canadians, only thirty-five thousand of whom really speak our language, you will be tempted to lose interest in their future. But if you say that these sixty thousand are present throughout the province, the importance of the geographical fact will give the poor ethnic reality exceptional dimensions. It is no longer a question of whether they speak good French or whether they truly share

French culture, it is enough to be aware that the only nation always present, just as is the anglophone element, is one of the co-founders of this country: the French Canadian nation.

AN UNEXPECTED EXPERIENCE I entered Saskatchewan, then, at Lloydminster, by Highway Number 5. I could have chatted for a long time with Barbeaus, Grégoires, and Élies. Farther south, at North Battleford, Doctor Gérard Breton would have been able to introduce me to dozens of French Canadian families. It would be like this until Prince Albert, and the whole length of my journey down to Saskatoon. All the pictures I have kept melt in my memory today into a single vision, a climate, an ambiance. It is called Domrémy. It is tiny, little more than a hamlet. The silos of its co-operative announce it from afar. I had made appointments, which I would miss. Here I was attracted by Domrémy, God knows why.

I knew no one there, and if by chance I entered into conversation with the old people of the place I would have trouble explaining the precise reasons for my visit. One must have reasons and they must be precise. That one comes from Quebec isn't necessarily a passport. There is an accumulation of grievances against Quebec in these little French Canadian centres, and a good deal of apprehension about the present direction of our province. And there was always the risk that my status of writer might close mouths just as they were about to become loquacious. For the moment I wanted to fill myself with an atmosphere without any precise end in mind, simply because I felt at ease at Domrémy. Try to make them understand that. They would think I must be one of those journalists who write alarmist articles about the condition of French Canadians. I would confuse a peaceful life with poverty, simplicity of manners with ignorance, peace of heart with lack of ambition.

The sun struck down hard on the village; it was early afternoon. I decided to leave my car in front of the church, which is always a good point of reference. Lunch-hour wasn't yet over at the high school across the street. Young boys between the ages of ten and twenty gathered together to help manoeuvre the Martian that had somehow got lost here. I walked straight towards them. Their ranks suddenly grew sparse until there were only two adolescents left to confront this stranger that was I. Our conversation commenced rather limpingly. Yet these young people spoke a French whose quality surprised me. They addressed me through an invisible door, that door one shuts against salesmen. But they were quickly made to understand that I had nothing to sell them, that on the contrary I was in search of new friendships, new images of my country. And we came together in a climate of mutual sympathy. Now they hid nothing from me of all they knew about Domrémy. No, all the young people here did not speak as perfect French as they did. In their case it was a sort of accident. They weren't just sure why. Their parents had insisted. When they were children they had been denied dessert each time they sinned too gravely against the French language. I had heard this same refrain around Maillardville, and it made me feel very sad. They went to a public high school, and, as in all the public high schools, French was taught for only an hour a day. Otherwise one had to learn at home. But as one young person in two has to find employment elsewhere when he grows up, the little settlement is of course obliged to give first place to English. Otherwise the responsibility would be great: cripples would be cast into the labour market.

So . . . in a small village as in a big city, the problem is posed with the same sharpness: attachment to French language and culture is just as gratuitous and unreal as it was in Quebec at the time of the conquest. But it exists. It is utterly unlikely but it exists, and we have an obligation to take account of it.

A bell was heard: lunch-hour was over. My two companions took leave of me, extending their hands spontaneously in the best French tradition. Language isn't only a means of communication, it is also a way of thinking, a behaviour, a state of soul, a sensitivity. I would not soon forget that handshake I had done nothing to solicit.

I walked and walked in the dusty streets of Domrémy. Not a soul stirred. Everyone must be having a siesta. Well, no. Curtains quivered in windows. I saw heads and eyes here and there, crests of a wave of curiosity that moved as I moved. I stopped in front of the *Caisse populaire*, to read the notice of the hours of business. In these French Canadian hamlets the manager of the *Caisse* is ordinarily, with the curé, the best source of information. I already knew that the curé had gone on mission for the entire day, and I saw now that the manager would not be back for half an hour. But wait! I hadn't knocked on the door and I felt it suddenly alive. No doubt my approach had been spied, and someone would come through to meet me from the apartment I guessed to be at the back. Well, I would not knock at the door for I had had another idea. A moment before, as I passed the windows of the general store, I had noticed a man watching me pass with an open, rather troubling hostility whose reason I must now try to find out.

I retraced my steps. The man was still there, and now his wife was with him. He hurried behind the counter as soon as I commenced to climb the few steps that separated me from his observatory. His wife, who was still young and beautiful, drew back slightly and blushed like a young girl as I came in and addressed her in French. She admitted later that she had taken me for a government inspector. An inspector of what? I ask you. One might believe that these little French Canadian hamlets suffer from a bad conscience. Or perhaps they feel there is something illegal about their very existence.

As soon as I had introduced myself, the young woman became pleasant, relaxed, and smiling. Her husband refused to raise his eyes from his newspaper. He remained bowed over the counter, wearing an absent-minded look, but he did not miss a word of our conversation. I spent a quarter of an hour there by my watch but he never raised his eyes from the news item that seemed to fascinate him, though he wouldn't have fooled anyone. From time to time the young woman spoke his name to ask him to answer some question I had just put to her. Then he sighed heavily and muttered a few words in an incredible accent made up of Swiss, Belgian, and Canadian tones. But he always slipped soon into English, which he spoke a little more intelligibly.

They were from Europe. I merely wanted to know what was behind a hostility so open and gratuitous. I found out finally, or rather I was in a position to have an inkling. There was more in it than peasant timidity, which takes all possible forms, according to the place and the hour. No, this was something intimate and very intense. He was revenging himself upon me for his frustrations. I realized that this man had never managed to get himself accepted by the village, because he did not belong to the few families with which it was stocked. He was a graft. Everyone was willing to buy his merchandise, but he would grow old in his solitude. And I was once more confronted with a fact that I would find in almost all hamlets and villages, whether they were English, French, German, or Ukrainian, in Canada or some other country: the man had come, as city people often do, to attach himself to one of those little places, the apparent serenity of which enchants us. What we took first for a smooth and peaceful existence is only a spider's web. At its centre are those that quietly watch their prey and others that are slowly nibbled.

I took leave of the little man in a tone I hoped showed some of the sympathy he aroused in me. He finally raised his eyes and looked at me, and a brief smile passed over his features. And his horrible little face became for that moment very beautiful. All human beings who suffer have a treasure in their heart and the better to protect it, they cover it with unpleasantness.

PORTRAIT OF A PIONEER   If I had never strolled through this lost little central Saskatchewan hamlet, I should never have made the acquaintance of Henri Baudais. 'Just turn to the right,' I was told, 'up by the cemetery.' The last was said rather meaningfully, as if to tell me that Baudais had chosen to bury himself alive. He was seldom seen any more in town. He lived alone in his big house, did a little gardening, watched his fields and his crops, without putting his heart in it, for he was now retired.

I expected to meet a sort of wild man, a misanthrope, but there before me was a highly civilized person, who still carried the weight of all humanity. He was well informed about all the international problems. Physically, he belongs to the type of the western pioneer. He displaces a great deal of air as he passes. He is massive and enormous, with a stentorian voice. He could absorb a pint of bad brandy without being any more deranged than after a cup of tea. He still has some property, a farm, some income, the result of relentless work after a seemingly hopeless start. He is sixty-seven years old.

His father arrived in Saskatchewan with fifteen dollars in his pocket. It was 1900. He settled his family in a shack and began to clear the land, and his life was organized in the atmosphere of improvisation that you can guess. Soon came the Baribauds and Duvals from Quebec, the Blondeaus from the Jura, the Guillets from France. They all helped one another and agreed to the division of the land. This was the beginning of Domrémy. Everything was going fairly well when along came the Dorion Policy, as it was already known at Duck Lake. 'You must legalize your situation, make your request to the land office, which will give you a lot of so many acres for a ten-dollar fee, renewable every three years.' And so the squatters obtained colonist status.

The stories of that time are all very highly coloured. Baudais told me dozens. I have remembered only the one about Père Amyot. He was a real old fox. The proprietor of the general store at Duck Lake, he held a great part of the neighbouring population under his tutelage by means of credit. Suddenly he had a brilliant idea. Anyone who wanted could have ten cows in return for half the calves obtained by the valuable help of these innocent beasts. Just imagine the size of the Amyot herd in a few years. Without knowing it, Amyot had reinvented the serfdom of the Middle Ages. When he took half the calves, he also took back his ten cows, and the wheel began to turn again. It was this system that permitted Baudais Senior to start in business. He finally won his independence with a great struggle.

Baudais told me the story of his family in snatches but without the slightest complacency. He gave me the impression that all the people in the village could tell as much. He kept his moments of euphoria for the description of the building of the first bridge, near St Louis, at temperatures of 50 below zero. But he reached his greatest heights when he flung out, in a voice that would have been enough to discourage Alexander Graham Bell from inventing the telephone: 'I saw them laying steel at Wachaw.'

He was only thirteen in 1910, when the Grand Trunk first appeared in the region. With steel came what Baudais called the era of 'automation'. The word startled me, but he did not notice. He meant that rail transportation changed the habits of the most remote regions, flooding the area with tractors and the whole range of machinery so well established today. The only difficult moment, with which so many stories had made me familiar, was the seven plagues of Egypt that struck the central part of Saskatchewan with particular violence: the depression of 1930, drought, grasshoppers, and so on. Beef sold for four cents a pound, pork for two and half, a bushel of wheat for from twenty to thirty cents, oats for from four to six cents a bushel, barley for twelve cents. On the whole, the selling price recovered only a part of the costs. And this did not take into account the work. But it was necessary to produce if one did not wish to die of hunger. Some fled from Saskatchewan. Many made their way to British Columbia. The Baudais family dug in, the war came and with it prosperity, a measure of prosperity. Baudais paused. I could feel that to his mind this prosperity brought by the war had settled nothing at all. I respected his silence. He poured himself a generous hooker of brandy and swallowed it at a gulp. He laid down his glass with a click of his tongue.

He looked at me and declared, 'The war wasted everything. Wars always waste everything.'

He was thinking of the young. Since the war, the young people have been lost to the farms. They dream only of sports cars, the city, the movies, pretty girls, and easy living.

'Yes, monsieur,' he insisted. 'The young got a taste for the outside.' And he added, 'Take a walk in our fields. You will see far more old men than young fellows on our beautiful tractors.'

I believe that Baudais is exaggerating. And even if his reproach is well-founded, serious anxiety would be uncalled-for. If the young men from the country are deserting the prairies, city people have quickly jumped on the tractors they abandoned. For since the opening up of the Chinese and Russian markets, the grain elevators have been filled only to be unloaded into freight cars. Not only are wheat and oats good business, they have become the two trump cards in our foreign trade.

And in our central provinces, you had better not express the slightest reservation about the Diefenbaker régime. Baudais for one would be quite capable of putting you out of the house. For him Diefenbaker is a sort of God — the one who dared to break the vicious circle in which our wheat sales were caught. This might be debated, but not with Baudais.

SEAMEN OF THE LAND   I resumed my journey to Saskatoon. I had been told so often that I would find the landscape monotonous because of its flat expanses and its uniformity that I felt I was driving through a luxuriant region. The slightest hill seemed a mountain peak, a grove of trees took on the dimensions of a forest, and if by chance the road approached the banks of the North Saskatchewan, I believed I was somewhere in the Chaudière valley. This was certainly an optical illusion and endured only as long as I did not find a perfect coincidence between the vision I expected and what I found. When I drove about the southern part of the province a few days later, I saw very clearly that Saskatchewan offers not the slightest foothold for the alpinist. For many miles I saw nothing but field after field stretching into infinity . . . and one trembles at the thought of what it must become in winter. Nothing here could contain the unleashed winds of our winters. One could die of cold if one did not see the storm approach in time. And people do die of cold on these roads, in the middle of the twentieth century, in big ultra-modern cars.

The wind, the sky, the winter storms, and the splendours of the sun haunt the literature of Saskatchewan. These conquerors of the prairies are seamen of the land. Their childhood unfolded in the infinite. The eye looks into the infinite, the wind blows from the infinite, the sun rises out of the infinite only to perish soon in the infinite. But we do not find the same tragic sense in their writings that we do among the Russians, who are sometimes at grips with the same violences of nature. In the literature of Saskatchewan and the other prairie provinces there is a sort of familiarity with forces that everywhere else are considered scourges. I remember a certain page by W. O. Mitchell in which he describes a snowstorm with a certain fellow-feeling, so that it is not easy to tell whether he saw this grandiose spectacle from the stage or from a very comfortable loge in the theatre: 'A tin can rolled in the street, a newspaper plastered itself against the base of a telephone pole' — the description begins like a simple, almost friendly thing. And he who has seen the wind is finally very much closer to the characters of Lamartine than to Shakespeare's universe. And yet there can be doubt that a storm on the Saskatchewan belongs to Shakespeare's universe. The rest bears witness in its own way to man's incredible resources for adapting himself to his environment.

THE DISCOVERY OF SASKATOON The trunk of the western maple is deeply carved. The design of the veins stands out as cleanly as Moorish lace. The indentations of the leaf are open to the stem. The leaf of the western maple spreads like a hand. It is this magnificent tree that abounds on the banks of the South Saskatchewan River where it runs through Saskatoon. Its sustained green gives a rhythm to the whole of the river landscape, which is accentuated by groves of poplars, aspens, and elms.

I am not quite sure what I expected when I arrived at Saskatoon. The cinema has neglected this little city, writers do not speak of it, its name is unknown to poets, and it is not precisely the centre of events. Is it because I was unable to imagine it ahead of time that I felt such affection for Saskatoon? It has broad avenues, little shady streets, and above all the river, which flows right through the centre of the city without losing its rural look. Saskatoon is called 'the City of Bridges', but I do not believe that its bridges are its chief interest. Several centuries of civilization are needed to integrate the silhouette of a bridge into the rhythm of a landscape. No, let us admit it, these bridges are of a pleasant ugliness. And yet they have not managed to mar Saskatoon. So what does this little city possess? Nothing, actually. Not the smallest mountain as a backdrop, the architecture of the houses is nondescript, the audacity of some of the modern buildings contrasts gracelessly with the general heavy, English style, and yet you will be captured by the city's quiet, peaceful, and harmonious charm. And there is the word that fits it best: Saskatoon is harmonious. It is a healthy plant, a polished stone, a sparkling window. This harmony is present all along the river, where you could walk for long hours in those shady avenues only a few minutes from the centre of the city. It is present also in the faces and in the expressions. Here is an active city that does not yet know the faults of the great metropolises. The comings and goings of people and cars have something muted about them. The noise is not irksome. The haste of pedestrians has nothing hysterical about it. You know you could interrupt the general movement at your will without creating the least congestion. The air was dry in this first week of June, as it is in all the prairie provinces, but the sun penetrates it without burning. I do not believe there is pleasanter air to breathe anywhere in the world than in Saskatoon during the first weeks of June. And then Saskatoon has the Bessborough, and without that it would lose an essential dimension.

SUCH A PLEASANT HOTEL   Till now I have never mentioned the hotels where I stayed except to amuse myself a little. Not deliberately but because they are so utterly extraordinary. Those huge stone and brick châteaus that our railways have scattered over most of Canada are unreal, rococo, but very comfortable. Most of them would be 'in red' in the Michelin Guide, because of their comfort, the quality of their service, and the pleasure the traveller feels from the moment he arrives. I don't know one that is comparable to the Bessborough of Saskatoon. It is the newest in the CNR chain of hotels. But this is not what gives it its interest. Its charm perhaps comes from the role it plays in the social life of the city.

One is suddenly aware that, alongside the functions it fills for visitors and conventions, it has been adopted by the population of Saskatoon for its business meetings, its study groups, its occasional dinners, even its chief social affairs. When I happened to be unable to reach an acquaintance by phone, I had a good chance of finding him in one of the public rooms of the Bessborough. In the course of my investigations into other matters, I learned that during the winter the ballroom of the Bessborough becomes a sort of private club every Saturday night available to the entire city. Its restaurant is of exceptional quality. Limits to the consumption of alcoholic beverages are as capricious as elsewhere, but easier to bear: they are applied without any trace of sadism, with frank apologies, and I predict that Saskatoon will be one of the first cities of western Canada to free itself from servitude to an archaic puritanism.

I open the window of my room: it overlooks Kinsmen's Park, the river, and beyond, slightly raised, the university city, built of grey stone from the bed of the Saskatchewan River, which at the end of day takes on the tawny hues of Moroccan murals. It is all discreet, secretly animated, and it enchants me.

LIFE BEGINS AT SEVENTY It is a well-known phenomenon that western Canada takes care of its old people. There are no more fitted-up barracks but real garden cities. Everything has been devised to keep the spectre of death at a distance. I have known some who have experienced the pleasant things of life for the first time at seventy.

At Saskatoon there is Mount Royal Lodge. It is a model of its sort, probably borrowed from the great American achievements. I do not believe Mount Royal Lodge has its equivalent anywhere in Canada. And I understood why everyone had insisted upon showing it to me. I felt not the slightest desire to see it. The image of old age is melancholy, because it is promised to us. We who walk with a brisk step will also know muscular pains, shortness of breath, a mist over our eyes, humming in our ears, even if we escape the more bitter sufferings of old age. For Mount Royal Lodge is not a hospital but a resort. Theoretically only old people in good health are received there. There is a central building where the widowed and single live — men on one side, women on the other — and almost a hundred ultra-modern apartments grouped by twos in attractive houses. All this is on a rise of land, overlooking one of the most beautiful parts of the city, and the air there is of the purest. There are common-rooms, television, a library, an amusement program, bridge tournaments . . .

This is a kindly idea, but is it as humane as it seems to be? It is still too soon to judge. I only know that while I was visiting it, my heart was in pieces. And I could not help thinking that all these old people had been crowded together into the anteroom of death. Anywhere else they might have been able to forget it. Here, as soon as they go into the corridor, they see the fatal work on the features of their neighbours. But it is a kindly idea, for Mount Royal Lodge is a private institution, entirely non-profit-making; the directors are elected each year and offer their professional services without fee. But there is a certain obliviousness and a good deal of insensitivity in these American formulae. I still prefer the Scandinavian institutions that leave the old people their entire individuality. They are provided with apartments at a modest rent and protected from insecurity, hunger, cold, and illness. But they are not forced to live a community life.

In Mount Royal Lodge I see yet another sign of that process of socialization that is continuing in our capitalist societies. The concept of the individual has been tossed to the four winds.

Here old age is an abstraction. This institution corresponds perfectly with the needs of old age but not of old people. Is this good or evil? I could not say. I only know I should not wish that anyone dear to me, or I myself, should end his days in one of these magnificent old-age inns, where the inmates travel towards death together in the luxury and comfort of a first-class carriage, without being able to forget for a moment the place of destination. These institutions will finally be equipped with a secretariat run by funeral directors to which the boarders will be invited to come to choose — at their ease — their oak coffin or cemetery lot. I am not exaggerating very much. These places are haunted by all sorts of preoccupations that would seem sordid if they were addressed to an individual. Their nobility or their generosity can delude us because they have reference to a social class that we have too openly neglected.

THE CAMPUS OF GREY STONE   The English have the expression 'Bricks before Brains' to express the idea. The containers are often more remarkable than the contents. Publishers prosper before writers, art galleries attract more attention than painters, university campuses exist long before students and professors, and I have seen very poor faculties operating in ultra-modern settings that the great European universities are not yet in a position to offer. The phenomenon is particularly verifiable at Saskatoon. The city wasn't yet a year old, and the whole province not yet three, when the government decided to establish a campus of thirty-two hundred acres on the banks of the Saskatchewan River. It was the 3rd of April 1907. The campus now contains 6,900 students, and fifty buildings, only a few of which belong to affiliated institutions. A third of these buildings have made their appearance in the course of the last fifteen years, and a half-dozen others are about to be added as part of a program of expansion that aims to absorb the growing flood of new admissions, of the order of eight thousand in 1967. As I write these lines, I have visited all the university campuses of the West. The one in Saskatoon is not the biggest, nor the most important, but it is the most harmonious — a word that comes to me often and without effort when I speak of this little city — harmonious because most of the buildings have been built of a local stone, taken from the bed of the river, the 'greystone' whose tints vary with the light. The style is collegiate Gothic. I like those windows made of little squares enclosed in metal, I like those gables and turrets. It is as if dozens of manor-houses had met together on these lawns among all the varieties of trees and flowers.

THE MOST UNEXPECTED INCIDENT OF MY LONG CANADIAN PEREGRI-NATION From the outside the Intercontinental Packers plant looks like an immense army barracks. It is a maze of one-storey structures, except for the administration building, whose rise dominates the whole like an observation post. As you enter you are struck by a persistent odour of fresh blood. There is an air-conditioning system, but when it is time to kill the cattle, all the installations of the factory are more or less bathed in those ex-halations, to which it seems our nostrils very quickly become accustomed. Young secretaries come and go, type documents, work electronic machines, stop for a moment to tell a neighbour about last night's date or week-end plans, seeming not in the least disturbed. Perhaps we are all born murderers. Even dogs could not remain more than an hour in this atmosphere without nausea.

Before I was shown around the plant, I was to be presented to Mr Mendel, the owner. He has his office on the second floor. Wide doors were opened and I saw a simple staircase, which reminded me of certain European apartment houses, but I had no time to examine it; my glance was caught by an incredible profusion of canvases hanging on the wall, sometimes in several rows. There were Fashbenders, Poliakoffs, I thought I recognized a Suzuki, a painter I had known in Japan and for whom I feel the greatest esteem. Frankly it took my breath away. I had come to inspect an abattoir and here I was in a museum. Nor was this all. At the top of the stairs a series of three art galleries formed the antechamber to the boss's office. I had not eyes enough to see everything. There was a magnificent Riopelle, one of the first canvases he sold in Paris after he had ruthlessly renounced the figure in favour of rhythm and colour; there was an Estève of 1952, one of the most austere painters of the French School, whom only a great connoisseur would have bought in 1952. I saw a Buffet of the first manner, a Marcoussis, a Dufy, another Dufy, a Max Ernst, a Venard, and in another little adjoining hall some Canadians: a Morrice, a Lakson, a 1915 MacDonald, an Emily Carr.

The owner surprised me in the midst of my euphoria. Introductions were easy and pleasant. Mendel is seventy-five but he has the eyes of a youth of twenty and he is as supple as a hare. Though very short and slim, he has the gift of presence. He has suppressed any notion of size. If he wishes to give a haughty look, he does not rise up on his toes so we can see him better. He ordinarily directs his glance downwards as if you were even shorter than he is. And in this one trait of behaviour, he told me his whole life. One must have learned to dominate everything around one in order to dominate oneself with such ease. He has none of those rather pitiful little devices of all the short men I have known. He is in no hurry to have you sit down. Seeing my interest in his collection of pictures, he offered to show me all his treasures. They are innumerable.

In passing I noted Chato's portrait of Colette. In another room there was an unusual Van Dongen — unusual at least in the price one could obtain today for this canvas of 1903, when Van Dongen was amusing himself painting horses. All the rooms were filled with marvels.

Before the war Mendel raised horses in Hungary. Like all the rich men of his country, he spent several months of each year in Paris. In this way he made his discoveries, for they were real discoveries. Certain of these canvases, which are now worth small fortunes, he obtained for ridiculous prices. He possessed the most essential quality of the collector: flair. As we went along a poorly lighted corridor, I noticed about fifty canvases, carefully and somewhat obsessively portraying various sorts of food. There were sausages, hams, potatoes, roasts of beef, depicted with an incredible attention to realism. There was a roast of lamb you would be glad to put on your table. I might have burst out laughing if Mendel had not told me the sad story. These paintings are the work of a young Austrian painter, Eric Schmidt, who was literally dying of starvation in Paris. Finally, because of his deprivations, he developed a real neurosis. He could no longer paint anything but food, the permanent object of his desire. Mendel met him and systematically bought all his canvases as soon as he finished them. Schmidt's circumstances improved, which quickly helped him free himself of his obsession. I have seen his most recent canvases, of which Mendel is not the only purchaser. They are joyous but now abstract. They have great style. Schmidt is considered one of the hopes of the French school. This story is enough to show not only Mendel's flair but his generosity. We will see that he had genius.

He is a Hungarian Jew, who found himself in Paris when war was declared in 1939. He was returning, I believe, with his wife and two daughters, from the New York World's Fair and had intended to journey quietly back to Hungary after a few weeks in Paris. Instead he abandoned all his possessions in Hungary and returned at once to America. Possessors of great fortunes can always count in moments of distress upon some holdings outside the country. But in 1939, when Mendel and his family gathered together in New York, it was no longer a multimillionaire, it was not even a rich man who must begin his life over again at fifty; it was a man of goodwill, who could count only on some valuable connections. He was later able to save his collection of paintings and some liquid assets in Switzerland. He had no more news of his Hungarian ranch, his property, or his relatives. He was on another planet; he knew French better than English, and I repeat that he was fifty and had as his only resource the will to begin again. After innumerable fruitless attempts, and only four years after the beginning of his exile, he was in Saskatoon, at the head of a small business that would become in a few years the very important Intercontinental Packers Ltd.

His success has surpassed his hopes and I do not see what could threaten him. Thanks to him, the raising of beef cattle has developed in the whole Saskatoon region, which was formerly engaged solely in the production of wheat and oats. The plant was soon to be doubled in size to meet the staggering growth of the production centres. He needed great ability to achieve this result in the fiscal universe of the postwar period. The great American fortunes were all made before the thirties. Dupont, Ford, Rockefeller, and Kennedy needed only courage and good ideas. Mendel fought alone in a system based on the redistribution of wealth and the greatest good of our present economy. If he still managed to create a great fortune, one could deduce without the slightest inquiry that he has at the same time enriched those around him. In other words, his millions came to him almost by accident; the important thing to him was to carry the enterprise he had founded to its limits. I had a chance to speak to some of his employees. The firm has the reputation of paying the best salaries in the region for equivalent work, and the establishment of the union was approved at the time by all the directors. Mr Mendel understood.

The most interesting part of Mendel's story is his artistic career, though he is one of the least discussed persons in the city. The new Saskatoon art centre is his work and bears his name. He is also its sponsor. Its architecture is very daring, designed by Blankstein, Gilmore, and Hamca of Winnipeg. The building includes concert halls, an art centre, a conservatory, and a library. I suspect that Mendel has bequeathed it his very important collection of canvases, to which he is so attached. I shall never be sure, for it would be difficult to ask such a question of a man of seventy-five. Though perhaps you could with him, for I have never met anyone so defiantly alive.

This man has visions of the world and of life that I like, because they are grafted on his own experience. When our conversation detoured for a moment towards Paris, he made an unexpected remark, dully angry, filled with as much desire as frustration. 'You should never fall in love with Paris. Never. Paris is a whore. I almost fell into her trap once, but I escaped in time.' And I realized at that moment that he would give his profitable business for a little apartment in the fifth *arrondissement*. When we reached dessert we were exchanging those cheerful absurdities that can sometimes define us better than the most profound confessions. Mendel, for instance, admitted the three great passions of his life, which his seventy-five years have only displaced in order of priority. Formerly he was fascinated by women, horses, and painting . . . and now he is fascinated by painting, horses, and women.

He said to me suddenly, with his unforgettable accent, 'I do not live. I bite into life.'

It was a man of seventy-five who said this, in a tone I shall never forget — a tone that haunts me sometimes when I am very tired, a tone that helps me gather my energies together to continue on my way.

BATOCHE TODAY   A little church, a modest presbytery, its façade still marked by bullet-holes, a few houses, a valley as green as in a corner of provincial France — and today a blazing sun and silence. It was just a few days before the opening of the tourist season. I was very lucky, for I would be alone here with a few swallows. A young Métis, handsome as a god, smoked a cigarette in the doorway of the presbytery, which has been turned into a museum. He was a government employee, a civil servant. There cannot be many Métis on the payroll of the federal government.

He watched me, smiling, while I read the words on the commemorative plaques: 'Here, on 15 May 1885, after a battle of four days, the Métis under Louis Riel surrendered to General Middleton, commander of the Canadian force,' and 'This building — the presbytery — is still as it was in 1885, when the village and the neighbouring region became the last stronghold of the Métis led by Louis Riel . . .'

I went over to the Métis and we talked for a long time, first of Batoche as it is today and then of the rebellion. It was impossible to believe that this place, now so peaceful, could have been the theatre of bloody events. Batoche was founded by Oblates in 1881. At the time of the rebellion Father Végreville was in charge of the mission. Some old people in Batoche still remember those times. The whole village remains impregnated with this, the most important historical event of the Canadian West. Today the 285 members of the parish of Batoche are almost all Métis, like the young employee of the museum. He pointed out to me that the museum's official texts avoid using the word 'rebellion'. There have been incidents, even very recently. For the population of Batoche, and the greater part of the French Canadian nation, Louis Riel and his supporters were not rebels but patriots. They did not revolt against the government but took up arms to defend their rights.

I left Batoche, that delightful village, and drove down towards the Saskatchewan River by a dusty but infinitely poetic little road. A light current, just enough to enliven the landscape, floated upon the surface of the river. At the end of my route was a flat boat, big enough for two or three cars. Here and there along the Saskatchewan you can cross the river by these ferryboats of another age. You detach them from the dock and they drift towards the opposite shore. The motive force is the current, and the cable to which the boat is attached is enough to keep it in the right direction.

A man was for the moment invisible, and I did not catch sight of him until I had driven my car on board. I saw him coming then, mopping his forehead: it was a Métis, a big strapping fellow. He set the craft in motion in silence, after a merely formal greeting. How did it begin? We were suddenly in animated conversation. While the boat took us across, we settled all the problems of the world. This thirty-year-old Métis spoke correct French and had obviously received a good education; he read everything he could find and was passionately interested in politics. His mother was born in Batoche. His grandfather knew the rebellion of 1885. So there we were again. I thought that now I could get some authentic details. But he immediately fell into a fathomless silence.

It is incredible that after eighty years, young Métis 'who are perfectly assimilated' as the Olympians would say . . .

REGINA GETS ITS SECOND WIND Regina has aged rapidly. Despite my repeated attempts to become acquainted with all its marvels — and its parliament, some of its parks, and certain avenues are indeed worthy of the veneration with which they are surrounded — I could never completely get away from the impression of desolation the city first gave me. But let us trust in the years to come, for Regina has just launched upon a rejuvenation program, which plans not only to renovate the civic centre but to rezone the whole city and build the entire new university campus now in course of construction. As the result of this full-scale town-planning effort, Regina will have a new face before ten years have passed.

The one it shows us today is little in accord with the idea we have of it. One would swear the city had scarcely recovered from the celebrated cyclone of 1912. The truth is more prosaic. The city was built very quickly, and as recently as 1950 no one believed it would ever become a very significant city. And then suddenly the population began to increase rapidly from one year to the next, new industries have multiplied, new buildings sprung up here and there. Today it has a new airport; it is the central city of twenty trucking companies, an important stop on the CPR, a stage on the Trans-Canada Highway; it is considered by experts one of the best situations for small and medium-sized industry; it has two petroleum refineries and its own electric company; its water reserves are sufficient for the moment and will become limitless when the great dams on the Saskatchewan and Qu'Appelle are finished.

Regina has become aware of the new dimensions of its future and is trying to model itself upon the prosperity that seems promised to it. It is rather as if having been confined so long to its politics — excellent politics that have brought the western provinces more rapidly than the rest of Canada to various social security measures, by a sort of natural process based on the desire to resolve problems peculiar to themselves — Regina had suddenly taken the measure of its industrial future. We are witnessing in this city a bursting of the limits it had set for itself. If you attempt to learn the underlying reasons for this, you will be offered dozens, but most frequently the recent discovery of potash. The first plants are in construction in the Saskatoon region, but the whole province will know a 'boom' comparable to that brought by the discovery of petroleum in Alberta. Till now the province has shared only crumbs of the industrial prosperity of Alberta, and its important grain production does not give it sufficient protection from bad years.

Since the drought and the grasshoppers, everyone watches the barometer with unhealthy anxiety. Newspapers and radio and television give long and frequent weather reports to the point of nausea. Sometimes the approach of rain is the excuse for an eight-column headline. If it doesn't rain for a few days, there is talk of drought and you will be offered alarmist pictures of the forthcoming wheat or oats crop. Regina had to emerge from this vocation for insecurity. And then came potash. Now Regina can look its future in the face. You will tell me that the exploitation of potash, like that of petroleum in Alberta, will be ninety per cent underwritten by American firms. Why make a tragedy of it? Millions of dollars have begun to fall on Saskatchewan and will bring hundreds of supplementary industries into being.

It is curious, and very reassuring, that potash was discovered in Saskatchewan just when the great sociologists and eminent philosophers were becoming concerned about the world of 2000. The hour was approaching when hunger would exist everywhere. The children of America would in their turn have the swollen bellies of the undernourished. It seemed that the generation of the end of the world had been born and that when we built our fine houses we had unwittingly prepared our orchestra-seat for the day of the great cataclysm. Suddenly news came from Saskatchewan that the subsoil of the province contained substances capable of fertilizing all the world's deserts. At the time there were only timid news items. Even today some people will reproach me for putting these remarks under the heading of my stay in the legislative capital. I have not described the beautiful marble halls of the parliament building and here I am talking about potash. We have more imagination for unhappiness than for beneficent visions. Too bad! Nothing can stop my considering this little city of one hundred and twenty thousand inhabitants in the centre of the prairies as the great capital of a great province that, on a certain day in 1943, will have helped the world free itself from the spectre of hunger. And that seems to me more important than describing its main street, with its poor little big stores and its air of a small town that is not yet sure where it is going.

Unlike gold, silver, diamonds, or petroleum, potash has never that I know of made man dream or even aroused any secret avarice. Yet it is a valuable substance, more important by far than all the precious metals combined. It is present in all nature, in the life of plants, men, and animals. But it vanishes from fields that have been intensively cultivated for centuries and must be put back in the form of chemical fertilizer. Along with phosphorus and nitrogen, potash is an essential element of fertilizer. In 1950 there was concern in the western world about the dwindling of its reserves. Hope suddenly came from Saskatchewan. When the inland sea that covered that part of Canada more than three hundred and fifty million years ago withdrew, it left a thick bed of potash salts over an area three hundred and fifty miles long by a more or less continuous breadth of fifty miles. Similar beds may exist in several countries of the world, but the advantage here is that it extends under the surface to a maximum depth of five thousand feet and can be extracted by the ordinary mining techniques. It is, moreover, of exceptional purity, demanding a minimum of treatment.

A very little province is coming to grips with a colossal future. The production of potash will become the sixth mining industry in all Canada in a very few years. But above all, the world's hunger will have lost the game, theoretically at least, for two thousand years.

Regina was for a long time the headquarters of the RCMP . . . then the North West Mounted Police. Now that the force has been transferred to Ottawa, Regina remains the principal training centre. Here is a fact that is not likely to awaken my lyricism. But veneration for the police officer and the priest is the prerogative of the pure in heart. And I was apparently surrounded by the pure in heart. The RCMP quarters — who would have believed it? — are Regina's greatest tourist attraction.

THE QU'APPELLE VALLEY Everyone had told me, 'You mustn't leave Saskatchewan without taking at least a bit of a jaunt into the Qu'Appelle Valley.' And everyone was right, for this is indeed the most harmonious landscape the province can offer. Not the most imposing or the wildest, but truly the most harmonious — rather like the Laurentians reduced. I am using the word 'reduced' in its strongest sense. You will think you are suddenly driving through mountains, when they are in reality only little hills. The illusion comes from your long journeys over flat lands. Here at a turning of the road a ravine yawns but it is only a gradient of a few feet. The Qu'Appelle River broadens, thunders like a real river, though until now it was just a little stream of erratic disposition. And you will finally find some real lakes, real woods, all drawn by the hand of an artist.

There are Indians everywhere in this region. No sign on the road will enable you to discover them easily but there are several reserves of different tribes, linked with the tar-surfaced road by sandy dirt tracks in which, in bad weather, your fine car will sink. This happened to me so often that I can personally testify to it. But each time young Sioux or vigorous Crees appeared out of the driving rain to help me on my way. Just where did they come from? Was there still an Indian behind every tree-trunk as in the time of the first explorers?

This trip off the beaten paths enabled me to penetrate into the Sioux reserve of Standing Buffalo in the company of two impromptu guides who led me straight to the old sage known throughout these regions by the name Obey. Perhaps this was his first name. At any rate it seemed to be the only name he had.

The houses in Standing Buffalo were just like all the houses in western villages — except Obey's, which was a wretched shack. Why? Because Obey deserted his Cree reserve many years ago and came to the Sioux of Standing Buffalo as a guest. Guests have the right not to die of hunger or cold, but not to a house. I learned later that he built his shack himself and also the stable in which he still carefully tends a thoroughbred horse. I learned also that Obey suffers no harassment in this reserve but is treated with the respect due to his age and wisdom.

For the moment the shack was empty. We had made this arduous expedition in the rain over impracticable roads only to knock on a hermetically sealed door. My two young guides did not own themselves beaten. They were both in their twenties. They had learned a little French at school and a good deal of English at their work. We understood one another quite well by going from one language to the other at the slightest breakdown of vocabulary. One was a Cree, the other an authentic Sioux. But they had both left their reserves. They work at Qu'Appelle, are very popular with girls, and drink tons of beer every day in the village hotel. I was to know something about this, since they proposed to take me to Qu'Appelle to find Obey.

For that was where he must be, they insisted. Since he wasn't in his shack, the old man was meeting his friends at the hotel tavern. How could I refuse? Even in this flood of rain, we could see from time to time Indians with their raincoats over their heads driving happily along on their motorcycles.

We arrived at the Qu'Appelle hotel where we found almost all the Indians we could wish for, except Obey. My two guides proposed to wait for him. I couldn't see any way to withdraw without losing face while they were filling the table with an incalculable number of glasses full of smooth beer. I have never seen so many glasses of beer on one table. They had the property of renewing themselves automatically. They were eternal glasses — or eternally filled at least. Here was a harsh test for one that has an inborn resistance to this gassy nectar. Well, I would have to prove myself equal to the occasion, for my two companions seemed to be preparing for a long and joyful evening at arms. It was no use my pointing out that since Mr Obey was not here, this perhaps meant that he was somewhere else — arguments of this sort seemed to have no pertinence for them. And the surface of our table continued to adorn itself with glasses of golden liquid, the sight of which, I will confess, became less and less antipathetic to me.

And then these young Indians had a story to tell me. It is not worth repeating, since it is identical with that of all the young Indians I have met. The young Indian who has decided to burn his bridges back to the reserve — and this is a more and more common phenomenon — finally seeks refuge in some artificial paradise. I began to realize that I must extricate myself from here before I found some charm in this sordid tavern. I knew I would have to take leave of my young companions with all possible circumspection, for I sensed that they were on the edge of some second stage of drunkenness, or that a very definite hostility, come from some ancient well of rancour, was beginning to tinge the euphoria that had marked our relations until now.

I turned back to them from the door to give them a farewell wave of the hand. The two faces were smiling pleasantly, but their eyes were cutting as steel. I learned later that a brief scuffle had erupted a short time after my departure. About what? No one could quite say. I learned only that my two young Indian friends had been thrown out the door like dogs. God protects writers . . . or perhaps it is the devil.

I finally found the old sage, Obey, in a little restaurant, a sort of *comptoir-lunch*, as we call it in Quebec. I saw nothing but Indians, not only at the tables but behind the counter and beyond the double swinging door that opened into the kitchen. The old man, who had been advised of my coming, was awaiting me at the back of this little place. Everybody would be witness to our conversation, for at eighty-two the old man was half deaf and I should have to shout my questions. Obey was no longer a man . . . but the mere presence of a man, an ethereal symbol of humanity. I had the feeling he might evaporate if I were to raise my voice a notch. He hadn't a tooth, but his white hair was still luxuriant and his eyes were twenty years old. His whole appearance displayed an exquisite sensibility and a certain refinement. He must have been very handsome. He spoke correct English. I was soon able to lower my voice for I saw that he practised lip-reading. By then he was used to me and we were finally able to converse.

His story is fascinating, at least it fascinates me. Here was an authentic hunter who had worked for long years exclusively for the Hudson's Bay Company. He never sold to any other company because its agents had won the confidence of several generations of his family. He received a dollar and a half for each fox and was able to trap about five hundred a year. But along with this, he was an active sportsman from the time he was twenty. For seventy years he played baseball, lacrosse, and football. He attracted attention particularly by his exploits as a runner. He cited several of his best times to me, which I am unfortunately not qualified to appreciate, but which I have retained for the interest of enthusiasts: one hundred yards in ten seconds, a quarter of a mile in a minute, half a mile in two minutes, a mile in four minutes. Is this extraordinary? Specialists will know.

His wife died about fifteen years ago, but he has two daughters and a son who have given him twenty-four grandchildren and sixty-eight great grandchildren. But I feel sure that his great passion is the racehorse he bought two years ago with the savings of many years, including his old-age pension. I looked at the old man and found it remarkable that he should be at grips with a real passion at the age of eighty-two — a passion that made his eyes shine. He told me about the horse's day, and described his character and the walks they take together every day now that the old man is no longer able to ride. The image of that miserable shack, a shack planted in the middle of a naked field near a stable — that image I had glimpsed under a driving rain, with a twist of the heart, returned to my memory less hauntingly. There is sun sometimes, there is the friendship between a man and an animal, and especially the great brotherhood of the Indian with nature, a brotherhood of which books had often informed me but the real breath of which I felt for the first time in this dusty little restaurant in Qu'Appelle.

INTELLECTUAL SEGREGATION   Right beside the little town of Qu'-Appelle, I was surprised to discover one of the largest centres of fishery research in Saskatchewan — research but also culture. For here you will find millions of specimens of fish of all species and sizes in reservoirs where the water flows at temperatures varied according to the nature and age of the young fish. I saw, for instance, that attempts were being made to acclimatize a French river trout. Last year about a hundred lakes and streams were stocked with fry.

To those who think of Saskatchewan only in terms of prairies, let us say that one-eighth of its territory is made up of lakes and rivers. There is commercial fishing as well as fishing for sport. Is there need to emphasize the utility of a centre of this nature, since they exist in all the provinces? One need only recall that of each hundred fish in our lakes, sixty-one will die in the course of the year, die of natural causes. So we must be able to replace them, at the same time as all those that are fished for pleasure or profit, while taking account, of course, of the colossal reproductive efforts that the different species themselves practise in the field, not always with the same fortunate results.

I could cite names, figures, and accomplishments, but it was not this that held my attention today. I was distracted by an incident that had nothing to do with those creatures whose stupidity has deprived us of all pity. They will continue to die slowly for hours in our baskets and our boats, without any risk of the SPCA's concerning itself with their fate, which is the least enviable in creation. No, what mobilized all my attention today was the attitude to my two young Indian companions.

They were perfectly sober this time. They had been anxious to accompany me, obviously because of their evident pleasure in driving my car. They took the wheel in turns, and in this way I was able to inspect the region through the eyes of young Indians.

After various expeditions the young Indians brought me to the Qu'Appelle fish-breeding centre, which I had indicated a desire to visit. There was no one there. The doors were open but it was lunchtime. I should have preferred to wait docilely for the return of the caretaker, but the young Indians were familiars of the place and undertook to guide me around the equipment and the reservoirs as if they were the owners. They furnished me with valuable information, speaking with dreamy eyes of the pleasures the rainbow trout gives fishermen because of its extraordinary fighting qualities. They explained the varieties of young fish, and their journeys, and were as fascinated as I was by the foreign species they were attempting to acclimatize to the icy waters of the Saskatchewan lakes.

But suddenly we heard the sound of nervous feet. A man appeared with two assistants. They stopped motionless in the doorway. This was a perfectly normal reaction: we might have been almost any sort of wrongdoers and, in any event, had no authorization to wander about these places in the absence of the guards. But my distress came after their first stupefaction had passed. For I received a polite, almost deferential treatment but my two Indian companions would have been hustled out of the place if my presence had not imposed a certain caution. The two boys were very correct in their behaviour. They had been the first to cover themselves with all sorts of excuses: since they had been employed by the research centre, they had imagined . . . The white men didn't even listen to them. They were deprived of the right to exist. I am not saying this treatment is currently accorded to Indians at Qu'Appelle or elsewhere. I am telling what I saw and what I felt at that moment. And it was an infinitely sorrowful experience.

The two young Indians had won the right to my friendship. And I proved it to them. For little by little I was able to make them indispensable to our conversation. Finally the white men were consulting them as experts. I knew they would be grateful to me. They made a careful note of my address. They wished to send me a Christmas card.

The true integration of the Indian will take place first in our minds and in our hearts. And this form of integration is the only hope for the future. They will bring our society a richness that would be the envy of many European countries. If Canada is finally to give itself a face and a definition, it needs them. Any plan for the future that does not take account of the two hundred thousand Indians in our land can only be a misrepresentation.

Manitoba

WHERE WAS I NOW? I always leave a province just when I feel
most attached to it. My only consolation is to find it in part
elsewhere. So Manitoba seemed to me at first an extension of
Saskatchewan, before I became aware of its own personality,
which is composed almost equally of characteristics of the East
and the West. We often speak of a place as a crossroads, when
that is not the most appropriate word. But as soon as I arrived
in Winnipeg I was conscious for the first time of the presence
nearby of Ontario and Quebec. And while I was settling myself
in, I did not feel as elsewhere the sense that I must get through
several days of adaptation.

My agenda was filled with urgent instructions, which I must
attend to as soon as I arrived. I did nothing about them but
granted myself a holiday until next morning. I had taken measures to arrive alone and to remain alone, at least for the first
hours of my stay. I wished to stroll about in the city and absorb
some of those useless pictures and fugitive impressions that are
what I value most. I intended especially to take my bearings a
little.

To begin with, Canada had seemed to me a vast formless thing that no human being could grasp in its entirety. In practice, the same vibration and similar rhythms are carried from one province to the other. Because the provinces are faced with the same problems, the same attitude — but so vaguely still — is beginning to take form. The innumerable ethnic groups that had seemed to me to form at best a bizarre mosaic are secretly permeated with a similar awareness of our realities. They do not suspect it, but they are above all Canadians, even when they hasten to call themselves Germans, or Ukrainians, or French, or Italians. And then, this country is a paradise of personalities. They believe that the whole world is similarly peopled with giants. They could be accused of everything, but not of mediocrity.

Our history is only beginning. The new generations have an important challenge to meet: to show themselves equal to the superhuman destiny our ancestors assumed with a simplicity that today constitutes our greatest originality. There is no example in modern history, except the United States during its first hours, where the practice of the exceptional has become more natural, more commonplace, than here. Every day I had been told fantastic stories in the tone used to describe banal incidents to which no one attaches any importance. I believe it was this that had finally begun to cast a spell upon me, really cast a spell — the certainty that my country, right down to its most unknown individuals, completely escapes mediocrity. One might place signs at every instant: 'Pass by. Little Gods at Work.'

All this is lyrical, immoderate, unfounded, and a shade ridiculous, but it was what I was thinking on this evening of my arrival in Winnipeg. How many times had I felt a deep sadness at finding along our frontier institutions and structures set there by our neighbours to the south. I was letting myself be taken in by mirages. Canada has kept what the United States has necessarily lost in completing its cycle of industrialization and under the weight of its demographic evolution. The game we are playing is not won. Twenty million human beings have undertaken to mould a territory — a task that four hundred million, for all one knows, might not be sufficient to accomplish. For many decades each one of us must do the work of ten. This is what the western pioneers have done, and their line perpetuates itself, sometimes under the guise of middle-class comfort.

So I walked aimlessly this first evening through the streets of Winnipeg. And I was easily captured by the charm of Portage Avenue, one of the great commercial avenues, not only of the city, but of the Canadian West. In the afternoon one does not need to wonder for long which side of the street the big stores are on. The crowd jostles about on a mile of sidewalk, while the opposite pavement is almost empty. In the evening Portage Avenue almost achieves an equilibrium. On both sides of the street movie theatres, restaurants, and bars set blinking in equal number their multicoloured, multiform, and on the whole rather aggressive neon signs. I felt a sort of inward exaltation, having known so many dismal evenings in the other cities of the West. Here one could imagine that the population might have other desires to satisfy after work than playing cards or looking at television. On all sides there was animated talk, laughter, the movement of lively groups. I was very pleased to find again some suggestion of our great cities of Quebec and Ontario. Elsewhere in the West I had seen the eternal notice on the doors of clubs: 'Ladies with escorts'. Here there was nothing of the sort. But even so you must not think . . . The girls have begun to come rather timidly — in groups of two, more often of three or four. They settle themselves at a table, and only very bold young men can manage to drag them away for the space of a dance. In theory they come to dance, but they are still little accustomed to their new liberties.

May I be pardoned for frivolous preoccupations, but they are invested in my eyes with an importance not always possessed by beds of potash and enormous dams — the streets of Winnipeg appeared to be full of pretty girls. Was I the victim of an illusion? I seemed to have come suddenly out of a long tunnel, empty of such sparkling smiles as I saw around me, by such hair piled high in the latest cinema style, but especially by such eyes ranging so strikingly between grey and indigo. I told myself that all these beautiful girls must adorn the streets of the other big cities, whether Vancouver, Calgary, or Edmonton, and that I had simply been too inattentive to notice them . . . well, I was mistaken. An expert in such matters, and Winnipeg possesses several, was to inform me with abundant documentation that the mixture of races in this city has been practised so freely that a number of specimens of rare beauty have resulted. With a little application, you would be able to spot Italian eyes in a Ukrainian face, adorned with a head of Scandinavian hair. Imagine such combinations as you please, and they have some chance here of corresponding with reality.

The population, which is approaching the half-million mark, is made up of almost all the ethnic groups I had encountered elsewhere. But no one of them is predominant. It is remarkable that Winnipeg has achieved that process of integration spoken of a great deal elsewhere without convincing proof of it ever being given. Here, whether one is of German origin or Ukrainian, one is above all of Winnipeg. Even St Boniface, directly across the river and the most significant French Canadian city outside Quebec, feels itself to be an integral part of Winnipeg.

YET TOURISM IS A SERIOUS INDUSTRY Winnipeg has a certain number of so-called tourist attractions, as have all the cities of the West, of the whole country, of the continent, and of the world. Everywhere else I had travelled out of season. But in Winnipeg it was July, right in the middle of the tourist season. I had the choice of making the tour of these attractions on my own, with the chance of tangling in each spot with one of those groups of tourists that are the despair of modern times. I decided to join one of the groups rather than encounter them all in turn.

And so it was that with death in my soul I took my place in one of those superb air-conditioned buses, full of elderly rheumatic Americans, young students breaking out their blue bermudas, a few happy innocents embarking on the venture in the belief that they were sharing in some deserving expedition, and at least two experienced travellers, who were not taken in by anything and were preparing to question the guide on subjects about which he knew nothing — that is to say, all subjects without exception. For it is a characteristic of our guides in the West and elsewhere to know nothing beyond the patter they have memorized, which includes more American-style wisecracks than strictly historical facts. They all have the air of saying, 'You haven't come this far just to be bored.'

This guide began gloriously; there wasn't a word spoken for the first hour of the trip. This was so much gained. He was too busy driving his enormous bus from one hotel to another to collect his clients of the afternoon. In this way I visited all the hotels of the city. On all sides I saw Banks of Montreal and Wheat Pools; when we came back along this street at the end of the day, I was informed that there were in fact several Banks of Montreal and several branches of the Wheat Pool in Winnipeg.

The bus was suddenly full, the guide adjusted his voice to the microphone and began to talk. He never shut up again. Forgive me for this violently descriptive expression but I cannot think of any other. And we were to obtain, along with a deluge of dates and historical facts, some very humorous remarks about the longest street in Winnipeg — the Trans-Canada Highway, which is five thousand miles long — and other witticisms to delight our hearts. The itinerary carried us in turn from the Grotto of Lourdes to the 'beautiful St Boniface Cathedral' to the RCMP barracks, and through Assiniboine Park to the zoo — 'the most important in western Canada'. We were taken next to St Jacques, to the residential quarter of Silver Heights, and of course to the marvellous and 'typical' parliament buildings.

Well, here we will make a long pause, for I wish to take the opportunity to point out one of the evils suffered by all the cities of the world but which I never felt with more embarrassment than during this visit to the Manitoba parliament. The depressing appearance of the tourist species, with its dangling cameras, its multiform hats, its bermudas, and its guileless grins, is not always a true index of the quality of its intentions and its cultivation. When the first shock was over, I engaged in conversation with two professors, who would have deserved a treatment more commensurate with their education. Here was an example of the most deplorable mania, which we have inherited without discussion from the United States — that of taking everything down to the lowest common denominator. Yet it would be so simple to assume that a person who has chosen to make a first general contact with a city on a suffocating July afternoon instead of staying pleasantly in the coolness of his air-conditioned room has the right to a little regard.

After a spectacular semi-circle, then, the bus drew to a halt on the parliament square, and the guide announced a piece of happy news, which fell like honey on our smarting ears. For this important visit we were going to be entrusted to a young student who had had the happy idea of earning her university tuition this way. Once we were settled into this climate of good conscience, there began the most unexpected of circus acts.

Like most of its fellows of the West, the Winnipeg parliament seems to me a little overdone with its immense marble halls, its Greco-something style, its offices with the Queen's portrait and its gigantic debating halls — these often to settle the legislative problems of populations of less than a million. Each time I found myself before one of these parliaments, I said to myself, 'It's the federal House of Commons. It is impossible that for such a little province . . .' But it was indeed the legislature, built and set in place and inaugurated, sometimes before the number of members and the parliamentary structures had been decided. Despite everything, I am willing to consider them all equally beautiful, fully justified, and admirable. It must be made clear that we all belong, by direct, indirect, or circumstantial bonds, to the most important parliamentary complex in the world, the Commonwealth itself. From Victoria to St John's, Newfoundland, our parliaments all cry 'Present' with a powerful voice and pretend to believe they are not being complacent about it.

But this group tour began with some rather odd but fitting details about the two enormous bronze bisons that guard the great marble staircase. Immediately afterwards, before the entrance to the temple, the frail young girl used the same phonographic tone to tell us about the bronze Queen Victoria, seated on a throne, likewise of bronze, with an air of great satisfaction. To link with the same tone descriptions of bisons and the Queen, isn't that rather verging upon lèse-majesté? But it was terribly hot, everyone was in a hurry, and the frail young girl was anxious to have done with this group and attack the next . . . the last, perhaps, of her afternoon. We climbed the great marble staircase, the frail young girl ahead of us, everyone racing so as not to risk having our ranks invaded by a group of schoolchildren. Let us recall our curious journey up to this point: Queen Victoria, the two enormous bisons. Now without the slightest warning we were in a Greek temple.

In the most natural tone in the world, and without psychological transition, the frail young girl began to explain the mysteries and protocols of ancient sacrifices. There we all were, packed like imbeciles on a circular gallery, built around the span of a superb dome and providing glimpses of the ground floor below, while the itinerary of the high priest and his acolytes, the exact situation of the altar, the procession, the oracles, and all the rest of it were explained to us. I will not lie. Among the crowd of tourists, I saw several pairs of large admiring eyes. No doubt these people envied the Canadians of Winnipeg for having known ancient sacrifices. And they plied the frail young girl with questions, to make quite sure of the precise position of the altar with respect to the spectators and to find out the content of the oracles. It is not these people I was thinking of when I spoke of the circus act. They had come here seeking emotions and would have them at all costs. They were overcome with joy, when with a negligent gesture, very sure of her effect since she had achieved it so many times, the frail young girl indicated on one of the walls the fossil of a crustacean no less than five hundred million years old. Those that had already made the construction of the

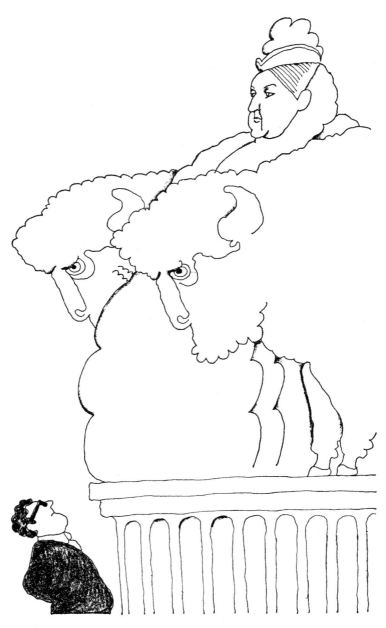

To link with the same tone descriptions of bisons and the Queen, isn't
that rather verging upon lèse-majesté?

parliament date from the time of Pericles almost fainted with happiness. Here indeed was a well-preserved building.

Meanwhile the great doors of the assembly had just opened. At last we were going to hear about the parliamentary function of this admirable structure. Would you believe it? I was told about all the statues, all the Greco-something figures in the frescoes, the ashtrays, the candelabra, the inkwells, and the oaken speaker's chair, which a boy tried out to the great diversion of the learned assembly, while the frail young girl burst into a holy rage, which permitted her to abbreviate without explanation the time she was supposed to devote to us. But at the exit, she drew upon her ultimate resources of goodwill to toss us her little piece about the Golden Boy.

I offer my excuses but I hadn't noticed him. I had taken him for some sort of weathervane; without knowing it, I had come very close to sacrilege. He is a little gilded personage, also borrowed, of course, from Greek mythology, thirteen and a half feet high, two hundred and fifty-five feet above the ground. For amateurs of such things, we were told without a smile that this is the highest point in the city, and one of the highest in the province. He has been immobilized in full flight. In his right hand he carries a vaguely Olympic torch and in his left hand a sheaf of wheat, which is gilded like all the rest of his graceful person. The attitude of the body, the tilt of the head are loaded with symbolism. The entire figure is supposed to show the spirit of enterprise and eternal youth, a theme one finds in almost all the symbolism of the province.

And now the turn was over. We got back into the bus. I was distressed and anxious. We are the youngest tourist country in the world. And we enter the game with a piece of foolishness . . . or perhaps stupidity. When will the government look into the very important matter of tourist visits?

BRIGITTE BARDOT WOULD BE DELIGHTED Was it appropriate? I thought constantly of Brigitte Bardot during my visit to the big abattoirs near St Boniface, which are reputed to be the largest in the whole British Commonwealth. I thought of Brigitte Bardot, especially on the upper floor, where every day experts cause dozens and dozens of splendid beasts that have committed no crime against humanity to depart this life. Brigitte would be happy to see what care is taken to make all these fine creatures safe from the blows of fate. Give us our daily steak but permit us to eat it with a good conscience.

I was disguised as an astronaut, or almost so. So was there some danger involved in frequenting this place that I didn't know about? Indeed, yes. It seems that these quarters of a thousand pounds might fall on your head in the course of your peregrinations. I was to see, in fact, that in certain sections of the plant entire steers travelled overhead, attached to assembly — or rather disassembly — lines. The closer they got to the huge refrigerating plants the more they resembled those carcasses that adorn your butcher shop.

The story began with my six-floor trip by elevator in the company of an enormous sow. It was not that she was a disagreeable companion. She seemed to be of an amiable disposition and a certain breeding, for she drew back politely to leave me as much room as was possible. But did she suddenly guess the fate that awaited her? We had only reached the third floor when she began to give piercing cries, which continued to increase in volume until we reached our destination. A moment before, while I was walking along a gangway suspended above the cattle-paddocks, my companion had sworn to me that the animals did not in the least sense the approach of death and that everything that was said on this subject was completely grotesque. When we reached the sixth floor I was convinced this enormous sow was a flagrant exception. She was determined not to leave the elevator. She had entered with a firm gait, lively eyes, and in cheerful mood. And now look at her. She was frantic, her eyes glassy, violent spasms shook her body. She had smelled the abattoir and the blood of the abattoir, blood that would soon be mixed with hers. It took three men to drag her out and direct her towards the anteroom of death.

My guide drew me in the opposite direction and we entered an immense hall, full of those disassembly lines of which I spoke. The steer arrives here on foot, leaves well tied up in cheese-cloth, and is put in the refrigeration plant. On his journey, he has lost his life, his hide, his blood, his guts, his entrails, and his viscera . . . this is a good many things to lose in a few minutes. Scores of employees work on the line, performing a single opera-tion as the animal is presented to them, suspended by a hook. The abattoir is generally situated on the uppermost storey so that all portions requiring special treatment can travel to the lower floors by an arrangement of pipes. The hide, for instance, goes right down to the basement. Everywhere, powerful jets of water are at the disposal of the employees, who manage to com-plete the cycle of operations in an atmosphere of cleanliness that was my keenest surprise so far. Even odours are suppressed. And everything I saw wore shades ranging from white to pink to red.

GENTLE DEATH   Three by three, the steers were led into a metal corral, which was then closed behind them. A man approached them and from a high ramp pointed a curious pistol at their brains. A light detonation, as from a child's gun, and the steer collapsed. It had not been killed by the explosion but by the plunging of a steel shaft into its vital centre. It is the principle of the *descabillo* in the Spanish *corrida* but with the difference here that there is plenty of time to aim the shot, unknown to the beast, since it does not see its attacker. I swear to you, Brigitte, that the beast has no time to suffer, even for a fraction of a second. The executioner went on talking to me while he com-pleted his task, and I answered him. That is what was new for me. I answered him. Yet God knows that the sight of death, even the death of a skunk on the road, has always perturbed me. Here it didn't in the slightest. How can I understand this? Per-haps I had been expecting such horrifying visions, because of my ignorance, that before this death that one could call clean . . . discreet and unspectacular . . . yes, it was surely this. The proof of it was that I found the man rather congenial. Now that I have withdrawn from him a little, his work fills me with the keenest repulsion.

STEINBACH, AN UNEXPECTED DISCOVERY   Canada is a writers' paradise. You never know what to expect. It is useless to draw up a precise itinerary for yourself, you will change it constantly, according to the varied pulls of the road. I was preparing to set out for the tourist paradise of Whiteshell when I heard for the first time of Steinbach, the Mennonite town.

An unprepared traveller might go through Steinbach without suspecting that this was one of the oldest white settlements in Manitoba, founded by adherents of one of the most rigorous religions in the world, pilgrims of the absolute who have journeyed for more than four centuries in quest of the promised land where they would be free to practise their beliefs. And always the cycle repeats itself: new countries, in need of colonists, give them prior assurance of the liberties that to their eyes are essential — for instance that of educating their children as they wish and exemption from military service — but comes the development of the region, the province, or the emerging country, and difficulties begin — pressures, and attempts at integration, which go most often to the point of harassment or even persecution. This is in bulk the history of the Mennonites in the world, since the first exodus of the Anabaptists from Switzerland in the fifteenth century, to their migration through Germany, Russia, and finally Holland, where they experienced their golden age. There were several hundreds of thousands of Mennonites in western Canada. How many are there today? Only those that are willing to speak English. The others have fled the difficulties that all lie more or less in the compulsory attendance at public schools.

At first sight Steinbach is the town of the automobile. The main street, which might be that of a metropolis, is lined with garages, gas stations, repair shops, salesrooms, and stores. All the big companies are represented and you could buy a Mercedes as easily as a Chevrolet. The most knowledgeable buy their cars not in Winnipeg but in Steinbach. Yet the total population does not exceed thirty-five hundred, and away from the main street you would search in vain for the slightest activity. Everyone is a Mennonite here, but they belong to various ethnic groups, the most important of which are Dutch, German, and Russian.

I talked with several residents of Steinbach: all spoke with a pronounced accent of their national origin. They were willing to learn English but it is obvious that for them English is only a means of communication and that they speak their mother tongues at home. You will seek in vain for a bar, a tavern, or a restaurant with a permit to sell wine or spirits: Mennonites do not drink. Well, down there, in a little street, there is a place where the young men sometimes go to have a beer. Beer is permitted to them, but the elders do not approve: this is the beginning of assimilation.

On the counter of a grocery store I noticed the local paper: *Carillon News*. A red two-column headline said 'General sale of cars to draw customers from the whole province.' Other headlines of the first page: 'Former Canadian pilot opens automobile sales,' and under the heading, 'Meet the men of Automobile City,' the subheading 'L. A. Barkman, our first Pontiac-Buick salesman, is the ideal mayor for Steinbach.'

I talked for a long time with one of the leaders of the town, the proprietor of an immense automobile salesroom, which he directs from a sort of glassed-in cockpit. He has a panoramic view of all the services and gives instructions by phone, televox, or directly, holding the door open with his foot. It's a marvel just to see him at work. I saw him dictate a letter to a secretary, ordering tires of a revolutionary concept, reprimand a mechanic, complete a sale with a hurried client, without forgetting the question I had asked him about the Mennonites and answering it, after he had finished, in a quiet voice. The whole thing began over again in a few minutes. And he always came back to me with a clear mind and intelligent and well-documented replies. I offered him a cigarette. He gave an astonished smile. I should have known by now that the Mennonites do not smoke any more than they drink. I invited him to lunch. Another smile of astonishment: he would not eat until evening. Most Mennonites eat only two meals a day. I asked him to recommend a good restaurant in the neighbourhood. The question seemed to embarrass him. Perhaps on the highway . . . though he couldn't be sure. Till evening, and with various people, I talked about Mennonites on an empty stomach.

AN UNUSUAL AND FASCINATING 14TH OF JULY Station CKSB announced great celebrations for the 14th of July at St Boniface and at St Claude. It was rather as if it were announced that there would be great manifestations on St Jean-Baptiste Day at Montreal and at Sainte-Rose-du-Dégélé. St Claude has a population of less than six hundred and is about sixty miles southwest of Winnipeg, 'in the mountain', as they say in those parts. In Manitoba, when the line of the horizon is slightly broken, it is a mountain. That the 14th of July in such a little place should hold such importance rather intrigued me. I set out for St Claude.

I was early. I found a little village with deserted streets and an impenetrable silence. It was six o'clock in the evening of the 13th. Several miles away, there would be a bonfire at nightfall, but the real celebrations would not take place till next day. There would be High Mass, followed by a parade of all the organizations of the region, and even of St Boniface, and in the afternoon a baseball game and an outdoor fête for young and old. Would there be a public dance? Dancing in the streets? Neither the streets nor the houses were decorated. I could not make this picture of St Claude coincide with what the radio and newspapers had allowed me to expect. It was clear that nothing of importance would take place here. I was wrong. Next day everything exploded with joy. More than ten thousand people attended the outdoor fête. It was a real 14th of July, above all for the young, whom their elders watched with fascinated interest.

I decided to spend the night at St Claude and I began by

looking for a hotel room. Nothing was easier. There were two hotels, whose rooms had clearly never been occupied by travellers. The hotel permit is bought so one can open an otherwise illegal beer parlour. The rooms are only flimsy justifications, perfunctorily provided with bed and towel. The one assigned to me was the most comfortable in the house; as well as the bed and towel, its furniture included a rocking-chair. A naked bulb on the ceiling, no cupboard, no wardrobe, no hook on the wall to hold my clothes. There were no toilet facilities in the room, but there was the common bathroom at the end of the hall. As I was the only customer of the hotel, I was not disturbed by this. I was to see in time that this common bathroom, which contained neither a shower nor a bath but simply a washbasin, was used by the household comprising the head of the house, his pregnant wife, and a couple of nymphets. Although it was fifty or so feet from my room, the plumbing was so indiscreet that I was perfectly informed about its hours of use. The key to my room could not be found. It had been put somewhere several months ago . . . 'and then, you understand, travellers so seldom come this way.'

I understood perfectly, and I was delighted. The one thing lacking to my happiness was a meal. I was hungry as a wolf, and here at St Claude, a French village, the wine would be excellent and the cooking marvellous. Bad news. The hotel was a restaurant merely in principle. The menu offered only omelette and a whole range of hamburgers, with mustard, with tomato ketchup, with gooseberry jam — unless that was the beginning of the list of desserts. As for wine, well, they weren't yet licensed for that.

'And anyway, most of the people in St Claude come from the Jura, and that was so many years ago that you see . . .' It was the pregnant woman who told me this. She was in the doorway of the kitchen and spoke to me with affectionate reproach, as if I were a capricious child. She had quite enough to do cooking for her husband and her two little girls. I should have understood that this hotel was above all, like all village hotels, a tavern pure and simple, and that customers shouldn't expect anything but beer. From my seat I had a full view of the other room: the proprietor was with a customer. Not ten, not five, one customer. And it was the evening before the 14th of July.

I swam in an atmosphere of unreality. I swallowed a little of this and that which my hostess was willing to put on the table, and then, while I was waiting to go over to Belle Isle for the big bonfire that had been announced for a week by the newspapers and the radio, I wandered haphazardly on the main street of St Claude, looking for some natives of the town. There was not as much as a cat to be seen.

In despair and to pass the time, I made an appointment by telephone with the curé. It was a brilliant idea. The curés of these little villages are wells of knowledge, they possess the archives of the region, and they have many stories to tell.

The Abbé Jean-Marie Gagné did not need to be begged to give me an interview forthwith. 'Just come when it suits you. I'll be reading my breviary while I wait for you.' I crossed the railway tracks and discovered a delightful wooden church, built after the model of the churches of the Jura. I learned later that it would soon be demolished when the new church under construction, which was much bigger but lacking in any character, was inaugurated. It's too bad. St Claude has a population of six hundred, but on Sundays as many worshippers come to Mass from the surrounding country.

I stopped for a moment before a sort of giant shed. It was the *salle des fêtes*. At last the first decorations. A young man was busy putting up the last flags. Upon inquiry I learned that the celebration was not for the 14th of July but for a wedding. The nuptial reception would be held here from eight o'clock till dawn. Almost everywhere in the West the religious ceremony is held at the end of the afternoon and the reception in the evening. The young man was fascinated by my story and finally without ceremony invited me to the reception. One more or one less. Everyone would be delighted to know I was there. He was one of the organizers.

Later as I was leaving the presbytery, after a very long conversation with Monsieur le Curé, I found myself in the midst of the throng of arriving wedding guests. The door of a car opened suddenly before me and I was face to face with the bride in her long veil. She smiled and spoke a few words that said a great deal about the speed with which news travels at St Claude: 'I hope you'll join us.'

She said this in a bird's voice, she was charming, I almost kissed her. Much later, at the end of the evening, when I returned from the St John's fire, I had to pass the *salle des fêtes*. The reception was in full swing. The doors were wide open to the night and groups of guests were taking a breath of coolness outside. Someone recognized my car and once again I was invited to come in. This time I accepted. I made myself as small as possible. I stayed only a few minutes, long enough to taste the wine. It was excellent. I looked around for the bride but she was no longer present. The bridal couple are not indispensable to a wedding reception.

THE CLASSIC ITINERARY THROUGH WHITESHELL   It is the standard excursion for vacationists. I did not feel a delirious enthusiasm as I set out — for several confused reasons, two of which were not in the least confused: I was not on vacation and I have a horror of holiday centres. Too many people on the beaches — too many ugly, fat, obese, and lumpish people. Adolescents and old men who dream of nudist colonies have certainly never set foot in one. And then I had already done enough driving in Manitoba to have exhausted any pleasure I might get from covering several hundred more miles of it. The network of roads is very well arranged in general, and it is rarely that one cannot get from one point to another by different ways, which is not the case in all the provinces of the West. But as soon as you leave the main arteries, you risk finding roads that are tired out by long and redoubtable winters, sections under repair, sometimes veritable quagmires. But this is not the worst. If you are driving at seventy or seventy-five miles an hour, which is already an infraction of the law, you will often be passed by a car you haven't had time to glimpse in your rearview mirror.

The Manitoba roads are full of daredevils. It would not be so bad if you had come from the eastern provinces where highway hazards are not essentially different. But if, like me, you began your journey in British Columbia, the motorist's paradise chiefly because of its excellent and uncrowded roads, you must make yourself a whole new road psychology and give your reflexes full play. Never slow down, for instance, to avoid a gopher. You will quickly learn that these little creatures are of an accomplished stupidity and will be crushed in any event. Never be too confident on curves. On the prairies the visibility is so great that very treacherous curves are needed if the motorist is not to believe them, and treat them as, a straight road. Never trust the advice given you in gas stations about the duration of some stage of your journey. This happened to me several times. You will be told, for instance, 'It's an hour's drive from here.' You look at your map and it shows a distance of seventy-five miles. You must drive at eighty or eighty-five miles an hour to cover seventy-five miles in an hour. At Steinbach, the automobile town, a Buick salesman swore to me at the news of a terrible accident that had taken place in the region the evening before, 'I never drive more than eighty or ninety miles an hour.' So how fast do the others drive? I have some small idea. May it do them good. I remember the comment of a group of young Indians in an old Plymouth more than twenty years old, 'They only need to forbid new cars. We can never go above fifty. The water begins to boil in the radiator.' There is a certain truth in this *reductio ad absurdum*.

INNUMERABLE LAKES Whiteshell is indeed a vacation paradise. There are a million acres of forests, lakes, and rivers, near the Ontario border. It is a provincial park, already very well equipped to receive thousands of lovers of fresh air and sun, and fishing and yachting enthusiasts, each year. There are numerous beaches of white sand, golf links, tennis courts, and so on and on. You can stay at delightful inns or in motels that go from hideous to the ultimate point in luxury and comfort with private beach, panoramic bay, flowered terraces, sterilized glasses, and a cup of coffee in the wall that you can heat up simply by pressing an ordinary switch; immense grounds are at the disposal of trailers or campers in tents. The conifers are small in diameter, the woods very airy, and the forest rarely dramatic. The lakes have the purity of crystal and are tender and very romantic simply because they are never surrounded by mountains. This was the first time I had ever seen so many mountain lakes, without the slightest mountain around. It gives a curious effect, in a way reassuring. You have the feeling you could go right across them without having to swim.

ONLY FOR THE EYE I am not going to speak of all these lakes. Besides, I have my favourite. This is Lake Falcon. There everything is harmony, calmness, and beauty. Nothing comes to shock your glance. A little town among trees. And the sand of the beach is of a milky white, such as you never see elsewhere except on the coasts of Africa, up near Agadir. There were several hundred bathers, but there could be twice as many without breaking the rhythms of this unspoiled landscape, so present to your eye and to your ear. The droning of cars does not prevent your hearing the birds, and wherever you turn your eyes the blue and green reflections of the lake, streaked only by a coming and going of little sailboats, will fill you with inner exaltation.

However, our paradises have forgotten that some travellers sometimes feel the legitimate desire to partake of a full meal. For the several days of my journey through what is considered the vacation paradise of Manitoba — and God knows the term is justified on more than one score — I suffered from hunger. By searching diligently and if you are willing to waste your days hunting them up, you can apply to certain theoretically private fishing clubs, where at certain hours and provided your credentials are in order you will be served a relatively decent meal. But do not search for a restaurant at Falcon Lake, for there are none. Oh, you will sometimes see a promising sign bearing the word that makes you salivate with pleasure. Go in and look at the menu. The Campbell kitchens are in charge of the soup, and the wretched Germans of the rest, via the United States, in the shape of hamburgers and hot dogs. As for the 'French fries', they have nothing French about them, they are only a carbonized parody. I have always been fascinated by how many people, young and old, sometimes in modest circumstances and most often of the middle class, are willing to eat so badly so consistently, in public at least. That this charming Lake Falcon did not offer me the smallest gastronomical inn in its own way defines a total behaviour. That no one here has yet had the idea of starting one means that the enterprise would involve risks. And that an enterprise of this nature involves risks in the midst of such varied refinements is in itself the chief reason for my concern. In this respect Quebec seems to me to be several centuries ahead of the other provinces.

TO EACH HIS FOSSIL   The Tyndall quarry is not at Tyndall but at Garson, the neighbouring municipality. So Tyndall stone should be known as Garson stone. But the name is so well implanted that even the citizens of Garson know and speak of it as Tyndall stone. This is because, long before truck transport, Tyndall was the only railway station in the region, which is directly north of Winnipeg. People said, 'Have you received your Tyndall stones?' and they have continued to do so.

I made a long visit to the quarry, which began to develop at the beginning of the century but contains prehistoric rocks. These are the stones I had seen in the great halls of the Winnipeg parliament, on the façade of the St Boniface Basilica and most of the buildings of the university campus, and which are to be seen at Ottawa and even in the Limoilou church at Quebec. They are more than two hundred and fifty million years old.

It was one o'clock in the afternoon; the sun was violent. I believe it would have been possible to grill a steak on one of the great flat stones with which the quarry is covered. A dozen employees were returning in small groups to their work. I saw them rise from every shady corner — behind the trucks, folds in the rocks, the sheds. The mercury must have climbed to nearly 90 degrees but the heat was dry, as is also the cold on the prairies, and I found it bearable and almost pleasant.

I had been told to ask for Mick Klimchuck. He took charge of my initiation. He is the crew chief. He was here from the beginning, when no one believed in the future of this stone. Today one could not say that it is recognized: it is still a luxury and its cost price is relatively high — for a relatively simple reason that Mick made clear to me as he led me to the bottom of the quarry.

I had the impression that I was going down the steps of an immense open-air Greek theatre, tens of times larger than the theatre at Epidaurus. We reached a central platform, surrounded by electric saws that could cut a house in two. In the middle ground a steam-powered saw, similar to the models in use during the first quarter of the century, was still at work, smoking like an old locomotive. Below, pumps flung up accumulated rain-water in a burst of jets that gave a holiday air to the entire scene. From here I could clearly see the design of at least seven different layers of stone. Of these strata, only two have a market: the surface stratum and that of the great depth. None of the intermediate layers are used in construction. They are accumulated in immense blocks of several tons on almost all the approaches to the quarry, and if you want them you need only help yourself: there is no market for these superb stones. The only two in demand, and these two have a firm market at forty dollars a ton, are the upper stratum, which is pale grey and contains fossils, and the lowest level, the blue layer, as it is called, likewise bearing fossils and one of the warmest, the most subtly shaded, and the most vital stones I know. And I will never understand why so many of our architects have brought marble from Italy at great expense when we need only bend to gather up this marvel, for which foreign builders would envy us if it were better known.

Fossils are to be found in almost all the geological layers. Workmen often detach a few as they work and take them home. But they don't know quite what to do with them. All the children of the district already have large collections. And even so they don't open a fossil shop for tourists. Seeing my interest in these fossils, Klimchuck gave me a chisel and a hammer and said, 'Help yourself,' adding, 'it's more fun.' He was right. It was one of the most entertaining moments of my visit, at least for the workmen who saw me in operation. I walked about avenues bordered by blocks of stone placed one upon the other to a height of about twenty feet and I had an embarrassment of choice between batrachians, fish, and invertebrates of the Silurian, Cambrian, Devonian or Carboniferous period, which bloomed here and there under the cuts of the saw. I chose four particularly well-modelled specimens. I was surprised to be able to detach them quite easily. And I could better understand why these intermediate layers have not found a market. They are as friable as chalk: a few blows of the hammer and the chisel penetrates the stone. There is no danger of destroying the fossil, whose firmness is of another age. The best method is to cut an outline around the fossil, draw the ball thus formed from the stone block, and then strike this mass. The friable stone comes away at once and you will be surprised to see the naked fossil emerge as by a cinema effect.

The four magnificent specimens I brought from Tyndall and that I extracted myself — 'it's more fun' — are part of my daughter's collection. Rather, they were part of it, for the little wretch likes nothing better than to gratify her little friends, complete with explanations that you will not find in all the scientific books. Only one seems to have survived. I noticed it on her work-table in use as a paperweight.

The allusion is not without its utility. Our behaviour towards these fossils is not far from that of children. If I am not mistaken, we have an attraction of rare quality in this Tyndall quarry.

What are we doing with it? A vague commerce. Not a hundred and sixty tons are extracted in a day, which saves the quarry from the least recession. It closed its doors in 1929 until the last war. And each year the sixteen employees must work elsewhere for the duration of the winter. Each spring they commence anew for a few months. If we sometimes give proof in our relations with tourists of an astonishing craftiness, we put a great innocence into it. And when by chance we possess, as at Tyndall, a certain justification for wishing to attract tourists, we are inactive, taken by surprise, shocked. A little like children who are given an elaborate electric train at Christmas that only their father knows how to operate.

Newfoundland

TO ONTARIO AND QUEBEC VIA THE ATLANTIC PROVINCES Newfoundland tomorrow. The weather report gave the temperature there as 45 degrees. It was July. At Winnipeg the mercury was climbing past the 80 mark as we boarded the aircraft.

When we were above Montreal, a voice was heard over the intercom of the tightly filled Vanguard: 'In a few minutes we will put down at Dorval.' This bit of news took the passengers by surprise. No stop had been scheduled for Montreal. At our departure from Toronto we had been informed that the flight would take so many hours — six, I believe — and would carry us directly to Halifax, then to Sydney, and finally to St John's, Newfoundland. The voice in the intercom resumed: 'Passengers are requested not to unfasten their seat-belts. The aircraft will taxi down the runway and immediately take off again.'

The aircraft landed, taxied to the end of the runway, made a complete turn, revved up its motors again, and immediately took off. Under the circumstances it was hard to understand how the passengers would have had the idea even for a second of unfastening their belts. And now we were airborne. We had time to admire Montreal once again as we described a lovely curve above it, flying at low altitude. But few passengers were in a mood to enjoy it. I saw set looks all around me and pale foreheads on which stood drops of sweat. The stewardesses had disappeared. When they returned, their faces were relaxed and smiling. They were perfectly in possession of themselves. Nothing at all had happened. Nothing at least that we would ever know. Was this in the orders? Wouldn't it be better to inform the passengers? Wouldn't the truth be more easily borne than everything we had just imagined? I don't know. It appears that these grave matters are settled at international conferences at which psychiatrists probably have a seat near the airline directors. In such a case, one must say this. In another, it is better for the passengers to know everything. In such and such another, it is better to tell them nothing.

For half an hour we would listen to the noise of the engines and inform ourselves as best we could. And then forgetfulness, the magnificent and rather stupid forgetfulness of people accustomed to flying, would settle upon us. The first luncheon trays were already being carried in. Whatever the menu might be, we would eat it all with a good appetite. Whole countries live happily on top of volcanoes. In Japan twenty-two-storey building are being built. There hasn't been a serious earthquake for half a century, confidence is restored. It was not this that most surprised me. I have known for a long time that we possess a faculty for forgetting that is perhaps the most valuable resource of the human spirit. What would we do, for instance, if we could not forget that we are born with the cross of death on our foreheads, as in Montherlant's colonies? No, my greatest astonishment had been the discovery that at least half the passengers, about forty, had been indifferent to the incident. The aircraft might have plunged to the earth like a dead leaf and they wouldn't even have glanced towards the windows.

Such people are the ideal clientele of the airlines. My neighbour belonged to this breed. He explained what must have happened. In his opinion the mechanism of the undercarriage had blocked, we had been flying with the wheels down, which would have braked us terribly. We could only unblock them by landing on the runway. It was a fanciful explanation, it seemed to me, but he defended it calmly, with the help of some valuable documentation from the *Reader's Digest*. It never occurred to him for an instant that the wheels might have been locked inside the plane, forcing us to make a belly landing. Such an idea would never occur to him. He had decided once for all to travel on these aircraft that go to their point of arrival without fuss.

And so had I.

EXCEPTIONAL DECOR   It might be Naples; it is only St John's. A play of gentle, very romantic mountains around a deep indentation of the ocean; a few little roads along the waterfront, on which scores of raw wooden houses, blackened by the winds and spray, trace their dark veins against new buildings which today blaze with whiteness under a cinematic sun. In the background new avenues and new neighbourhoods are woven slowly, like a spider's web, around the culminating point of the landscape: the St John's Basilica, an ugly but rather touching structure. You might believe a storm had carried away the upper half of the towers. Nothing of the sort. It was conceived that way and it is considered very beautiful here.

I hastened to climb to the heights of Cabot Tower, a sort of eagle's nest perched above the city, on the seashore. It is there one should make one's first contact with St John's. We will never be able to forget again that its situation is very exceptional and that people come from far away to admire it.

I expected to find Newfoundland under fog, and I glimpsed it under a Mediterranean sky. But I was glad I made good use of my first hours. In my whole stay, I would never see the sun again except in brief flashes. The end of July offered me only wind, rain, or haze. 'Is this normal?' I hastened to ask almost everyone as the days passed and the mercury very rarely rose above sixty. I received all imaginable replies, sometimes even from old fishermen. 'Perfectly normal. We have only two seasons here — winter and fall.' 'Absolutely normal. Our summer is short, but it is the most beautiful in the world.' 'The winter is windy and foggy, but the temperature never goes down below zero as with you. The Newfoundland climate is temperate.' All sorts of replies. Just the same I formed an impression. Let us say that in summer you are not likely to suffer from the heat and that on certain evenings in July you will see smoke rising from the chimneys. The beaches are not congested. A big swimming pool assures us that it is 'heated in all seasons'. A shop selling summer clothes is inconceivable: this little specialty occupies only timid corners of the windows of stores, which clearly depend on a more durable trade. And sales of suntan creams are not likely to enrich the few drugstores that offer you various brands, with the air of saying: 'We are able to satisfy all whims.' If St John's, Newfoundland, intends to launch itself seriously into the tourist business, it should reverse steam and say, for instance, 'Escape torrid, suffocating heat. Come and enjoy the benefits of air-cooled summers' and it could emphasize the absence of ir-ritating pollen, which makes this land a sort of paradise for hay-fever sufferers. I know what I myself would then add. The romantic nature of the setting. Mountains much higher than our Laurentians and sometimes as spectacular as our Rockies, and yet of a rounded shape with wild grass growing among conifers, as if these forests had been planted on English lawns. They should also speak of the sense of strangeness one receives from this population that is too newly Canadian to be so in depth, this foreign country just an hour and a half's flight from us. And the luminous quality of the summer mist on certain mornings. And the poetry of this small, lively, animated harbour in a country one might have believed completely uninhabited, when we observed it first from the air. When St John's makes up its mind to attract tourists, it will draw off one of the most interest-ing clienteles, experienced travellers in search of landscapes and emotions they have not known elsewhere.

TALKING STREETS   The city through which I was walking is the oldest in North America. St John's, Newfoundland, was an international port when New York was only a vague tract of land and you could buy Manhattan Island for fifty dollars. I had moved until now through the provinces of the West, where the cities proudest of their history had not had a century of life. Now I was in a seaport that became in 1583 the cornerstone of the British empire in America. In the course of its history it was successively under the guardianship of the Dutch, the English, and the French, and experienced an infinite number of raids and battles before America was even out of diapers. Its five centuries of history do not sound like a picnic. Nor do its winters. Nor does the daily life of its fishermen. This is not a land of ease, as you can tell simply by walking down the streets of the city. Not that the houses are crumbling. You would have to search for a long time to find one more than a hundred years old. For fire is also part of the general picture. And for every ten old houses of blackened wood, you will find a hundred that are not twenty-five years old. This city has little seductiveness, to tell the truth, but it has charm, that of a blazing fireplace. It warms the whole countryside, which otherwise would seem inhuman and abandoned. This is a deception, though. I did not yet know that few of our provinces are so marked by the presence of man.

Even the city itself is something of a miracle. For more than three centuries it was forbidden to settle there. St John's was to be only a base for the fishing fleets of the British merchants. Once the fishing season was over, everyone had to pack up and go home. Each captain had the order to bring back all his crew and his fishermen. Deserters were subject to heavy penalties and, at any rate, could count only on their own resources throughout the winter. The first deserters died of starvation and exposure. An entire series of regulations intended to prevent white settlement on Newfoundland was revoked only in about 1811 — that is to say long after the whole St John's area adjacent to the harbour had been inhabited.

CONFEDERATION BUILDING   It will be pointed out to you that this is the vastest complex of modern construction that has ever been placed at the disposition of a government in America. This is perhaps the truth and it matters little after all. It is the contents of a building that interest you. But be that as it may, this twelve-storey brick building will seem to you more appropriate than those immense marble parliaments in Greco-something-or-other style that have mushroomed across the country. And there is no danger here that anyone will play that Winnipeg trick of explaining the protocol of ancient sacrifices.

It is called Confederation Building for obvious reasons. It was born of the new obligations created by the union of Newfoundland with Canada in 1949. Here are grouped all the governmental and administrative services from the prime minister's offices to the cleaning department. The quarters reserved to the different services have not the luxuriousness we might be led to expect by the style and ostentation of the central hall, or of the legislative assembly. Here there is a rather unusual atmosphere: all the members are seated on the same side of the room, or almost so. Prime Minister Smallwood personally revised the plans of the whole building and this resulted in arrangements that show his astonishing care for efficiency. From his office the prime minister can go straight into the library of parliament or the cabinet room, or to his secretary, or to a private elevator that gives him direct access to the legislative assembly on the upper floor. There are doors enough in this one room to make a stage director dream. The allusion is not unmerited. Smallwood has a keen sense of theatre.

Since the building is built in the vertical, the windows open on one side upon the ocean and the harbour of St John's and on the other upon the mountain. Everyone comes and goes here, especially in the big entrance hall, as if on a stage. They are beginning to become part of the scenery now and are scarcely embarrassed by the projectors. I often have this impression in our big American buildings, rather as if everything were taking place before an invisible audience. There is a certain way of walking, of sitting, of picking up the telephone, of knitting the brows, of protruding the lower lip between two sentences: it is perhaps the kickback from the cinema.

There was a time when the chief business street of St John's, on the edge of the harbour, was deserted by all good people. I was told that during the war, because of the proximity of two important American and Canadian bases, a considerable number of girls attracted by the military took over this little street each evening after six o'clock, putting the local population to flight. The authorities had to step in and dust off old laws against prostitution, but nothing availed. Today Water Street is calm and uneventful, as provincial as you could wish. A two-storey shop assumes immense proportions; the whole is so harmonious, discreet, and modest. How charming are these little cities at the end of the world which open up all day with metropolitan airs and close up again at nightfall like sensitive plants.

A few neon lights remind you of the presence of an excellent restaurant. Of a quite high standard, it has no serious rival. Newfoundland is not the land of gastronomy, as who did not know in advance? It is astonishing enough that a restaurant of this quality exists in St John's — a quality that the big kitchens of the Newfoundland Hotel, where I had stopped like everyone else, might envy. The Newfoundland is another of those big comfortable but pleasant nonentities of our railway chains, which operate at full capacity all year. Perhaps this is what prevents them from sprucing themselves up a bit, despite the huge profits they must make.

Soon after I arrived, it was invaded by cabinet ministers, ministers' wives, ministers' secretaries, and ministerial advisers, who blew away all the people with whom I had made contact. And then I heard in the hall — you would have had to be deaf not to hear it — a spoken French that made it clear that Quebec was participating in this conference. It was a native product, no doubt accustomed to open spaces. He was introduced to me and I was carried along with a group into the last of a series of rooms

where travellers gather to talk. I was surprised to see him maintain his voice at a pitch quite at odds with the size of this
muffled room. But he proved a resourceful companion, whose
loose attachment to the ministerial delegation allowed him innumerable hours of leisure, and he took charge of the first hours
of my local education with consummate science. He began in a
spectacular fashion by letting me taste the native drink, a little
fallen from popularity today but long a great favourite, in the
days when pure rum came from the Antilles, legally or not, for
a song: it is called calabogus. It is a mixture of rum and spruce
beer.

Notice to specialists: with the best will in the world, I am sure
I am in no danger of over-indulging in calabogus.

PICTURES OF ST JOHN'S   Nothing happens in this little city quite
as it does elsewhere. Some people have all the time in the world,
and others are in a tremendous hurry. I had to tell my story
countless times in the course of my first walks through the city.
In contrast to this, you will meet a high civil servant, surrounded
by half a dozen telephones, who had his dinner the night before
last at Teheran, slept at Rome, lunched at Lisbon, and returned
to St John's in time for dinner last night. Because of the time
difference, he went to his office after only three hours' sleep and
will be off tomorrow for Boston.

There are those that have time like Judge Higgins, who speaks
to you familiarly at the exit to his office in what Newfound-
landers still call the 'Supreme Court', and those whose time is
money, like the businessman who is building new motels here
and there in the interior of the province, before any travellers
have even ventured that way.

Among those that had time was the proprietor of a shop with
a promising name, at least to me: 'Au coin français'. I took up
as little space as possible in this establishment devoted to fine
lingerie and trinkets. A sort of giant, rather like Harold Mac-
millan, came to the rescue of his employee, who was disturbed
by my speaking to him in French. He himself spoke several

words in our language, with that very pleasant accent that Europeans sometimes have, and continued in English when he knew enough about me to feel authorized to do so. He spoke that excellent 'English' English that I heard almost everywhere here, not only in the hotel, the public places, and the streets, but on radio and television. It is this that gives Newfoundland some of its exoticism.

Mr Steven is a teacher of Scottish origin. With a great deal of humour he told me of his journey from his teaching days to this ladies' shop. I learned all sorts of rather personal details, for I was already almost one of the family. His wife, for instance, was spending her holidays about two steps from here, at the Newfoundland Hotel. He described her to me. I certainly must have passed her in the corridors. He went to join her at dinner, whenever she phoned to invite him. I did see the two of them together, in fact, later on. After a fortnight she would return to her place 'Au coin français' in excellent form, as if she had spent her vacation at the other end of the earth. This was the first time I had ever heard of such an arrangement. It seemed to function admirably.

AS MANY VILLAGES AS THERE ARE INHABITANTS   You have a curious sensation after you consider a detailed map of the province. On the east there is a complex of four peninsulas forming the letter 'H' and joined to the rest of the island by an isthmus. You might imagine that only these four peninsulas have had time to develop during the last century. You will be surprised to see fishing villages spread all along the entire six thousand miles of coast. It is quite unimaginable — there are almost as many villages as there are people.

This is scarcely an exaggeration. The entire population of Newfoundland is not more than half a million. If you subtract the population of St John's, about 80,000, and those of the towns of the interior, like Grand Falls and the new industrial town of Corner Brook, opposite St John's, not far from the Gulf of St

Lawrence, how many thousands are there left for those innumerable fishing villages that have mushroomed in all the coves, the inlets, the basins, and the bays? It cannot allow a very big average per village and I have in fact seen places of only ten or so houses.

When a son marries, a big house is built for him — the fishermen's houses are often spacious, because long months are lived indoors — and it is built if possible in a neighbouring cove so as to assure him of a perfect autonomy. And in this way it came about that all the habitable coasts very quickly became inhabited. And so you have the unexpected result of never feeling at the end of the world in this huge, thinly peopled island. Now that communication is no longer entirely by sea and a considerable network of roads is being developed, you will never drive more than a few miles without coming upon a village, or even a little town. It was this that most struck me as I undertook my excursions in almost every direction from St John's. This island of often naked and spectacular mountains is warmed everywhere by the presence of man.

I drove thus for several days, amid rain, fog, and wind, with very rare breaks in the clouds. The weather changes constantly in Newfoundland, and it often happens that you experience all four seasons in a single day. At every instant, the coastal road offers you glimpses of ocean and mountain, to which the mist or even the rain gives a romantic, mobile, and slightly unreal dimension. You cannot quite believe that at the end of this road there are houses, men, women, a school, a church, television aerials, big cars, smiles, tears, and life. The road changes abruptly into a quagmire, plunges into a thicket of spruce, and at once emerges gloriously upon a little village drawn by a dreaming child, with all the houses placed just so on a cove protected by a flat rock that juts deeply into the ocean. This is Flatrock. The wind is up. The fishermen are not on the ocean. We will have plenty of time to meet them.

The cod trap is made of a sort of squared net, held to the surface by floats, and extended by a vertical net against which the cod flings itself. It will naturally follow this net to the openings cut in both sides of it at the entrance to the square trap. It then begins to circle without ever finding the exits. The traps are emptied between five and seven o'clock in the morning and then the whole thing begins over again. For this work, which in many cases does not take one very far from shore, flat-bottomed, locally built boats are used. The Newfoundland fishermen are great boat builders; they have developed techniques completely adapted to their needs. Near Port-de-Grave, I had occasion to chat with a champion, who can build a trawler in his improvised boatworks as readily as a dory. The keel is made of Douglas fir and all the rest of spruce, the most abundant wood on the island.

Below the main street of Flatrock, which climbs in a straight line to the church — everyone has a view of the ocean here — there was a little family business in operation. For the first time I watched preparation of cod, from the time it left the boats until it was put in the freezer as fillets. This is usually done in big plants. The small enterprises, and they are innumerable, sell the green cod to the wholesalers for about three dollars a hundredweight. This is less lucrative than dried cod, by twelve to fifteen dollars a hundredweight, but green cod requires a minimum of preparation. Though the fishing villages differ greatly from one another in their surroundings, it is evident that the same mode of living and working is found all along the coasts. But the duration of the season varies, depending upon whether the port is open to the ocean or more or less enclosed. At Flatrock they take out the boats for only two or three months at the most. A few miles to the north, Port-de-Grave, which is naturally protected, has a five-month season.

A haunting image, one I found everywhere — the doors of the houses are whole, blind, without even the smallest pane of glass. That sight alone is enough to make us aware of the violence of the winter winds. Not the cold, for I had heard it repeated too often for it not to be true that the temperature rarely goes below zero in Newfoundland. But cold less intense than elsewhere could make certain winter days unbearable here because of the wind, the fog, and the damp.

A cow browsed quietly at the side of the road. She was a privileged creature here, as in India. The village has seventy sheep and six milk cows. Beef is very seldom eaten and then it is imported. The Newfoundland livestock is limited to sheep. Everything else comes from elsewhere. But because Newfound-landers are great consumers of fresh, smoked, and dried fish, and most of the little villages are assured of a certain autonomy in food production, every day is Friday here — which might cause trouble elsewhere but not at Flatrock, which is of Scottish and Catholic origin. And besides, some of these Fridays can be turned into Sundays. The Newfoundland housewife is very resourceful, and fresh cod is delicious — fresh, that is eaten right after it leaves the boats. So only fishermen know fresh cod. And it makes all the difference. I myself encountered this horror only in the form of codliver oil in my childhood. I scarcely felt drawn by the thought of tasting it. However, I went from surprise to surprise. But you must be lucky enough to eat cod in a home and not count too much on restaurants, large or small.

WHAT DO THE YOUNG PEOPLE DREAM OF? I went from one little fishing port to another up to the northern extremity of the 'H' I spoke of earlier, which is composed of the four principal penin-sulas attached to the island of Newfoundland. Of course I do not intend to describe each one in turn, though I am very much tempted to do so, for the surroundings change before your eyes and the cove you are about to discover is entirely different from the one you have just left. The villages are also different, and the populations — sometimes Scottish, sometimes Irish, some-times English — are never the same. I shall simply evoke a few memories that seem to me to cast some light upon one of the most engaging and most romantic provinces in Canada.

On the way to Pouch Cove I picked up a young man who was walking in the rain. His truck had broken down a few miles back and I don't know how far he had travelled on foot in search of a gas station — and without success. While I busied myself with his problem, he talked to me freely about the existence of the young people of Newfoundland. He was about twenty-five. He had served two years in the army, in various parts of Canada, chiefly in British Columbia. Why? By choice, because he had wanted to travel a little. For a time he had fancied making it his career. And then his father needed him to help in his general store. He came back, found his old friends, including a girl who had now grown up and wisely waited for him to specify certain plans for the future. When I asked him if he believed he would remain in Newfoundland all his life, he said 'Yes' with a sigh and after a dreamy silence.

It is true that his truck had broken down. When he continued on his way shortly afterwards he was able to smile again and of his own accord showed me a photograph of his fiancée. One does not really believe in a marriage in those parts until after the young couple have left the church on their wedding morning. Many young men spend two or three seasons fishing and set out for elsewhere with their nest egg. More and more of them do it. For this reason the government is endeavouring by every means possible to create new jobs each year. As for the successors to the old fishermen, it is no doubt possible, and even probable, that they will be found, but I don't believe in it. Television and films, which are present wherever electricity goes, have put the young men in touch with a universe that is fascinating and so much easier. Their dreams are quite similar to those of all the adolescents of the world: in short, big cars, money, life.

A lad of fifteen explained all this to me beside a black rock, where his father and two brothers were struggling to raise the baskets of cod to the vertical with the help of an arrangement of cables.

He concluded with a smile that took on an indescribably pathetic quality here, at just this moment, 'I'm studying. I'm not ever going to do that work. I'm going to go away.'

THE CHIEF PROBLEM Education is one of the chief problems to which the Smallwood government has applied itself since 1949. Before that the principal centres had their schools, and elsewhere the local priest took over the responsibility for the education of the village with assistance from an elderly spinster, but several generations were never able to set foot in a school. Thousands of men, women, and children could neither read nor write.

In fifteen years schools on the primary level have multiplied at a comforting rate. And fewer and fewer teachers must instruct the entire eleven grades, sometimes with only one or two pupils in each. A certain number of regional secondary schools have also been built to give young people the opportunity to have access to administration, business, office work, and all the new technical disciplines, as well as to university. For the young Newfoundlanders, a leap of several centuries has been accomplished in less than fifteen years.

Study bursaries have become an institution; a greater number are distributed each year in Newfoundland than in all the other provinces combined. Otherwise there would be danger that the magnificent vocational training centres, the government's most lucid effort to prepare the new generations for industrial development, would be empty. Too much cannot be asked of fishermen's families, the greater number of which just manage to survive. That they consent to be separated from a child, almost drawn by lot, for the whole period of his studies, is itself a sort of miracle. It is fine that they see the value of it. Though this is not the case with all families. Some have refused, without discussion, a scholarship won by the oldest son, still a minor. This phenomenon is fortunately rare enough that there has been no thought of taking official measures against it. But that the phenomenon exists, somewhere among us, is enough to give one a touch of nausea.

Everywhere that the still infant highway system permits, school buses carry the children to school. In certain regions, the same classrooms serve two or three different groups in the course of the day, to assure the maximum use of the available space.

LOVE AT FIRST SIGHT FOR PORT-DE-GRAVE I see them again on the approaches to the dock. There were about ten of them sitting in the sun, on sacks or wooden benches, their backs against a cement wall. They were smoking their pipes, reading the paper, or talking. Some of them were old but there were others that weren't yet thirty. The day was over. There were still some good hours of leisure before night. The latecomers were busy washing the dock and dismantling the equipment that had been used to prepare the cod. On fine days this work is done outdoors at Port-de-Grave.

The village is widespread and the houses are grouped snugly one against the other on the flank of a hill, along a single street. The port is natural, protected along its breadth by a series of rocks, which rise up regularly and close together, like icebergs. Between these rocks are corridors wide enough to permit the passage of a fishing trawler without perilous manoeuvres. The effect is striking, as if it had been designed by a man's hand and set in place by an army of slaves. All around Newfoundland nature has worked like this for the fishermen for millenia. I felt the same sense of the infinite here as I did in Polynesia at the entrance to the natural passages cut in the coral reefs before each of the largest bays, as if God had said to man, 'Here you will build your city.'

There are villages where contact is direct, open, and irresist-ible. Here at Port-de-Grave, I was aware, I should have to pass an exam. I had left my car at the end of the village and now approached the fishermen with the innocence of a solitary walker. A lovely clearing had succeeded the fog and the rain; it seemed as if the sun had at last decided to settle down in New-foundland for several days. There was good humour in the air, and they watched me come as if I were the messenger of the king. But from the beginning I realized sharply that these ten fishermen had gathered into a single person before the stranger. I could still ask my questions; they would reply only in groups or through the voice of a spokesman after several moments of silent consultation. This was clear to me; they were forming a monolithic block, and this gives one a curious sensation. You feel that you are in the wings, now you are on the stage, the curtain has risen, and you must do your little turn. Well, precisely — I hadn't anything prepared, and I think they were grateful for this. After two fragments of rather foolish conversation, I kept silent as willingly as they did, and like them I looked at the sea. One of the younger men got up and began to ask me a great many questions, while giving the impression that he was replying to mine. The whole group listened with an open and frank attention. I was passing my exam. And then I turned to an old man with mischievous eyes, who had not yet uttered a word but had not missed a single one of my gestures or syllables, and spoke to him in calculated admiration of his pipe, an unusual enough object to find in the mouth of a Newfoundland fisherman. It must have come from China, at any rate from the Orient. I had chanced on the right subject. There was a great burst of laughter that I can still hear and that warmed my heart. From that moment the game was won. I was introduced all round, and I might still be at Port-de-Grave if at the end of the evening a lad had not come to tell me, quite unperturbed, that my car was blocking the way of an enormous truck.

If I have tried to reproduce a little of the climate of certain, sometimes rather delicate approaches, it is because, in its own way, this defines a manner of thinking. Only an exceedingly pressed and hurried traveller would read timidity into such behaviour. A much more profound feeling is involved, a feeling I found again like a watermark on my conversations in even the most advanced circles. A little as if people were reasoning within themselves: 'You are a stranger to Newfoundland. So whatever you do, however sharp your powers of perception may be, you will never understand anything of what we are or of what we have done under conditions that would have driven you to despair. You will settle the whole matter by telling everyone that we are poor, without seeing that we have given proof of an

*I turned to an old man with mischievous eyes and spoke to him in
calculated admiration of his pipe.*

almost superhuman tenacity.' This, more or less, was the un-
spoken backdrop to all my Newfoundland encounters. And I
know now that it is an important spiritual reality upon which the
traveller must embroider his pictures. They will have no value
otherwise. They will shatter into pieces.

THE RISING CITY If you go right to the opposite end of the Trans-
Canada Highway, you will end up at Corner Brook, a real city
and still rapidly expanding. It is situated back from Island Bay,
which opens widely upon the Gulf of St Lawrence. The total
population does not exceed thirty thousand, but it is the centre
of a vast region of forest, hydraulic power, and minerals. Its rate
of growth accelerates each year, and with the development of
Labrador and the west coast it is still impossible to predict the
extent of its expansion in the course of the next quarter century.
It is not unfeasible that it may dangerously rival St John's and
some day make the centre of gravity of this new province swing
to that side. Yet its beginnings were modest. Christopher Fisher's
little mill became in the course of years the vast Bowater Organization, one of the largest pulp and paper industries in the world,
which ensures permanent employment to at least three thousand
in the locality. But let us look at what is new. A cement factory,
a hundred and fifty employees. The government set it up in
1952 and hastened to hand it over to a private company as soon
as it had found a taker. The same is true of Atlantic Gypsum,
which gives work to two-hundred-odd employees, specializing in
construction materials suited to the present needs of Newfoundland. The intention, in both cases, was to prove that Newfoundland is in a position to utilize its own resources on the spot. But
all this would remain rather slender without the mysterious
bonds that seem to join Corner Brook's destiny to that of Labrador, its rich neighbour across the way, which some day might
well make a noisy entrance onto the Canadian scene.

It has become a rite: each province will soon be the richest
and the most prosperous in the country. In Alberta it is oil, in

Saskatchewan potash, but I confess that I did not expect to hear the same refrain in Newfoundland.

All this is a sign of good health. A big country like ours can develop only by competition. We are just studying for our matriculation. But Newfoundland? You have counted without Labrador. When you bring up some problem that seems to you a dead-end street, the reply will come, 'Oh, but have you thought that in Labrador . . .'

Nova Scotia

The DC-8 went into a dive through a thick layer of clouds. It will soon be Canadian autumn in all its splendour, I thought. But we came out of one cumulus only to enter another. Perhaps the whole earth had liquefied and we would emerge from the other side and head for the moon. This idea was in some way reassuring just at this moment. I was always seized with the same panic when I was about to undertake the exploration of a province of which I still knew nothing.

Now the autumn blazed wherever I turned my eyes. I had believed the sun was indispensable to it. But there were fragments of light around lakes and on the slopes of mountains. It seemed to me that the sun would spoil this festival of light, which welled from the earth. I was often to have this sensation as I travelled around Nova Scotia.

What did it come from? Perhaps accounts of the 1917 explosion or year-end reports of the harbour activities. . . . I had imagined Halifax as an ugly, smoke-laden city, hysterical and slightly frenzied. Compared to the picture I had formed of it, I found it charming from the outset. In the first place, one has access to it by a suspension bridge that has no reason to envy its colleague at the other extremity of the country, Vancouver's Lion Gate. Named for the celebrated prime minister of Nova Scotia, Angus L. Macdonald, this superb structure represents the third attempt to link Halifax to Dartmouth, its neighbour across the way. Halifax is in fact a prisoner of its peninsula and its development can spread only to the opposite shore. Dartmouth is profiting fully from this situation and is at the moment the expanding city. But thanks to the Macdonald Bridge, a single future joins the complex, and even though municipalities are multiplying, it is evident that all this region will some day bear the same name. The bridge dominates from a great height one of the most beautiful ports in the world on one side, and on the other Bedford Basin, a sort of inner lake where scores of fishing trawlers still take refuge at the approach of storm.

The checkerboard of streets towards which the bridge was rapidly bearing me was outlined in trees, and this was not the least of my surprises. If all the streets of the city had been as bare as I had imagined them, its desolate architecture, the wretched brick of its business streets and the sickly stone of its old buildings would have made my first contact with Halifax rather cheerless on this rainy October night.

OTHER PEOPLE'S WARS   Halifax is above all the Citadel. You are not likely to forget this, for its walls rise over the city, and to get from one district to another you often have to drive along the flanks of the hill it overhangs. It is a real citadel with its arrangement of walls, its bastions, and its handsome cannon. It has just one peculiarity: that of never having served.

The war waged by France and England for the possession of North America passed around, wide of, and at angles to Halifax, but never made the slightest pause there. One might say, on the contrary, that wars, including the last one, were profitable to this city and that for it the world's sufferings have expressed themselves ultimately as the tinklings of cash registers. Reread the stories of the capture of Louisbourg or Quebec and you will see that at Halifax the sounds of festivities and gala entertainments cover the sound of cannon.

From the strategic point of view I believe that the Halifax citadel is in a very sorry state, but it is a pretty place to visit. Its lawns are as English as lawns can be when they take the trouble, two museums tell you about battles that took place elsewhere, and several paths up the hill become the willing accomplices of lovers on summer evenings. With a tear of nostalgia for its brilliant wartime soirées, the Halifax citadel fills the same tourist and romantic functions as does the citadel of Quebec, and as do all the citadels of the world probably in this era of supersonic aviation. One small bomb, and all these splendid structures, yesterday still impregnable, would dissolve in a cloud of medieval dust.

I know where I stand. I shall never like citadels. Those that have been used upset me. The others seem to me deliciously absurd.

Quite by chance, during one of my walks around the harbour of Halifax, I suddenly found myself face to face with the *Bluenose*. She is the second specimen, the property of a local brewer. I counted on seeing her only around Lunenburg, that little town of German origin where her builders are well known. But one never knows where the *Bluenose* will next appear. Her owners, or their friends, or the friends of their friends, always have plans that assure her a fairly eventful day-to-day existence. She was being unloaded at this moment of empty crates, which told in their own way that she had been the scene of a fashionable reception.

Bluenose II is the exact replica of the first of her species, which bore off four international championships in the North Atlantic. What a lasting shock it was to catch sight of her like this, without warning. There are children's dreams behind such triumphs of ship-building. And this is her principal charm.

After travelling across our over-structured America, what a sudden delight to be confronted with such delicious, useless things. They are part of the mythology of childhood, which the rest of us find only on Christmas Eve, but happily some of our millionaires still know how to provide for themselves, between two banking operations.

HOSPITALITY . . . AN ART OF LIVING   A provincial civil servant decided that I had still seen nothing of his city. . . . 'Have you seen the silhouette of the devil in the third window of St Paul's Church? Have you attended a session of the city council? Have you visited our yacht club? And Dalhousie University?' Yes indeed, I hastened to say. I was intending this very day . . . But there was nothing for it. He picked me up in his own car, put off his appointments for several hours, and decided to round out my education.

He is an appealing personality. There are many such in Halifax. 'He pushes his own goods,' as they say of a good salesman, but he puts style into it and wields humour in a diverting way. He was a pure-bred Scot, like hundreds that must exist in the streets of Glasgow. He pokes gentle fun at the flag of Nova Scotia, the only Canadian province that has possessed its emblem by royal charter since 1621, pokes just enough fun so that you will be able to get out of the trap he has set for you so elegantly. For you will understand that for him, as for all his fellow-citizens, the Nova Scotia flag is a serious, solemn, and deeply rooted thing.

In the same way he will have done what is necessary to get you enrolled in the Order of Good Cheer. You will not quite know what it is, but he will hand you a sort of diploma engraved in gold, on which your name appears in Gothic letters. This is an honour theoretically reserved for visiting personalities. You will blush with confusion when you understand that it is not a hoax. The Order of Good Cheer, of which Samuel de Champlain was the first Grand Master, was founded in 1606. At the time the colonists of Port-Royal had passed two rather hard winters and saw the approach of the third with a good deal of apprehension. Champlain then had the idea of this new society. Each day, a member of the Order of Good Cheer had the duty of providing the food and inventing games. This was the occasion for royal feasts almost every evening of the long winter. A ritual was established, recipes were invented, and the chroniclers wax lyrical in their praise of moose-pâté pies and beavers' tails en casserole. Today the Order of Good Cheer has several thousand members in all of North America, but only a little nucleus continues to maintain the tradition on the spot, that is to say at Halifax. And this tradition frankly takes on a tourist character. Why not? And of what importance is it?

I was interested only in the reaction of my guide. For him this was much more than a pleasant story of times past. For him the Order of Good Cheer defined the personal character of Nova Scotia, as did its flag, its tartans, the bagpipes, and the entire arsenal of folklore. There is a breath of the artificial in all this that might irritate you if it were not so innocent, so frank, and ultimately useless. For Nova Scotia could leave all this gimcrackery in the hands of the manufacturers of souvenirs; the real charms of this province are elsewhere — in its landscapes and especially in its people. They joke among themselves, as do the Scots, about their thrift, which often shows itself in little things. But there are few provinces where so open and simple a hospitality is practised. I who have made it a point of honour to invite all my interlocutors to my table, had now to defend myself from an incalculable number of invitations. Everywhere else I had no trouble respecting my agenda. Here, I had to turn it upside down repeatedly in order not to disappoint my hosts of an evening. Each time these were delightful moments. These people scarcely knew me, they were very little concerned about that far-off province, Quebec. This was simply an occasion for a moment of pure hospitality and the pleasure of talking with someone who had come from afar and brought news of the world. These people had opened the doors of their hearts to me before they opened the doors of their houses.

FIRE, A PERMANENT ENEMY   My impromptu guide had a story. He was a volunteer fireman. They train several hours a week, after a very serious period of initiation. Recruiting is easy in this city that has known so much tragedy.

Everyone is sensitive to the permanent danger of fire. Everyone obscurely dreads the always possible catastrophe. Throw a cigarette butt on the sidewalk, even when it is streaming with water, and the foot of a passer will extend with a circular movement to put it well out. . . . Who has not heard of the terrible explosion of 1917? Who will not find the occasion to tell you what he remembers of it? It was more spectacular, more deadly than the San Francisco earthquake or the Chicago fire. Sixteen hundred dead, the greater number of them burned alive in the conflagration that followed the collision of two ships in the port, one of them, the *Mont Blanc*, loaded with dynamite. Eight thousand injured, forty thousand without shelter on that December morning of 1917, in wartime and during the harshest winter Nova Scotia had experienced in more than twenty years. There have been other catastrophes at Halifax, many others though infinitely less tragic. In short, my companion knew why he was a volunteer fireman. He belongs to a generation that could calculate the terrifying supremacy of fire over man. There will never be a sufficient number allied against it.

He had devoted several hours of his leisure to the brigade when one day during practice, while he was at the top of an eighty-foot ladder, the mechanism suddenly loosened, the ladder abruptly folded, precipitating him into a fall that caused him an incredible number of fractures. . . . He told me all this with a certain humour, as if the accident dated from the Middle Ages and concerned someone else. In fact, he had just left the hospital after spending four months in a plaster cast and experiencing a thousand sorts of agonies. Shortly afterwards, when we got out of the car, he gave a demonstration of walking and trotting to show me he hadn't suffered any serious handicap.

PROGRESS CATCHES UP WITH THE PAST He spoke to me of other things, that is to say of the super-supermarket before which we had just stopped. He was affecting detachment but I could see that I would have to be openly admiring if I did not wish to disappoint him.

This 'supermarket' trick had been pulled on me so many times during my visits to our cities, great and small, with natives that I should have acquired the right to be not only amused but even irritated. For what is more like one such 'whatnot', as some of the great of this world call them, than another whatnot of the same sort? And yet I had no desire to laugh. This man, otherwise adult and very intelligent, this man who had travelled widely and had just recovered from four months of immobility with profound ideas about life, this man who had talked to me about his city with that particular humour by which modesty most often expresses itself, was visibly very attached to this super-supermarket, and I honestly wished to try to understand this. So I did my utmost to visit the place with the same happy gait and see it with his eyes.

We raced through interminable passages, lined on both sides with shops and green plants; we came out onto the eternal little inner square, decked out with a fountain, a few reading benches, and an aquarium. We climbed staircases to obtain bird's-eye views of the festival of light that was taking place on the ground floor. We even went down to the basement to find the bowl-o-drome, as certain people call them. Well, I saw an immensity, a universe, a galaxy of bowling alleys, where people were amusing themselves knocking down pins, the newest of which have vaguely the shape of policemen's batons. This, it seemed, might well be the largest bowl-o-drome in the province, perhaps in Canada or even in America. The players have a choice of various counters to restore their souls or, if they care to, they can even treat themselves to a pause at a tavern or a cosy bar. But I hadn't seen anything yet. There was also a movie theatre, a children's nursery, and an infirmary for emergencies. We went back up, this time by escalator, to find the precise spot where the podium is erected on evenings when there are concerts. No trifling music. Mozart and Beethoven have been offered here.

And then suddenly I understood it all. Below I caught sight of some adolescent boys, books under their arms, who had stopped to make conversation with some girls. There were five of them, all blushing. Beyond them, some animated groups might well be discussing politics. Slightly withdrawn, on a bench, an old man smoked his pipe and watched the fashionable people in the central avenue. He might have been at the hotel in Dawson or on the front stoop of his own house, in his village. Shortly before we had met a young man, the rising alderman. He had scarcely had time to shake hands with us for he was already late for an appointment with a colleague at the super-supermarket restaurant. Yes, I understood. I understood that with this formula we have re-invented the market of Athens, of Pompeii, and of Rome, all the marketplaces of Europe. We have adapted them to our new needs, we have protected them against the rigour of our winters, we have equipped them with all the little cossetings of American life. They have become the faithful reflection of a society and a period, or at least a moment of that society. For they will refine as we do. The decorations will become less aggressive, the lighting more sober, the showcases better arranged, the window-dressing more harmonious, and the catalogue of our resources wider and less directly dependent upon American invention.

Before I saw them through the eyes of my companion, places of this sort had always seemed to me rather depressing, even at peak hours, when they might have been expected to draw me into their rhythm by their deafening bustle. They have become transformed with time. Young people have discovered love here, conflicts have been settled, others have been secretly hatched. These places have become, like all the true markets of the world, a point of encounter, a convergence, an accord with life. They have become humanized.

FIRST NON-SECTARIAN UNIVERSITY In all the Atlantic provinces Dalhousie University enjoys the same prestige as Laval, Montreal, or McGill. Even the Acadians sometimes prefer to take law, medicine, or science here. The campus, which is in the middle of Halifax, is much more suggestive of England than all the broad, beautiful campuses of our new western universities, which have so visibly been taken in tow by American concepts. Here, everything is compact, modest, functional. A quality of austerity rules, as does red brick.

I talked with a few students. Inquiries of this sort have nothing rigorous about them, nor are they scientific, and I don't want to present them as such. I might have chanced to fall upon giddy enthusiasts. These students were not. They complained of material conditions, of the poorness of some of the equipment, of the fees, of the cost of living. Students here cannot find as remunerative summer jobs as can students in the West, or in Ontario, or even in Quebec. Cars on the campus are not as numerous as I had seen elsewhere. The daily lives of the students seem rather drab, they have little money for entertainment.

But in them I felt a wonderful confidence in their institution . . . more than that, pride — the sort of pride not always possessed by the students of the big western universities, except perhaps in the marvellous equipment of their campus. Here the students seemed openly to admire the professors. In the West they boasted about the architecture of the buildings. I would not mention this if I had not noticed the phenomenon increase as I approached our oldest universities of the East. This is a state of mind that seems to me more in accord with primary realities.

MOOSEBURGERS As I drove from Halifax to Windsor, the radio of my car had a great deal to say about 'mooseburgers', to give them their English name. They were being offered at Dartmouth,

Halifax's 'rising' sister city. As the sale of moosemeat is forbidden, they were free. Once you were on the premises, ways would be found to make you give a generous contribution towards the building of a new medical centre. But how exotic this is! In what other country in the world is one in a position to hand out 'mooseburgers' for three whole days to thousands of people?

In a little restaurant somewhere, I said to the waitress as she brought me the steak I had ordered, 'What I would give to have a good moose steak today!'

'Be quiet,' she whispered in my ear. 'That's exactly what it is.'

THE MAD TIDES   Windsor is a charming little city, situated at the juncture of the Avon and Ste Croix Rivers, certainly among the most unusual rivers in the world. They form a natural harbour, which at high tide can receive ocean vessels safely. And then, suddenly, after several hours, the ships stand high and dry on a reddish silt and cannot continue on their way until the next tide. The same phenomenon is repeated more or less around the Bay of Fundy, which is celebrated the world over for the extent of its tides, whose differences in level sometimes amount to about forty feet.

At Windsor there is a sort of terrace, near a railway bridge, where it is recommended that you stop to observe the phenomenon under the best conditions. You have only to set your car at a certain angle and wait. A detailed card tells you the hours when the tides come in and go out every day of the year. Provided you do not mistake the month or the day, you will be almost certain in advance of the length of your wait.

When I passed that way a little shiver was beginning to ascend the river. Beside me a door slammed and I saw a tall American leap onto the terrace with his binoculars. His state of excitement had no relation to the mildness of the spectacle. To see him, one would have believed a typhoon was approaching. His young wife joined him, took the glasses from him, and concentrated in her turn. Their conversation was animated. The spectacle had begun. It would continue for four and a half hours.

I did not hesitate to involve myself in their celebration and then I understood their enthusiasm. They had been awaiting this moment for about two hours, and they had been on the point of giving up when suddenly in the distance . . . We were strays, completely out of season. Behind us a cluster of half a dozen native Nova Scotians observed each one of our reactions. For them we were the phenomenon.

It was cold. A fine but icy rain sprinkled us and we would see just as well from our car. And precisely what were we waiting for? However, I do not regret my conversation with my American couple. Here were people who would take a plane to witness the northern lights, who would spend hours watching an ant-hill, who stay up late on certain July evenings to participate in the games of the stars. We always say 'American' to characterize a certain behaviour. This means strictly nothing. These people were like all the others I have encountered across the world who have a passion for the phenomena of nature. They form a sort of nation, unknown to themselves. I am not one of them and I regret this. And I envied them for a moment as I left them. I would not have the courage to wait three hours more to see the enormous trawler, towards which the waters had begun to creep, finally float free. The only natural phenomena that interest me are those whose outcome is not known to me in advance. Speak to me of a good storm or a cyclone.

But I was wrong. My young couple had returned to their car. They put on the heat and wiped the mud from the windows and took sandwiches and a thermos of coffee from the glove compartment. They would stay. And they would see that the level of the water really climbs some thirty feet in four hours. They would not have to speak from hearsay. I shocked them a little by leaving the show right after the curtain rose.

NOT GUILTY   They do not know it, they do it without the least provocation, even with great innocence, but it is the English that sell 'Evangeline' at Grand-Pré and in the entire region made celebrated by the Expulsion of the Acadians. And this strikes your heart curiously. I should not be any happier to be offered Evangeline by the descendants of the deported. The commercial exploitation of great and small misfortunes has always made me shiver a little. I must reason at odds with others, for I see that this tradition is firmly planted in all latitudes. At Pompeii I was sold Vesuvius and at Tinos Miraculous Virgins. But let us acknowledge that at Grand-Pré, out of season at least, there is a certain discretion about it all. And apart from the eternal and frightful souvenir shop, which is practically its entrance door, you can invoke memories of Evangeline at your ease in the little Grand-Pré Park.

Many Acadians returned, but considerably to the south, spreading their villages in a line towards Yarmouth along a coast that everyone, the Acadians themselves first, calls pleasantly 'French coast'. For the moment we are in the land of Evangeline in the smiling Grand-Pré valley. It is true that Longfellow's heroine never existed, but her face and her beautiful love story are indissociable from the tragic expulsion of 1755 and perhaps correspond to more living realities than all those evoked by grave and angry historians. There were very certainly a great many Evangelines. There still are. I met several of them.

I MET EVANGELINE   I remember one of them. She was twenty-two, pretty and frail-looking with great sea-coloured eyes. A princess. I see her still in her white diner. She was selling an infinite variety of ice-cream dishes. I had driven until too late. In this corner of Nova Scotia I would not find a restaurant open at nine o'clock in the evening. So as I had not eaten, I ordered an enormous concoction, filled with ice cream and milk and vanilla essence, and I talked for a long time with Evangeline.

Standing at a counter by the side of the highway, in a terrifying silence, broken only by the sound of the waves that could be sensed nearby, in a low-ceilinged night pierced only by the weak glow that came from within the diner, Evangeline told me her new tragedy. And it, too, was a love story. Here was an exquisite person better endowed at the outset than was needed for a real woman's career in a more evolved society. Born on the 'French coast', she had remained a child of the sea. It had never occurred to her to go to a city in the interior. There she would die of loneliness. Each year she watched the approach of the long winter with unutterable dread, but it was possible to believe that she needed this provocation. Each time she took stock of herself as she awaited the return of the summer sun. She was well acquainted with the festival of spring on the sea and in the meadows. But she had just made a terrible discovery. Till now she had only dreamed her life. Two years ago she had entered her twenties, she would be thirty in a few years, and she shivered at the thought. At thirty, here, women are already aged and solitary. I felt a panic within her that many women of fifty have not yet known in our big cities.

Languishing Evangeline, at certain moments you sighed in a way I know well, sighs that seemed to tell of an imprisoned and burdensome love. You told me everything and you must have regretted it later. One does not say such things to a passing stranger. I was following my trade, which was to listen to you. But I could have said to you, 'Stop . . . I will continue,' for you were reliving Evangeline's long search. You will seek him everywhere and at last you will wonder if he ever existed. You will forget the colour of his eyes, the shape of his face. He will melt into the phantoms of your subconscious.

You were able to smile again for a moment as you said, 'You know . . . the young people know how to entertain themselves here, sometimes.' But you did not see the expression in your eyes at that instant. It still follows me. You had the eyes of Vulcan, sweet Evangeline, eyes that accused your early family environment, your convent school, your country, and the whole world. I too became suddenly suspect, and you enclosed yourself in your interior universe, seated yourself a short distance away, and turned the dial of a transistor.

After an endless silence you said suddenly, 'The worst thing is that we don't know either English or French.' You did indeed speak French with an accent I had never heard, made up of a

succession of uneven sounds, at times outrageous, almost inhuman, and at other times musical, gentle, and as moving as a
confidence. Your remark struck me in the face like spray that
leaves behind it the iodized scent of the sea.

This was my first real contact with the roughest Acadian
accent, the one most deprived of a future now that French-
language radio and television provide models daily. I had not
even an instant's desire to smile. Those that make fun of your
accent have understood nothing at all. In its own way it expresses your deep suffering and your isolation. You are right.
You cannot speak either English or French correctly, you have
been taught only to suffer in silence behind an artless smile. And
you are not the only one, I have known others, many others
along my way. And now that I have met you, I do not feel the
least desire to remove the dust that covers Longfellow's *Evangeline* on one of the shelves of my library.

The Expulsion of the Acadians belongs to our childhood. It is
one of the passages of our history that struck us most and that
we found easiest to remember. The teacher's voice swelled at
certain moments, he rolled his eyes, he became partisan. Strangely, or so at least I have been told, there is a great deal of pathos
also in English schools in connection with what history has remembered under the title of 'the Expulsion of the Acadians', a
pathos that often takes the same direction as ours. Why? Perhaps
because in this tragic episode the Acadians provide perfect victims.

THE HABITATION OF PORT-ROYAL   Even out of season I could not
pass close to the celebrated habitation of Port-Royal without
going to see it. If it were closed, I would walk around it, I
would breathe its air, and that would be that. Besides, the little
road leading towards it is delightful, edged on one side by the
river and on the other by green slopes. Here and there were
clusters of prosperous middle-class houses of a vaguely high-
presbytery style, where, in the absence of a breviary, it would

be very pleasant to read the newspaper on what we in Quebec call the gallery.

Port-Royal seemed to have closed to visitors the great doors opening onto the inner court. Was I really disappointed? Simply to set eyes suddenly upon this black-painted quadrilateral against its frame of green gives you a little shock. It is as if magnificent granaries in mourning clothes were playing puss-in-the-corner. All the wooden walls appeared to be coated with a thick soot, which had been carefully applied with a brush, so it should not fall on the lovely lawns. I was alone, completely alone for dozens of feet around. And then suddenly I heard a tune on a harmonica that seemed to rise from the ground. A melody I had never heard and quite unreal. This must be how ghost stories are born. If I had immediately fled, I could have claimed that at Port-Royal that day with all the doors shut, Champlain's ghost had returned to his former haunts to play the harmonica.

The truth is always simpler. I pushed the great door. It was open. And my harmonica-player was no other than a young guide, who took a long time to become aware of my presence beside him. Given over to his dreams and his music, he was deep in a happy solitude that few travellers were likely to disturb now that the tourist season was over. I spoke some suitable words. He jumped, threw his instrument on the table, rose, clicked his heels, and stood at attention. I did not require this much, and to give him time to come back from his musical stratosphere I praised the musical talents which I had had time to appreciate — fortunately, for these were apparently the only talents that this curious young man would be in a position to display. For his ignorance about everything that concerned the remarkable institution he had the duty to show me was wonderful to see.

We went by the inner court from one building to the other. He opened a door and said, 'These are the kitchens.' I saw only an empty room, adorned with a large fireplace. Another door opened upon another almost naked room: 'This is the dining room.' And so on. Did the governor take his meals in the common room? Don't know. What wood is this table made of? Don't know. Pine? Yes, I think so. Or would it perhaps be oak? Yes, it's oak. How many visitors from June to September? The answer came promptly: Forty thousand. Were you here then? I was just beginning. We shouldn't be too cruel towards beginners, but just the same . . .

The present habitation is of course only a reconstruction, but it is so faithful to the original that it hides nothing from us, except perhaps the furniture. The whole recalls the big farms of the north of France in the sixteenth century. All the buildings are arranged around an inner court with platforms for cannon, protected by palisades, at the south and southeast angles. There is first of all the entrance of squared oak with walls of board siding, the building method in use in France at that period; a small building described by Champlain in these terms: 'a little house where we put the tools unloaded from our bark, and where the Sieur Boulay lodged when the Sieur DuPont returned to France'. The panes of the windows are encased in lead. The roof is covered with pine planks. Next door is the forge. The iron was brought from France but the artisans made by hand the hardware needed for the doors, the windows, and the hearths. Next is the kitchen. In his history of New France Lescarbot reports that the chief foods were peas, beans, prunes, rice, dried cod, salt meats, oil, butter, mussels, lobster, and crab. Then in succession come the bakehouse and the reception hall where were held the festivals of the Order of Good Cheer, of which I have already spoken.

You will still find the lodgings and dormitory of the artisans, the chapel, the missionaries' quarters, the storehouse, the cellar, the trading hall, the guardroom, the well, and finally the governor's lodgings, which are scarcely more luxurious than the others though very much larger and constructed with particular care. Champlain made use of his stay at Port-Royal to draw the first detailed geographic maps of the Atlantic coast. He was by far the most illustrious guest of Port-Royal, and it was above all as a monument to his memory that the habitation was reconstructed. The task has been executed with a certain piety.

A CORNER OF FRANCE — BUT WHICH? On the door of the little general store on the French coast were the eternal Coca-Cola, Pepsi, and Robin Hood signs, and a French name, Léger Gaudet. The outer walls were little different from those of a shack in the woods, but you had no sooner stepped over the doorsill than you were squarely in the middle of a general store in a film. For the moment a silent film. Ten pairs of eyes turned towards me, conversations were interrupted. Everyone waited for the stranger to do his little turn. Where did he come from? And what could he want of us at so late an hour? He had no sample-case in his hand, but perhaps he was a salesman from Quebec, a 'Canayen' as they say. At the counter stood Léger Gaudet, a handsome black bear, before him a heavy blond young man and an old woman with glasses and a pointed chin, and behind, in the back-shop, an arc of leathery faces, baked by the winds of the open sea. There was rather the atmosphere of a family party, which I had unwittingly disturbed. I had the sense that I had, through carelessness, committed an act of trespass.

I no longer remember the ironic comment I made about the marvels of their climate — it was raining in torrents — but suddenly everyone's confidence was restored, the conversation resumed in the back-shop, the old woman put down the bottle of ketchup she had been holding all this time in unstable equilibrium, and the blond young man dashed towards the soft-drinks dispenser he saw me approaching and politely opened it for me. We quickly became old friends. Soon they would know where I came from, where I was going, what I did in life, the age of my daughter, and perhaps even the colour of my wife's eyes. For if I concealed anything, I would remain a slightly suspect stranger.

How many times I had to compose in this way a sort of police report without obtaining anything in exchange but some information of doubtful interest. But the traveller gives more than he receives, and if at certain hours of his schedule he has to acknowledge that he has received a great deal, this is because he has given even more. Or on the other hand you feel that you

have become a sort of municipal, provincial, or university employee: your interlocutor intends at all costs to make use of you.
This time you will receive much more than you asked, but the
knowledge will have been rammed down your throat with a
pile-driver. You considered yourself very intelligent, but you
were just one more goose to stuff.

At Léger Gaudet's that evening I rested. In truth we didn't
have much to say to one another. And we said it badly. This was
the second time I had come in contact with this roughest of the
Acadian accents — there are several and some of them do not
lack charm — and very clearly Gaudet was listening not to what
I said but to how I said it.

He announced at one moment: 'I'm surprised that you come
from Quebec. Because in Quebec they usually speak a sort of
French that makes me sick.' He was charming.

No one replied directly to my questions. My mildest expressions of curiosity bumped into an obstinate silence, as if I were
conducting a police inquiry. God knows that during my travels
across Canada I had had to practise an infinite number of approaches, right up to the subtlest — not to have one at all. I can
still feel intensely what I later experienced repeatedly in Acadia,
though much less strongly — the sensation of conversing through
an invisible wall. Perhaps it was simply a matter of language.
Our vocabularies did not tally. Words did not mean the same
things.

But I believe now, in retrospect, that a much more profound
phenomenon was involved. The Acadians of the 'French coast'
are the heirs of several centuries of solitude. Their behaviour, at
any rate, seemed to me on the whole very different from what I
was to encounter in the Acadian milieus of Cape Breton, New
Brunswick, and Prince Edward Island. In the villages that trail
from St Bernard to Yarmouth the sea and its rigours are everywhere present — even if a good many, not to say the greater
number, of the inhabitants have now abandoned the difficult
life of the fisherman for trawler-building or lumbering. Certainly
there are some that break ranks, have their boys and girls study

at Collège Sainte-Anne at Church Point, the single French-language secondary school in Nova Scotia, the equivalent of the classical colleges of Quebec though with the power to grant its own diplomas. These families drive big cars, play bridge, and look at television. But at Gaudet's everyone was in modest circumstances, and the blond young man sketched a picture for me of the average life in these little villages. It seemed to depend upon a single issue — the tourist trade.

I was granted a great honour. I was invited into the little back-shop to hear the stories of the pipe-smokers. I did not understand all the words, some of which emerged rather gratingly from toothless mouths. But I understood enough of them to know that these stories weren't at all innocent. And I was able to carry away with me waves of laughter that warmed my heart.

VERDICT ON OUR HIGHWAY RESTAURANTS How good are our highway restaurants? I mean the restaurants along our main roads that are not intended for tourists but subsist throughout the year by the custom of truck drivers. I have often had occasion to stop at one of them, in Nova Scotia or elsewhere. They are not essentially distinguishable from the tourist restaurants, except in their surroundings, nor do they differ much from one province to another. In general they do not have a liquor permit, and one drinks coffee or pop with one's meals. The highway restaurant is a modest and functional place with a long counter at which one sits and a few, usually unoccupied, tables. Places are set directly on the plastic surface of the counter, before an islet of bottles and various receptacles containing salt, pepper, sugar, mustard, ketchup, H.P. sauce, and paper table-napkins. The menu is simple in the extreme, and hamburgers and various combinations of bacon and eggs are the great favourites. But you can also order turkey and green peas with a sweet green sauce I have never managed to identify, calves' liver and bacon, and different sorts of 'steak'. You begin your meal with tomato juice or tinned soup and finish it with 'homemade' pie — that is to say, homemade at a commercial bakery that sometimes serves an entire province with its fleet of trucks.

Prices are lower than elsewhere, but the quality is of a disturbing standard. And that is as well, for the regular customers cover the main dish with such a quantity of ketchup that it would be superfluous to trouble about the flavour of the food. People don't come here to eat, but to eat quickly.

But these places manage to become humanized by the simple process of receiving the same clientele. The truck driver enters, greets the comrades he always finds there on that particular day at that time, exchanges news with them about their respective districts, calls the proprietress and waitress by their first names, tells the latest anecdote, discusses the news bulletin he has just heard on his dashboard radio, and all this creates an atmosphere such as the staging posts must have had in former days.

I had stopped on this particular day at the Golden Pheasant just outside Yarmouth on Highway 3. Let us pick up the scene again at the point when the truck driver enters and finds the Thursday noon regulars . . . plus a man of about forty, who seems not to be from the district, who is wearing dark clothes, and whom he will come to sniff out from time to time, as if to make sure this isn't a Martian.

The stranger was myself. The truck driver took time to settle down and, God knows why, he finally called me 'the preacher', before hearing what I had to say in my own defence. So I had become the preacher, and he made this his first conversational springboard. For some minutes more he called me to witness his statements, purely as a matter of form, without being really concerned with my comments. 'The proprietress is a lot thinner' . . . 'Jenny' — this was the waitress — 'has been absent-minded for several weeks.' She was in love. I learned all about her love affair in a few sentences. Then he forgot me completely, which delighted me, for he became more himself and his humour less forced. This enabled me to hear a somewhat incredible story. Somewhere in Yarmouth a woman found a snake on her lawn. It was brown and two feet long. She rushed for a hatchet and cut the reptile in two. And behold, out of its belly came a multitude of little snakes about six inches long. Experts deduced that in a moment of panic she must have swallowed her young to protect them from some sort of danger. One of his friends then told about the lion. This happened at Quebec and had just upset the whole city. A lion, kept in the house like a dog, had crushed the skull of a three-months-old infant through the bars of its crib, probably trying to caress it, who could know? Next came a ghost story. And then it was my turn. I must now pay for my observer's post. Conversation had caught fire all over the restaurant, and wherever there were customers we were all a single happy group. The so-called preacher was now able to identify himself, which obliged me to reply to a rather annoying, unfair, and bitter questionnaire about Quebec. But the essential element was there, we were all united by a current of sympathy. And when we separated we had to leave subjects that were still warm and very much alive behind us on the counter, where they would slowly die, in spite of the efforts of the proprietress or Jenny to restore them a little.

All this while, and unknown to the assembly, a little drama had been played out between the waitress and me.

First scene: I was very hungry and ordered what the menu called 'Porter House steak', a piece of beef of about sixteen ounces. For the last few days I had been eating scallops, cod, and lobster. Just bring me anything with the colour and texture of beef and I would devour it.

Second scene: Anything was precisely what I was brought, though it bore the sonorous and promising name of 'Porter House'. I had ordered it rare, almost raw, but it was hard as calf leather, thin and very wide, accompanied by salad, tomatoes, cucumbers, peas, and french fries. I was well aware that the mere intrusion of a knife into this alimentary jumble would create a scene of havoc around my plate. In course of time I have perfected the only technique suitable. I always begin by conscientiously gulping down all the loose bits and pieces, from the peas to the sliced radishes, which seems to me to smack of perversion.

Third scene: I pointed out mildly to the waitress that, in spite of my earlier insistence, my 'Porter House' was not only over-cooked but of a strange texture, very much closer to that of stewing beef than to sirloin or even round steak. I saw her turn pale and she seemed plunged suddenly into such tragedy that I hastened to reassure her. There was no question of my returning the steak, so I decided to learn a little more about it. She was back at once on solid ground and able to complete my education. And here I learned a bewildering bit of news. The steaks served in our highway and similar small restaurants — under the names of fillet, t-bone, porter house, and other lofty titles — are cuts specially prepared by the big packinghouses from various parts of beef usually dedicated to more modest ends. She also pointed out, quite rightly, that prices are charged here that have little relation with those of the big restaurants.

Fourth scene: The waitress's mood, which had been restored for a moment, was dark again when she returned from the kitchen. In the pane of glass set in the door appeared the head of an old woman, who was looking at me steadily. The situation was clear. In vain had I taken utmost precautions and used all the diplomacy of which I am capable as I made my remarks. I had just dealt the establishment a deadly blow. Of this there was no doubt. The old woman, whose head was still framed in the window, was not angry. She was suffering. The waitress for her part was nursing the bitterness of defeat. I was to understand why.

Fifth and last scene: When all the other customers had de-parted and I was alone before a cup of wretched coffee, I forced the waitress to confidences. I had, after all, played the part of complaisant victim, I had no intention of leaving the premises as an accused. Well, I learned a bit of news that was even more bewildering than the first. This was the first time in the twenty years of the restaurant's existence that anyone had made the

In the pane of glass set in the door appeared the head of an old woman,
who was looking at me steadily.

slightest complaint about the food. What would you have answered? I couldn't think of anything. I congratulated her.

THE MOST SCOTTISH TOWN   I already rather liked the name: Antigonish. It is an Indian word that can mean almost anything you wish, since the translators have never managed to reach an agreement. For some it means 'a river in the form of a fork', which is quite a good description of the town's situation, midway between Halifax and Sydney, almost at the door of Cape Breton Island. For others it means 'the river of fish'. A third version is 'the place where bears tear off the branches of the beeches to get the beech-nuts'. For me, Antigonish means City of Traditions. Nowhere else in Nova Scotia did I encounter such a worship of tartans, bagpipes, and Gaelic culture, or of demonstrations of folk-dances and folk-songs and annual festivals.

It is true that in certain milieus of Halifax, Yarmouth, and Sydney I saw families that had their own tartan, their complete family trees, and a real passion for everything that could link them to the old Scottish traditions. But in Antigonish this is not an upper-middle-class privilege. Enter even modest houses and you will see all those handsome, often-read books telling of the antecedents and lineage of the family, festival costumes in the cupboards, and on the upright piano a book of ancient songs. Listen above all to the conversations and you will not be sure you are in Canada, you might be somewhere in Scotland.

Certain people will tell you, and it was told to me more than once, that all this is fabricated, that Antigonish is in the hands of a very active Chamber of Commerce and of a Historical Society openly playing for tourists. Visitors now come from a great distance to see the two-day festival put on each year in mid-July by the Antigonish Highland Society. There are even certain people that spend the entire year preparing for this event. It is true in a sense that Antigonish has fabricated itself from the festivals that today are a healthy part of its life. But this little town had the time, the culture, and above all the sensitivity needed to preserve the entire folklore of Nova Scotia.

At once the entrance to and exit from Cape Breton Island, Antigonish offers a varied and romantic setting, with discreet openings upon the sea between the folds of very gentle mountains, in the midst of meadows and glens. It is above all a cultural centre, and it is this that gives the little town its special climate. Its population scarcely exceeds four thousand, and yet you will find two thousand boys and girls studying at its various educational institutions, the most important of which is, of course, St Francis Xavier University. This excrescence of students and professors physically marks the town.

You are not likely to pass the campus of St F.X., as it is called, without seeing it. It occupies about a hundred acres on the edge of the city, with some twenty buildings apportioned among the various faculties. In all, a hundred professors and fifteen hundred students. It is a Catholic institution and was founded in 1853. At the outset it was a fairly faithful replica of the classical colleges of Quebec, but it is constantly raising its standing. It now offers master's degrees in arts and pedagogy, and in physics, chemistry, and geology in the sciences, pre-medical and pre-dental courses, courses in economics and commerce. With time it will become a real university, which will be quite a performance for a town of 4,500 people at some distance from the great urban centres.

But for me its greatest originality is its faculty of Gaelic. The enterprise was daring. It is true that Gaelic is still spoken in certain parts of Cape Breton and there is even a Gaelic College at St Ann, offering unexpectedly successful summer courses. But to open in 1958, within the framework of St Francis Xavier, a faculty of Scottish Gaelic, history, and Celtic literature, smacks of those after-dinner plans when all difficulties blur in the euphoria of a good wine.

ANOTHER GIANT   But it is true that the faculty holds a major ace in its hand: C.I.M. McLeod. One of his friends almost forced his door one evening to enable me to make his acquaintance. Though we had torn him away from his great research books, he immediately declared himself delighted: he was not all that fond of work but always had to have a good reason before he could grant himself a little holiday.

McLeod is enormous in physique, but you sense that he could execute the lightest of dance-steps. He is valued as a leader in all the milieus of the town. He is a specialist in the bagpipes, an expert on tartans, an authority on every aspect of Scottish folklore. His advice is prized in university circles. Above all, his agreement is prized. When he is angry, the whole world knows it.

McLeod was born in Scotland and attributes his predilection for Gaelic to the fact that his father and mother always spoke that language when they didn't want to be understood by their children. In due course, he got his revenge, for he studied Gaelic so relentlessly that he soon became a specialist. After he came to settle in Nova Scotia, in about 1950, he served for eight years as an adviser to the provincial Department of Education. Came an encounter with St Francis Xavier University. The attraction was mutual and gave rise to the creation of the faculty that concerns us. At first there were thirty students. Now there are a hundred and fifteen. A six months' course. Examinations and diplomas.

Gaelic is dying each year with the old. Young people need to possess a good dose of romanticism to learn a language that has almost disappeared from their homes and will be of no use to them in their careers. In 1931, 30,000 people still spoke Gaelic in Nova Scotia. In 1951, exactly twenty years later, there were only 6,700. The same recessive curve can be observed also in Scotland: 130,000 in 1931 as against 92,000 in 1951. Such institutions as the Gaelic Faculty of St F.X. are neither more nor less than rescue operations. They are also part of a total plan in which the provincial Ministry of Education is actively interested. There are dreams of educating teachers who will address themselves only to adults, in order to maintain and improve their knowledge of the language and its culture; there is the wish, above all, to introduce Gaelic into the primary school curriculum as has already been done in four public schools in Cape Breton. In 1951 the Association of Scottish Societies of Nova Scotia was formed to harmonize and consolidate the common objective. Courses were later given on the radio and publications founded to augment the training program of St Ann College and the Gaelic faculty at St F.X. The old dances became fashionable, including certain ones that were included in the physical education course at my primary school. Two swords were crossed on the floor, and then commenced to music a series of very complicated steps that even the most skilful among us accomplished with an utter lack of elegance. The same persons and societies that have undertaken to save the Gaelic language have also increased the practice of the bagpipes. Today there are some twenty provincial groups with about two hundred and fifty players. They were the great attraction at the time of the inauguration of the Canso Jetty, which has joined Cape Breton to the mainland since 1955.

A MATTER OF HARMONY   I had often been told about the Cabot Trail. It is a standard itinerary for vacationers. But ever since I had travelled our Rockies in all directions, I had given up hope, more or less, of encountering similar emotions elsewhere. I was wrong. The spectacular circuit that goes right around Cape Breton has dizzying moments. It is not the Rockies, very far from that. It is at very most the Gaspé, a little more polished. The sun seemed to have settled in for a few days, the autumn forests glowed against an ocean background of unchanging blue. The harmony was almost breathtaking.

The classic route begins at Fort Hastings, that is to say at the southernmost door to Cape Breton. One can then choose to go up to the national park by the east or by the west. I chose to go by the west coast, attracted by several villages with French names — Belle Côte, Terre Noire, Saint-Joseph du Moine, Grand Étang, Chéticamp. I was to learn that for about thirty miles the district is populated by descendants of the Acadians, like that

'French coast' I had followed to Yarmouth. Here one also finds the same accent, though perhaps a little less harsh to the ear than in the land of Evangeline. The people live chiefly by fishing: lobster, cod, and mackerel according to the season. Everywhere there are co-operatives and everywhere branches of the Royal Bank, as in all the rest of Cape Breton.

Perhaps it was because I was so pleased to find the sun again, on the very threshold of the Cabot Trail, but it seemed to me that the houses were enormous, freshly painted, that everything wore an air of prosperity. I must have been mistaken. It is not possible that people here do not know the same problems as in all the fishing villages of the Atlantic provinces: scantiness of earnings, aging equipment, the high cost of new material, disaffection of the young, the difficulties of obtaining supplies, transport and education — not to speak of loneliness, isolation, and interminable winters.

THE SEA AS A PREMIUM.   It was called the Cabot Trail when it was really just a track on which only the most intrepid ventured. Today it is a fine autoroute that our cars can traverse at a hundred miles an hour, even on the most abrupt slopes. You climb almost two thousand feet in a mere few miles. And the descents are as rapid. Make the most of this, for your emotions will not last more than thirty or so miles beyond Chéticamp. It is this first part that is the most spectacular, and if I had it to do over again I would begin on the Ingonish side so as to end at the exit of the national park, the place where I experienced symphony movements terminating in prolonged melodic runs. Powerful chords on the kettle-drums, then solos on the flute. Minutes of vertigo that remind you of the Rockies — though the peaks here are not three thousand feet high — followed by romanticism. The surroundings soften, the mountains stretch out, roll up, melt into the thick fleece of the autumn. If the sea were not always at the bottom of the landscape, you could believe you were somewhere in the Laurentians.

As if by a cinema effect, thick clouds came up to hide the sun from me as I left the Cape Breton National Park and the rain began and would continue until I reached Sydney. It would never leave me again for the weeks I spent travelling through Prince Edward Island and New Brunswick, except for rare intervals. However, I had taken my precautions.

October is considered the ideal month for the road. Dry weather, very luminous sun, multicoloured autumn. Although one is not likely to experience all four seasons in a single day, as sometimes happens in Newfoundland, even in August, the weather in the Maritimes is infinitely capricious and during the most beautiful months of the year it is not unlikely for umbrella-merchants to do as good business as sellers of bathing-suits. One runs this same risk all along the Atlantic coast, whether at Portland or at Cape Cod. One must resign oneself. I for my part have succeeded in liking the rain. I had plenty of time to get used to it, it is true, but from now on, wherever I may be in the world, I shall not be in the least perturbed to see the sky darken or the most dramatic storms brew. All the uglinesses of our landscape blur. Poles and electric wires, factory chimneys, ancient iron steps, gas stations, monstrous trucks — all withdraw into the surroundings and blend together in impressionistic vibrations that give way finally to the fog. You are aware then of that vague sense of collusion with nature that is part of your best memories of the summer. At such moments the driver may turn off the radio and conversation slowly fades away around him. He thinks he is obeying an instinct for security. The road has in fact become much more dangerous. One might yield then to infinitely deeper, finally inexpressible impulses. One feels something of the euphoria that comes from a swim in the ocean, a walk in the forest, a stay in the mountains — the sort of feeling animals must also know, in their fields, at the first streaks of dawn.

I was alone. I travelled perforce always alone from one town to another, and I had all the time I needed to analyse my sensations. I know there was no feeling of insecurity in them. And I

know that one can finally love the rain and the fog for reasons
that can balance one's reasons for loving the sun.

AND SUDDENLY FEAR   I decided to pick up one of those highway
hitch-hikers so abundant in Nova Scotia. They are generally itin-
erant workers. They have perhaps just finished two months' work
in the bush cutting Christmas trees and are on their way back
to Sydney or Halifax to hire on for something else. The phenomenon is found all over America to varying degrees. Unskilled
work is very unstable and, whatever the city, several hundreds
of workers are constantly in search of higher wages. The nature
of the work matters little; they will accept it if the pay is good.
Some of them live in trailers with their families so they will
always be free to better their lot. At Antigonish, right in the
centre of the little town, I had been able to visit a real trailer
village. It was neat and slicked up, with curtains at the windows,
fences, and little gardens. But it presents a strange picture even
so, and takes a little getting used to. I have seen such villages
almost everywhere, even in the mining towns of Abitibi.

In Nova Scotia one must add the chronic unemployment.
Activity, whether in the mines, in industry, or in commerce, is
subject to such variations in the course of the year that day-
labourers have no protection against the caprices of production.
Men are being let out at one place and hired at another. For them
it's a question of being at the right spot at the right moment.
And they learn the labour chart by a sort of underground. They
discover more by haunting the taverns than by reading the newspapers.

The man I had picked up belonged to this category. But it
took me a long time to find this out, for he never opened his
mouth. If he had not said 'Thank you' at the beginning, I might
have believed he was a deaf-mute. He looked like a decent
fellow, but for the first half hour that we drove along side by
side he did not open his lips.

I had been looking for a companion for the road and I'd

chanced upon the sphinx. Bad luck. All this would have been nothing if I had not suddenly begun to feel afraid.

THE TROJAN WAR WILL NOT TAKE PLACE   You would not suspect it when you look at a map of Cape Breton, which shows only its general aspect without indicating the network of roads, but from Ingonish there are several different ways to go to Sydney. That there should be even one seems rather an exploit. The land here is as full of holes as a colander and is deeply penetrated by the sea. Arms of land extend like the legs of a crab all around one of the biggest saltwater lakes in the world, Bras d'Or. My companion claimed to know all the routes. I could have gone directly to Sydney by a paved road; he interrupted his silence for several seconds to direct me to side-roads, several of which turned into quagmires, amidst a setting like the end of the world. I had never seen such desolate landscapes.

My companion had sunk back into his silence, and I went on asking my questions to a tombstone. And then I in turn stopped talking. A troublesome idea brushed my mind; it returned, made a nest for itself somewhere in my head, as always happens when one isn't on watch, and now it was quite at home and scratched gently at the cells of my brain. For as far as I could see in my rearview mirror, there was nothing and no one. On the two sides of the road, there was no house, no human presence. We were the last human beings driving on an earth that had been abandoned to the fog and the rain.

I was not yet very frightened, but I was frightened. It seemed to me that my companion was not indifferent to this great solitude, that he had perhaps sought it. For he was a little more relaxed now that we had left the highway. And I observed how steadily he was scrutinizing the rearview mirror. He seemed to be passionately interested in the landscape by the road, though till now it had seemed of no importance to him. What was going on behind that filthy dirty face that had not been shaved for three days? I tried to resume conversation. I obtained only a sigh. His breath was uneven. He took a package of cigarettes from his pocket, tossed it unopened on the dashboard, immediately picked it up again, put it back in his pocket.

Why had I been so stupid as to put myself in such a situation? Why had I picked him up? Why him and not someone else? Why had I followed his road directions? Yes, there it was, one always believes that these things are only for others, that we have been granted a sort of immunity at our birth, that we will never ride in an ambulance, that we will never be face to face with a bandit, a criminal, a murderer, or even the most inexperienced of thieves. What should I do? Stop and force him to get out? He would take that badly. What grievances had I against him? But I would not be recounting this incident if I had not become certain during this trip at the end of the world that this man was seeking only the moment, and also the opportunity and the courage, to attack me — attack me stupidly as in a bad movie. I was frankly afraid, but I remained all the while lucid enough to examine my reasons for being afraid. They were countless and stemmed from an infinity of details that it would not be agreeable to describe. I know only that they were sufficient.

The play of circumstances chose that I should become quite well acquainted with my companion. And I learned then what he had lacked at the moment — the experience and, even more than that, the courage. He hadn't a cent in his pockets, he hadn't eaten for two days, he hadn't drunk a single glass of beer since the night before. At such moments courage is in direct proportion to the number of glasses of beer one has drunk.

The affair was cleared up around a restaurant table, to which I invited him when suddenly we found ourselves on a busy highway. There had been no calculation on my part, my hunger was as ravenous as his. It was only a little more recent. I watched him return to life, to conversation, to that friendliness that springs up sometimes between two strangers who know they will never really know one another. However amiable he gradually became, I could not forget that for an interminable half hour this man was on the point of being my attacker.

While we continued on our way to Sydney, he did his utmost to reply of his own accord to the questions I had given up asking him. I learned all about him, about his wandering existence and his constant search for work. We even discovered a number of common memories. He had once worked in the West at a ranch where I had stayed. The sphynx had become a very little mouse. He began to bore me.

At certain hours there is no solution: half the human race scares you, and the other half bores you.

Prince Edward Island

FOG TO PIERCE Ignorance sometimes helps you gain precious time. When I first set foot in Borden, on Prince Edward Island, I knew that I would not have a long struggle against prejudices: I had no received ideas about Prince Edward Island, no pre-formed judgements. I was in the fog — in every sense of the word. True, there would soon be Charlottetown, the cradle of Confederation. But what does that mean? One is interested in healthy adults. Confederation is a sickly child, a source of great anxiety to its parents.

At Borden the sky suddenly cleared and I saw for the first time those little roads of red earth cutting through a gently undulating landscape. In the foreground there was a modern autoroute such as I would not see again anywhere on the island. Borden is the principal entrance port and a very wide highway takes you in an hour and a half to the capital, giving you the impression of driving through a solid, well-established province. The true face of the island only appears later.

At certain places an asphalt road will take you across cultivated fields on a ribbon scarcely wider than your car. Without this will to be straight and modest, the whole landscape would lose its harmony. You will not see any of the middle-class houses from the road: they hide at the back of parks.

When I reached Charlottetown, I recognized it, though I had never seen it before. It conceals its American-style business streets behind a curtain of shady alleys worthy of England. On the main square stands an arrangement of cubic structures, naked and of a futuristic severity, next door to the very ponderous, very old, cruciform parliament building: this is the Memorial Building, Canada's homage to the Fathers of Confederation. For the instant I was shocked. It seemed to me that ugliness here had prevailed over the desire for severity. But the extensive visit I was permitted to make later would animate those cubes with a certain life that does not burst upon the view of the casual observer. And a few hours later the night illuminations gave it a real but curious presence: the surfaces doubled, planes danced, sometimes in leaps of very violent yellow light. It made one think of a carnival castle.

JUST LIKE THE MOVIES   I was immersed from the moment of my arrival at the Charlottetown, the city's big hotel, in a bustle I had not expected. And I was accorded minute attentions that are not indulged in to excess in the several palaces of the Maritimes.

'Have you had a good trip, sir? . . . The forecast is sun for tomorrow. . . . Cocktails are being served in the big hall.'

I was soon to understand. I had been mistaken for a banker. I was almost deceived, because the hall swarmed with the coming and going of young men with greying temples, into believing that all the portly and aging bankers had been pensioned off.

These personages are the real monarchs of today, surrounded with flattering veneration, pampered, preceded in all their travels by a hurricane of servility. This evening there would be champagne at dessert. Around the tables there would be about ten millionaires — perhaps several times ten, who could know precisely? And so as not to risk any blunders, the staff had clearly received instructions to treat all the delegates as millionaires. There is a great deal of talk about the prestige of money. No one knows anything about it who has not mingled with a conference of millionaires. Utter the most simple-minded comment, and you will release approving laughter and your word will be repeated with blushes of pleasure. Approach the reception desk and behind it there will be half a dozen rapt looks and attentive smiles. The girl at the newsstand forgets to take your money.

I experienced all these little indulgences and many others as I awaited my turn to register. I had no alternative then but to disappoint the help. Henceforth I should be entitled only to the treatment reserved for ordinary travellers. That I know well. And it is after all the treatment to which I am most attached. One consoles oneself as one can.

AN ANGEL PASSES She was truly of rare beauty, a younger Grace Kelly. I had been flung into her arms without the slightest reservation. I might have been vexed by this. Had I become an old shrivelled thing to whom people would willingly entrust their little sisters? I understood better later. This gracious person was not only a Jehovah's Witness, she was a minister, an accredited minister. You must not believe that such good fortune happens to young girls by accident. There is a long preparation, commencing in their tenderest youth. Her father and mother are ministers.

Jehovah's Witnesses are not very numerous in Prince Edward Island, but I was able to get an idea of their quality. And that there are even a few is astonishing in itself. The figures that are most currently cited on the religious chart of this little province of only a hundred thousand people do not even give any space to the denominations that one finds in such great number in the Canadian West: forty-five per cent Catholic, fifty-five per cent Protestant. It is true that everyone that isn't a Catholic should be considered a Protestant. So she was a Jehovah's Witness and she made so little attempt to convert me that I found myself full of curiosity about her beliefs. I had always imagined them to be insistent and eager. But she did not reply to my questions.

My status as writer frightened her. It was the offices in Toronto that were qualified to discuss matters with writers. She had been trained to instruct people. Her ministry is composed of study groups, prayers, but principally house-visits.

'To sell your papers?' I asked.

'Not at all. To preach the word.'

'You mean you knock on the door and announce to whoever answers that you want to talk to them about God?'

'Exactly.'

'And they immediately ask you to come in?'

'Sometimes. But mostly they leave us standing in the vestibule and just ask us a few questions for form's sake.'

'They never slam the door without even listening?'

'Yes, often.'

'But Charlottetown isn't a very big city. This means that most of the time you're going back to the same places.'

'We make a point of going back to the doors that have been slammed against us and we have the great joy of seeing doors open wide the second or third time.'

The 'joy' she spoke of was not a pretence. The girl was transfigured. Before me stood the Angel of the Annunciation. I had not deserved it.

THE CONFERENCE OF 1864 Our first pilgrimage: the great Confederation hall. A museum piece. The decoration simpler than I should have imagined. It is on the second floor of the old parliament. It was here then that in September 1864 twenty-four high Canadian dignitaries gathered together to lay the foundation for Confederation. Macdonald, Georges-Étienne Cartier, Tupper, Langevin, and all the names one learned by heart at public school without ever being able to recite the whole list to the School Inspector.

The affair began with some fifteen delegates from the Maritimes. Their plan was not simple: they had been given the task of studying a proposal for the union of the three Maritime provinces. It is probable that the conference would have failed had it not been for the arrival of the distinguished delegation from the rest of Canada. They were called 'the Canadians'. The centre of the country had just been united under a coalition government of Liberals and Conservatives, with the name of the Province of Canada. The 'Canadians' saw in the Charlottetown Conference, which theoretically did not concern them, an unhoped-for opportunity to further the advance of the idea of a federation uniting the whole country from one ocean to the other. So they had themselves invited and came.

The eight 'Canadians' had no sooner arrived than their status as observers was made clear to them. They must sit in the galleries during the opening ceremonies and were not to join in the discussions unless requested to do so by the gathering as a whole. But here is a thing that always strikes me and is still perhaps one of our most typical traits of behaviour, even in our own day: we forget protocol with as much ease and grace as we have put strictness into establishing it. The day after the opening, 2 September, the 'Canadians' were sitting with all the others around the big table, and the Maritime delegates were listening with united ardour to these princes of the word that had come to them from afar.

Now the official delegates were acting as observers, though gradually they felt themselves more and more concerned. Fundamentally, the idea had been theirs. And the 'Canadians' had only extended to the whole country the union they had dreamed of for the Maritimes. And soon it was simply a question of whether there should be a little more union, or a little less, or a little too much . . .

I turned my head. My angel was still there, at my side. She wore the same smile. Of what had she been thinking all this time? Perhaps she had prayed. I should have been delighted to hear the story of the Conference of 1864 as recounted by a Jehovah's Witness. At what moment would she have seen the intervention of God? When the Canadians invited themselves?

When the Maritime delegates installed them in the galleries with the status of observers and requested that they keep silent? Her replies would have been a valuable indication to me. God is never mistaken and he sees very far into the future. The God of the Witnesses seemed to me to be marked by a very prudent reserve.

THE CONTENTS ARE SUPERIOR TO THE CONTAINER   Even before it was completed, it attracted crowds; one imagines that it will be for several years the centre of interest for visitors to Charlottetown. I am speaking of the monument erected to the memory of the Fathers of Confederation. I felt an agreeable surprise at the interest of its inner appointments. Everything is vast, often lighted ingeniously, through the sides, or the roof, or both at once. I would like to see a Velasquez exhibition, for instance, in one of the galleries of the museum, where the sources of light are at the sides so that in certain parts of the room the rays meet in a single pencil and make the interior light of a canvas glow at various angles. An enormous Eskimo sculpture by Inniukpak finds a dramatic accent here it would not necessarily possess in the presbytery atmosphere so characteristic of some of our museums. Was this intentional? At any rate, it stands at the centre of a luminous eddy, and all the features of the Mother and Child are as if underlined. Art is not a matter of volume, and I am very much afraid that this enormous piece is not Inniukpak's masterpiece. But in this gallery it finds its climate of light. It is suddenly animated with a strange life . . . Some canvases die a natural death in these modern galleries, where the sun is the source of the illumination. Others come suddenly to life and burst like buds.

The whole collection does not give an impression of great riches. You will of course find Emily Carrs, Cogill Haworths, Holmeses, Bobaks, Rex Woods in factory lots, but there are important absences on the English side as well as on the French — to represent us one Suzanne Bergeron and one Lemieux. This is always the mark of a young country — the setting first and then we'll see. I always feel the same uneasiness before this phenomenon. One dreams of the day when we shall build our museums to shelter valuable and rare collections that are so numerous we no longer know where to put them, of the day when we will build our concert halls to give real concerts in them each evening, of the day when the beauty of our campuses will be consonant with the quality of our university instruction. These are no doubt the dreams of old countries.

But let us not quibble. There are indications that we may be able to make up for our backwardness on the cultural level. Things move quickly in America. One of the young directors of the theatre told me that before the coming of television, many of the island's farmers wouldn't have known the difference between a ballet performance and a broom. Today the most fervent audience for ballet comes from the countryside nearby. And as the countryside is always nearby on Prince Edward Island, I concluded that they must come from just about everywhere.

The Charlottetown theatre had scheduled a half-dozen big theatrical and artistic productions for the next season. The most important of them would come from elsewhere, and all would play at a loss. What did it matter? Charlottetown possesses a theatre or concert hall that is the greatest success of the whole complex. It should be used. Culture does not necessarily obey the laws of biology: with us, it is the organ that creates the need.

THE 'PERSONALITY' OF A PROVINCE This island has no factories, no mines, no forests, no water power. If you observe some immense petroleum tanks on the heights of the Charlottetown harbour, do not look for the refineries; there are none. You will rarely meet big trucks on the roads of the interior. Small streams are called rivers here, and all the electricity consumed on the island is manufactured in the Charlottetown generating plant, which is powered by fuel oil. It is true that the island's neighbour is Newfoundland, which will soon have electricity to spare. For the time being, when night falls, you can tell yourself that an entire island is fed its power by a generating plant. I did not expect to find this cottage-craft image in one of the most technically advanced countries in the world.

Also, this island, whose periphery appears to be a succession of little fishing villages, is in reality a farm. Agriculture is the economic basis and the principal resource of the island. The soil is well adapted to the growing of potatoes, hay, barley, and vegetables, especially turnips. The rocky base of the island — there are no floods here — is covered to a depth of twenty-five feet with a thick layer of very red, fertile soil. The climate is really temperate, with no very hot days in summer or very cold days in winter. It is the kingdom of the tractor; it may be that tractors have become more domesticated than elsewhere, for they perform the most specialized tasks. I have even seen tiny tractors hitched up to ploughs, much like the horses of former days.

This island, which had no real forests and no mountains, had no drinking water — an exceptional situation in Canada, where lakes and spring-fed rivers are so abundant that we do not know even half of them. In Prince Edward Island it was necessary to dig wells. Not far from Charlottetown you can easily locate the fifty-eight wells that provide all sections of the island with drinking water. It is pumped regularly by gas motors. The reservoir has a capacity of a million gallons. A new reservoir of twice this size was under construction when I was there. The water is of excellent quality, and abundant.

Mealtimes in the province are breakfast at seven, noon meal at eleven, and the evening meal at five, or an hour earlier. To these Acadians add *réveillon*, which is eaten at nine or ten in the evening, preferably with friends. They drink a not very alcoholic beer of their own making. I have tried it and it seems to me an honest perversion. Sometimes this rather bitter beer is accompanied with a piece of pie. It is curious — a matter of habit, no doubt.

A CANADA IN A TEST-TUBE   At Tignish, a spot on the northwest corner of the island, I found an English-speaking priest and curate who never preach in French in their church, though it is attended by three hundred Acadian, hence francophone, families. I had discovered the reverse situation — near Mont-Carmel, I believe — where the curé did not know a word of English. But in both and similar cases the phenomenon seemed not to cause any special difficulty. There are deep-seated reasons for this. The Acadians in Prince Edward Island are very different from those I encountered elsewhere in the Maritimes.

They seem scarcely aware of anything that distinguishes them from their anglophone fellow-citizens. Nor are the 32,000 Scots aware of any difference, nor the 28,000 English, nor the 18,000 Irish. One would say that everyone has accepted the mixture with good grace. The situation is very different from that in the other provinces, where the ethnic groups tend to identify themselves with a particular culture, tradition, and folklore; one might believe that everyone here has only one nationality, the one Prince Edward Island confers upon its inhabitants. It is on the whole an interesting spectacle. But its homogeneity is only apparent.

J.-Henri Blanchard, for thirty-five years professor of French and botany at Prince of Wales College, now retired, told me about the school situation among the Acadians of the island. It is absolutely staggering. And one wonders how such a system could operate without creating grave conflicts at every moment, or misunderstandings at the very least. Yet it operates without too many shocks, probably because everyone has formed the habit of getting along with the means at hand without paying too much attention to the famous law of 1877: All the public schools of the province shall be English and neutral, and the pupils shall depend directly upon the Board of Education for the province, thus upon the government. When the moment of surprise had passed, French continued to be taught in the Acadian parishes, and the Protestant schools remained confessional. There was tolerance on all sides, and no sense of irritability.

This has lasted for almost a century, although along the way there have been a few adaptations. For instance, the Department of Education has recently recognized the syllabus prepared for the Acadian schools, and the English schools theoretically teach French after the eighth grade. But the law has not been modified. The Acadians are still obliged to pass their examinations in English, so that at the slightest difficulty the schools are obliged to set the material in the French course aside so as not to risk bringing down the grades of the Acadian students. As well, the scarcity of French teachers means that the English children are taught a symbolic, almost ludicrous book-language. In both cases the language of the seventeenth century is gradually shedding its plumage and very little is left of it.

So it is here of course that you encounter the most wretched spoken French, I think, of any of the Acadian districts of the Maritimes. It is not a dialect or a patois, as the English often believe, without being able to grasp the difference between the notions. It is a language, a real language, the one that was spoken in the seventeenth century but has long since fallen into decadence. Some English words are mixed in with it, and very little of the beautiful vocabulary of the seventeenth century has managed to be transmitted from one generation to another. And then modern life has overtaken French and we have been obliged to keep the original label for everything that comes to us from America.

The real problem is lack of teachers. There are dreams of a French teachers' college at Moncton, for instance, which will undertake the training of real French teachers for the Maritimes. Once this problem is settled, I foresee another graver one for Prince Edward Island: the Acadians here are in a false situation. The more they demonstrate the wish to conserve, or recover, their cultural heritage, the more awkward the law of 1877 will become. One cannot build anything solid upon a régime of tolerance, which an alteration of mood might at any moment reverse. For the time being everyone seems to believe that this climate propitious to mutual concessions is everlasting. But suppose that tomorrow Quebec . . . but let us not suppose anything.

Many people here, including Professor Blanchard, are very much aware of the fundamental problem. Most of these leaders have travelled, express themselves in correct French, have set up certain defence structures, and have the confidence of the seventeen thousand Acadians of the island. But their action cannot assume the same character as in the other provinces. All problems seem to dissolve into the same nationalism. I have never encountered this elsewhere — a truly homogeneous population. Everyone is above all of Prince Edward Island, whatever his descent may be. If you want to understand a little of what happens here, you must never lose sight of the fact that ninety-eight per cent of the present population was born right here.

And the future of biculturalism in all this? That is a matter for experts. As a writer, I was seeing for the first time in a tiny corner of my country layers of population all looking in the same direction. And the sight interested, in fact fascinated me. I am not sure that the Cradle of Confederation has taken the road of complete bilingualism. I might even feel that the opposite is true. But for the first time I was exploring a real province. It is the smallest, and the least populous. What did it matter? Perhaps it is in this laboratory test-tube that, unknown to us, one of the experiments of greatest value to the future of our country is being conducted. Whatever comes of it, whatever may be our final evolution, we will perhaps some day need to draw lessons from Prince Edward Island.

THE KING OF THE FISHERMEN Would Rustico be marked on a map if it were in Quebec? I am not sure. Here, on the scale of Prince Edward Island, it is a natural stopping place on the way out of the national park, and you will have no trouble spotting it. It is very tiny, prolonged in the direction of the sea by another tiny place, Rustico North, where a few families still live by fishing. The others are farmers. Daily life unwinds here in an infinite peace, although it is only twenty miles from the capital. What a charm of another age has been kept by these little settlements that I was to encounter henceforth all along my journey to the point of Tignish.

I walked along the harbour of Rustico, watching the work of the fishermen. There is a little co-operative, which occupies the principle buildings on the wharf. Crates of mackerel are carried here from the boats. One by one these crates are laid on the platform scales. The representative of the co-operative notes the weight — several hundred pounds — he says 'hop' and the mackerel are emptied on the warehouse benches. There are tons of fish on beds of ice, which will make their way unceasingly to the United States.

I was soon attracted by some independent fishermen, who were just returning from their day's work. They use boats built on the island, called 'v-boats'. A layman would easily confuse them with the dories the Gaspesians use. I was soon able to talk to them. They were not too happy. Their catch was only five thousand pounds. A good daily catch for a v-boat with a two-man crew should be ten thousand pounds. Even so it was not too bad. The day had been better than they expected. Wind had been predicted, but it had passed wide of them. I pointed out that it had rained without stopping since the morning and that this rain showed no sign of ceasing. To see the clouds pile up, one could believe that the sun would never appear again.

'Rain doesn't bother us,' said one.

'Wind is the fisherman's enemy, not rain,' said the other.

My heavy shoes would smell of fish for several hours. I had to splash through puddles that you might describe as saturated with mackerel, but what did it matter? It was pleasant for me to help unload the fish, and the fishermen seemed to appreciate it. Since Newfoundland I had accumulated a series of little experiences among fishermen, which enabled me to seem not too much of an imbecile today. There was no danger of my asking 'How is the lobster-fishing?' in the middle of November. And I knew how to raise a crate in a single heave. This is quite a skill and I still sometimes managed to splash my neighbour, but I knew a few small things and they were aware of it. Although I came from far away, they considered me a little as one of the group.

They worked with a net, they were lucky. A little later I saw some fishermen arrive who cannot afford five thousand dollars to buy a net. They have lines with several hooks and a good knowledge of their trade, but their catches are never more than two to four hundred pounds. Ordinarily they return before or after the others. I talked to them too. I sensed that they were ashamed of their catch. They had that envious shine in their eyes with which kids on roller skates look at their friends on bicycles. They fling the mackerel into plastic pans; they don't need crates. They hang their heads. The net is triumphing everywhere, even in the little ports; no one can consent to hang his head forever, and I sensed that these men had already made their decision.

Later the great specialist of the place consented to speak to me. This was Becher Court. I may seem to be making an event of this. Well, no one ever disturbs Old Man Court. He has his own equipment, his wharves, his refrigerating sheds. It is an autonomous enterprise — not very large but autonomous — a family business. Court reigns in the midst of his five unmarried sons — strapping fellows that seemed not only to have the greatest respect for him but dimly to fear him. This man must have terrible rages at times.

Everyone had returned from the fishing, great tables had been set up on the edge of the wharf, and all set very rapidly to work preparing the day's catch. There would be work enough for everyone until nightfall. But I had already had an opportunity to chat for a long time with one of his sons, the oldest, and now he wanted to introduce me to his father. First he asked me to wait, he wished to spy out the land. From the distance I saw him approach his father discreetly. The old man was whetting an enormous knife on a grindstone. He was outlined cleanly on a background of fine rain and indigo, almost black ocean, motionless and still in the midst of an incessant coming and going. He put such concentration into his task that you could imagine he was preparing a criminal weapon. The son circled him for a moment, not yet daring to approach him. The old man seemed unaware of his presence. Suddenly the son said something. The old man kept silent, the son stopped speaking. I wondered what they were waiting for. And then the old man cast a searching look towards me. He nodded. The son came racing towards me, smiling broadly; his father was willing to speak to me for a few minutes.

I had a delightful interview with this still vigorous old man. We spoke only of things I had seen a hundred times in our fishing ports but I shall always remember the atmosphere, composed of delicacy and sensitivity. This old man was the last free man. I cannot say as much for his sons, who seemed subjected to him as to a god. But how should one know? And then they are old enough to defend their rights. They all lived together in a modest wooden house on the other side of the road. In the distance could be heard the continuous barking of the big black dog that no doubt had the mission of guarding it. He had not stopped barking since he saw me pass. At my departure, he bounded in my direction like a wild thing but was nailed to the spot by a single word from his master. This man knew how to make himself obeyed by everything that was alive around him.

FARMERS OF THE SEA   For the first time I encountered poverty, real poverty such as one does not expect to encounter in Prince Edward Island. It was not the poverty of the Orient, but even so . . . Nor was it the poverty of the American continent. There were no big cars beside the shacks and no television aerials on the roofs. I was in the Alberton region, but that had no special significance, for I was to find the same images of desolation almost everywhere on the island if ever I ventured outside the standard itineraries. Desolation, yes, for these were not even fishing villages. Just a few tottering houses at some distance from the little settlements. The people get along as best they can. Meat never, or very rarely, appears on their tables. They cannot read or write. They do whatever they can to scratch a living from the sea.

'You should have seen them fifteen years ago,' I was told. 'No electricity, the roofs were like sieves, the children in rags. No furniture but a bench and a table. People even slept on the floor. Today these shacks have running water, electricity, and heat, and if the daily menu isn't very varied, at least one eats one's fill.'

All these images had a quality of profound unreality, here on this little island paradise where it is hard to believe that even the workers are not eternal vacationers. The poor seem poorer than elsewhere.

So what was it that happened fifteen years ago? And how have these poor isolated people become a little less poor? I learned as I scoured the region a little. Here and there I found little commercial enterprises, such as I had already seen in Nova Scotia and would see again in New Brunswick, but which had not till now attracted my attention. It must be said that they are of a completely minor order and that their annual turnover does not weigh very heavily in the general economy of the Maritimes.

I am speaking of Irish moss, a sort of plant that grows on the ocean-rocks and that the sea uproots and casts up on the shore. Each storm provides an unusual harvest. The moss is gathered up with special rakes, but I have seen children collecting it by hand. If one is lucky enough to live near rocks or cliffs that are covered with it periodically, one can go and cut it with long scissors. It is then put to dry and taken to little plants, which press it, tie it in bundles, and ship it to Rockland, Maine, or even to Denmark. I am told that Irish moss has several commercial uses — in the manufacture of jellies, certain cheeses, blancmange, and several medicaments. True or false, it is enough for me that it offers a permanent market for these very poor families. It fetches six cents a pound. When the whole family works at it, they can make as much as twenty-five dollars a day in the week after a storm. Long ago a certain Toupin, of Montreal, began to interest himself in Irish moss. He even succeeded in extracting a sort of beer from it, which had its hour of popularity. But it was about 1941 when John B. Myrick undertook to exploit it for the United States market, much as has continued till today.

I witnessed the pressing in a little plant. You have to have very steady nasal papillae. In spite of all the explanations that have been given to me, I still connect this plant with the alga family. Even when it is very strong, I have always been able to bear the smell of algae. But I found it impossible to remain for more than a few minutes in this shed. How wonderful is the adaptive faculty of the human body. I saw that my two informants had scarcely wakened from a siesta in that very place, for the prints of their bodies were still fresh on a pile of moss. And they moved around in it as if they were in a loft full of new-mown hay.

The turnover for the last three months of this business: 750,000 pounds baled and shipped. It isn't Peru, but it is no longer a condemnation to destitution. The ocean is a nourishing mother of limitless resources. One of these days we will be preserving plankton.

END OF THE LINE: EVERYBODY OUT   I continued on to Tignish, the westernmost point of the island. Here the train stops and beyond Tignish the roads are absolutely deserted. One could pitch a tent right in the middle of the road. It is infinitely poetic, the more so as you are likely at any moment to come upon one of those wonderful roads of red dirt that make the fields of the province bleed as soon as you leave the main arteries.

A good part of the population of Tignish is of Acadian origin; you might suspect it when you notice the huge Catholic church. The church is flanked by a school, whose dimensions are rather surprising in this minuscule place at the end of the world. It is true that it serves the whole region, but you quickly scent something unusual. You will soon learn that it was founded by Sir Charles Dalton, ex-lieutenant-governor of the province, Tignish's most illustrious citizen. In two buildings you have the history of

Tignish, which is half Acadian, half Scottish. And as the people live in the most distant region from Charlottetown, they have had two hundred years to become used to living together.

I took my lunch, or my noon meal — I no longer know quite what to call that midday activity, since the most modest title seems too grand — in a place of the café type, with a lunch-counter and a small stock of cigarettes, chocolate, and news-papers. I could have eaten a little more suitably at Madame Gaudet's Inn, but this I learned too late. For the moment there I was in the midst of several dozen schoolboys and schoolgirls be-tween the ages of ten and sixteen.

The place was like a barracks gone mad. I was seated firmly at a table already adorned with a half-dozen blond and brown heads. Among them there were some budding Brigitte Bardots, and it was really very curious to find twelve- and thirteen-year-old Brigitte Bardots here. Clearly the movies have passed this way. As I looked at them a little more closely, I saw that they were American Bardots with streaks of black pencil at the cor-ners of their eyes.

In the end it was their menu that impressed me most. Before these lovely adolescents I saw only chocolate bars, pop, and other such delicacies. It seemed that it was considered much smarter to eat at the restaurant. The children that brought their lunch were confined to the school assembly hall like penitents. Others accepted the menu imposed by this little café — an enormous young waitress brought them soup and spaghetti. This was somewhat better. But today I was witness to the fact that choco-late bars won the gastronomic marathon.

After the afternoon lessons, they would all climb into the school bus, to be deposited at the four corners of this lonely region, and next day the whole thing would begin over again. There was talk of opening a canteen at the school. If I had been able to, I would have presented them with the necessary funds right then. Those Brigitte Bardots of the seashore had very pale cheeks.

New Brunswick

NEVER ON SUNDAY I drove from Cape Tormentine to Moncton, no longer in the rain but through a thick fog. I trust no one will ever ask me to describe the countryside. I saw none of it, I had trouble even making out the edge of the road. When the Maritimes treat themselves to a fog, you have the feeling that the surrounding air has been changed into a solid substance — solid but soft. You drive in cotton. Here and there, along the road, buses and cars were stopped every which way. Their drivers had given up. But where were they? The vehicles were empty, and no light and no neon filtered towards you.

Was I afraid? I couldn't say. I can only recall my joy when I finally reached Shediac, a little fishing port, whose charms I was later to have much pleasure discovering. For the moment there were ten or so young men to make sympathetic fun of me. This foggy weather was not made for fragile Québécois. I would find myself in the ditch with my scooter if I insisted upon going on to Moncton. They predicted a thousand deaths for me, and concluded by inviting me to accompany them. We would form a caravan. They had come to have a drink with friends and were about to go back to Moncton.

The rest of the journey took place without the slightest difficulty. They drove a bit fast for me but a caravan provides its own security. This first contact in New Brunswick was one of the warmest I had. I had been immersed in the good nature, simplicity, and rather loud but appealing camaraderie that I have always connected with the Acadian temperament. I had not found that much sung-of love for life in the Acadian milieus of Nova Scotia or Prince Edward Island. At Shediac it had burst forth quite unaffectedly, and it never left me again. Almost everywhere in New Brunswick it broke the surface at the slightest opportunity.

At last the lights of Moncton's main street put the night and the fog to flight. It was Saturday evening. There was dancing at my hotel. I registered in the midst of a coming and going of young adolescents, several of whom crossed the hall with bottles of Coca-Cola or orange pop in their hands. 'Strong stuff', as they call it, was served only inside the dance-hall, from which came yé-yé rhythms at each swing of the glass door.

I was led to my room and shown a bit of corridor where I should find one of those ice-cube factories with which all hotels with pretensions to modernity are now equipped. I was ushered into a spacious room with a view of a little park — I should not have asked for so much. Fifty-six lamps were lit, the radio and the television were turned on. I was shown how to work the shower (the same system, if you please, as in the Hilton Hotels), the dials of the air-conditioner were twirled . . . in short, I had for a long time understood: I was in the most modern annex of the oldest hotel in town. I would have slept that night in an attic full of rats and spiders.

I was delighting myself with the thought of being able to stretch out on one of those downy beds and my eyelids were already heavy when the telephone rang. It was my comrades of the caravan. They intended to take charge of my initiation to Moncton. I thought it a splendid idea but suggested perhaps tomorrow, or the day after . . . But one has seen nothing if one has not taken advantage of the very special atmosphere of Saturday night. It was the night of nights.

We spent a joyful evening together. Utterly stupid, but joyful.

ACADIAN CAPITAL Moncton almost did not exist. By this I mean that until the coming of the railway, it was only a tiny settlement. It was called the 'Bend' and then the railway made it a junction. Today it is an important city, at least forty per cent of whose population is of Acadian origin. You will learn this as you go along, for on the busiest avenues everything is conducted in English. But as you leave the beaten paths, you will encounter a francophone milieu that is very firm, structured, and autonomous, as is the whole Acadian population of New Brunswick.

The land of Evangeline is no longer Grand-Pré or Nova Scotia. It is New Brunswick. If there is an Acadian culture, or soul, or nation, it is here that you will take its pulse. As well, it is the Acadians that give New Brunswick its originality. Not only do they make up half the population, they constitute the most important and the most homogeneous ethnic group. They have a hand in all sections of activity. Their presence makes itself felt in education and economics, and it might even be considered that with the coming of Robichaud, they have achieved power, or at least political initiative. Though it is not quite so simple.

I was struck from my first days among them by their spirit of independence with respect to Quebec. Here I had no special status, I awakened no particular curiosity, even in the simplest environments. I never found myself, as I listened to them, untapping some suppressed suffering, sprung from a frustration of some kind — as for example not being perfectly understood by Quebec. To the Acadians of New Brunswick it is not of the least importance whether they are understood or not. They are sure of themselves. They have passed the stage of survival and are on their way to realization. They are not living among the English. They are perfectly at home.

The figures do not leave any doubts that the Acadians are at home in New Brunswick. At Moncton: 40 per cent. County of

Westmoreland: 60 per cent. Kent: 85 per cent. Northumberland: 50 per cent. Gloucester: 90 per cent. Restigouche: 85 per cent. Madawaska: 90 per cent. Thus a total Acadian population of about 220,000, more than half the province.

At Moncton there is the old Université Saint-Joseph and the new Université de Moncton. They are the same thing. Saint-Joseph is not a true university but much the equivalent of our secondary colleges. However, after years of delay and excuses the institution was incorporated, funds provided, work of construction begun, curricula established, faculties set up — in brief, the Acadians will have their own university, which will lack only age and reputation to rival the University of New Brunswick at Fredericton, which was founded in 1785. The Acadians have had to wait a long time for their university.

It was a fine battle, not only against the eddies of public opinion but in the wings. Edmundston or Bathurst might have claimed paternity with as much right as Moncton. You don't need to travel for long in this province to become aware of internal rivalries even in the Acadian milieu. I met some Québécois in Moncton who live in complete isolation. They have not been admitted by the group. I even saw some Acadians from Madawaska who after years in Moncton have not been accepted in local circles. If you are from Moncton you might very well have the same experience in Edmundston or Bathurst. The Acadians have truly passed the era of survival, they have reached the chapter of rivalries. Some young sociologists are concerned about this. I do not understand. All this seems to me, on the contrary, to be a sign of good health. Rivalry can well be a modest form of competition. At any rate, as far as the University of Moncton was concerned, as soon as the decision was made, everyone yielded, and the project continues with the blessing of all the Acadians of the Maritimes.

Since it still exists, almost in the heart of the city, I visited the old Collège Saint-Joseph, which will be kept in service for as long as the new campus on the outskirts of town is not in a

position to accommodate all the faculties. It's a red brick structure and its wooden corridors creak under your feet. There is a
whole little world in the midst of a constant coming and going
of clerical collars. The atmosphere is dusty, of another age, and
strongly suggests that of the free colleges of France. We have
the sense of penetrating into the world of Mauriac — or perhaps
that of Peyrefitte. This will quickly evaporate, for it is clear that
the contents have commenced their metamorphosis before the
container. Lay professors and deans of faculties exceed clerical;
the executive of the Bureau of Regents is ninety per cent lay,
and it is not necessary to read through many issues of the students' newspaper to guess that here and there, among its con-
tributors, are some of the most lucid minds of this little province.
I was not much mistaken, after all: in these long creaking corridors Peyrefitte goes hand in hand with Mauriac.

A FASCINATING PHENOMENON   Moncton is an amusing city,
sprightly and full of tourist attractions that finally make you
slightly forget its ugliness. For it is a very ugly city, I feel,
though it could have many charms, set as it is on the banks of
the Petitcodiac River. I have no special perspicuity in city planning but if I were provided with the means I would make this
city a little marvel. I know that there are urban plans on the
council table, but they are so timid. The buildings old and new
have sprung up no matter how, the railway tracks rip through
the busiest part of town, and there are grimy walls and long
chimneys everywhere, so that the tiny green spaces seem to be
in penance.

One of these is famous, however, in all America. It is there
you can observe at its best one of the phenomena linked to the
play of the tides in the Bay of Fundy, the so-called tidal bore.

It must be clear by now what I feel about most of our tourist
attractions throughout the country. With very rare exceptions,
they bristle with false representation. But the Moncton tidal
bore keeps its promise, provided you arrive at the right moment.
It is evident that the phenomenon is determined by the intensity

of the wind, and the extent of the tide, which ascends the Petitcodiac River.

First there is a distant rustling. The waters of the rivers are calm, very calm. Suddenly the rustling is intensified, and you see coming towards you a bar of foaming water, the height of which can vary from a few inches to five feet and which advances at a speed of seven or eight miles an hour and continues till about fifteen miles above Moncton, raising the level of the waters in its passage all at once. The fishing must be good all along its journey, for the tidal bore is accompanied by the greedy cries of hundreds of gulls that jostle one another on the banks and move along at the same rhythm as the bore.

This is not a unique phenomenon, as one may guess. At Caudebec, in France, the Seine offers tidal bores as invariably and for the same reasons, as do at least two rivers in England, the Tsien-tang in China, and the Amazon in Brazil. But to one that witnesses it for the first time, the tidal bore seems to me certain to provide a little interior excitement. It puts us back in communication with the great forces of nature, which we are inclined to forget. It is good for us to see this, for it restores our measure, our little size on this immense planet at grips with the humours of its age.

ON THE WANDERER'S AGENDA   How pleasant it must be for the summer visitor to drive about at random on the coast of New Brunswick, from the Bay of Fundy to the extremity of the Baie des Chaleurs . . . that is to say to the hinge with Quebec. The whole way is full of little villages, several of which claim to be historic and really are so, but this is not their principal charm. They are set in landscapes that form a synthesis of all I had seen elsewhere in the eastern part of the country. Sometimes I found Newfoundland, sometimes Nova Scotia, very often Prince Edward Island, and the whole prepared me for Gaspé.

Apart from Saint John and Bathurst, which are its two poles of attraction, you will not find a single large town along this coastal road. And if by chance you veer off into the interior, you will find forest. This province is covered with forest for eighty per cent of its territory. It is from the forest that it draws the best part of its revenue. But between the fishing villages and the forest you will often be surprised to see, strung out into infinity, farming villages. This is the case, for instance, in Kent County, immediately to the north of the Moncton region. To adventurous spirits it offers some of the most peaceful summer excursions, notably along the Cocagne River. To the village of Côte d'Or, for example, one of the principal lobster ports of eastern Canada. At Rexton there is one of the most unexpected of encounters: a monument erected to the memory of Bonar Law, Kent County's most illustrious son, of whom your teacher has never told you — Bonar Law, prime minister of Great Britain in 1922. And suddenly you wonder how it could have happened that that parliamentary factory, Great Britain, had to supply itself from this very little village, in a very little county of a very little province of a far-off country.

The more you climb towards Bathurst, the more the fishing villages forecast those you will encounter later in Gaspé, on the other side of the Baie des Chaleurs. The Bay of Heat in the summer, yes . . . but in winter the Bay of Wind, of Cold, and of Icy Solitude. An image that you have always found ugly else-where and that *is* ugly brings you some kind of solace here: on the roofs television aerials rise like lightning-rods of loneliness. So Michelle Tisseyre's smile will freely enter these houses, and Dubé's tales, and plays, and films, and advertising — the whole circus that the adults have built at great expense to conquer loneliness and fear.

TO SAINT JOHN . . . THE LONG WAY ROUND   You could, of course, go from Moncton to Saint John by the interior, where at every instant the road offers pleasant glimpses of very romantic moun-tain and forest landscapes. But you should go the long way round at least once — that is to say by the coast. You will see the celebrated Hopewell Rocks — 'the biggest flower-vases in the

world', as they have been called — after ascending the Petitcodiac River to the Bay of Fundy. You will then enter the national
park of the same name. Its area does not exceed eighty square
miles. You will not be likely to meet a bear or a moose at the
end of an avenue, and you can take your grandfather with the
weak heart for a trip here without the least apprehension. But
the park gains in harmony what it loses in grandeur. I can
imagine how lively it must be in season. It is above all a 'playground', as they say — a sort of vacationers' paradise with golf,
sea-bathing, campgrounds, little lakes for canoes, bowling lawns,
tennis, all open-air sports. But I was alone at the end of autumn.
However, the sun was present. I am sorry all travellers do not
have the opportunity to see their beautiful national park as I
saw it at this moment.

THE METROPOLIS   Saint John is not at first sight a beautiful city,
any more than is Moncton or so many of our other little cities
across the country. You have the impression of driving about in
a back neighbourhood of Old Montreal. Few trees. Brick façades
blackened by time and smoke. Very infrequent green spaces. A
few views of the ocean, but these so timorous. It is clear that
these cities were built at the time when the enemy came from
the sea. So they turned their back upon it. The enemy is still
there, it is winter. The design of the streets was intended to
protect the walker and the houses from winter's gusts. Except
in the very centre of the city, where the animation seems to
wish to crystallize around an attractive park and then to descend
abruptly to the harbour along a very wide commercial avenue.

Saint John does not give itself city airs; it is a real city, the
most important in New Brunswick and one of the most active
in the Maritimes. An intense harbour traffic, big factories, ship-
yards, oil refineries, big stores by the dozen, several excellent
hotels and restaurants, a very large group of hospitals, seventy-
six churches, an unexpected number of historical remains, old
residential quarters and others that are brand new with their

little trees on guard like an army of toothpicks. In short, a city of 93,000 inhabitants — if one includes Lancaster — that appears to have twice as many. And one no longer asks oneself whether it is beautiful or not, for it is extraordinary enough to find so lively a city in a part of our country that seems crushed out of season by a century-long torpor.

Saint John also knows how to wear all faces, according to whether you see it from street level or from the suspension bridge that links it with Lancaster. However, it is from the summit of Fort Howe, a desolate little hill in the very heart of the city, that you will have the most interesting views of the harbour. It is impressive. Saint John is a national port, that is to say one of the eight ocean ports administered by the federal government. Ferries for Nova Scotia mingle with the coming and going of the freighters that keep Saint John in touch with the various markets of the world. The big local enterprise is of course the Irving refinery. Those interested will not be able to miss it. The works occupy an area of seven hundred acres and give employment to several hundreds of skilled workers. And if by chance you are seeking the way to it, just let yourself be guided by the emanations its chimneys spit forth upon the city.

THE ENGLISH . . . BUT WHICH? Saint John has typical English traits of behaviour, right down to the smallest crannies of daily life. You will not understand if you do not examine its history. This is the very stronghold of the Loyalists. Their attitude towards the rest of the country is not so different from that of the Acadians. Compared to the other English Canadians, they were the first to live in our immense country. Let us imagine that the fortune of war had left Canada to France; today it would be they, and not the Acadians, that would consider themselves an autonomous minority, an ethnic group distinct from English Canada.

The French Canadians usually speak of 'the English' as if they formed a monolithic block. The hypothesis is useful, even perhaps necessary, for one who wishes to define himself in his own milieu. I only know that all along my Canadian journey I have found English Canadian communities that were very different from one another. And to me it seems as grotesque to say that the English are all rich and cultivated as it is to say that French Canadians are poor, controlled by their priests, and eaters of pea-soup. Here, in the Maritimes, the English seemed to me as close to their priests as the Acadians. And they did not speak the same language I had heard in other provinces. They had a strong accent, it seemed to me. Their big universities, sometimes mistakenly, have several complexes about Ontario.

Their economic situation is rather mediocre on the whole. And, like the Acadians, they are at the mercy of American capital. In the English milieus of Saint John and Fredericton, I caught some remarks that were more bitter and at the same time more lucid in this respect than in the young provinces of the West, which seem to care rather little about the source of capital as long as they keep the sense that Canada follows an independent policy.

Here, for instance, a very cultured man remarked: 'Canada is not a country. It is only an American branch-office. Our political independence is a sham. Even if it were real, it would be just because we don't disturb anybody. Canada doesn't exist on the map of the world. It's never on the front page of the New York newspapers.'

The speaker was an English Canadian from Saint John. I was to hear the same tune elsewhere, at Fredericton, for instance. Nothing more is needed to describe this difference of approach to our problems that I sensed among the English of the Maritimes. This difference may take all forms, but one must be aware that it exists. I am not far from believing that English Canada has its own Acadians. And this would be a stroke of luck — the chance of sanity. These people have suffered, and still suffer, from a status of inferiority with respect to the rest of the country. And frustrations give people ideas, many ideas.

THE PATH OF THE LOYALISTS   Imagine that your town held in the palm of its hand all the treasures of its three centuries of history. This is the case at Saint John, where an hour's walk in the heart of the city will show you in turn an old Loyalist house, the garrison church, the old courthouse, Trinity Church, a cemetery, the old marketplace, and sundry other souvenirs of the Loyalist era, of which we shall mention only the chief. In the tourist season the visit has been turned into a parlour game, a sort of treasure hunt, crowned by a certificate from the mayor. Fortunately I escaped these little treats from the Chamber of Commerce. I was alone and I had plenty of time.

The Loyalist house just escaped vanishing, like several of its neighbours, under the demolition hammers. At the last moment some citizens protested and created a climate favourable to its restoration. The result is remarkable. The whole, in Georgian style, diffuses an austere charm well suited to a period when the upper-class citizen was careful not to display any external signs of his riches. The house was built by a certain David Merritt, who settled at Saint John towards the end of the American War of Independence. Sheraton furniture was current then — as was also my guide, it would seem. He behaved like a son of the house, let me into all the little secrets of the time, and did everything but open the doors of the secretary to give me the master's love-letters to read.

David Merritt was part of the very first waves of colonists-in-spite-of-themselves. He was on his feet within a few years, but this was not the case with everyone. Most of them took time to free themselves from the various bonds that still attached them to the United States. Everything had happened so quickly. From one day to the next they were dispossessed, poor, without a country. Several returned to England. Others put themselves under the protection of the army, which had pledged by treaty to watch over their safety. And it was much for them as it had been for the Acadians at the moment of the Expulsion, even if the motive force and the circumstances differed. They were put on board transport ships and a course set to the north. In this way the first cargoes landed at the mouth of the Saint John River. Merritt was of the number. The city of Saint John was born. Other settlements sprang up along the river and in several other corners of New Brunswick.

This province was made, roughly speaking, of two sorts of deportees: the Acadians on their return from exile and the Loyalists at the beginning of theirs. It is rare that the ethnic groups of a little province are linked by the same sufferings. Hold such discourses as you like with me about Canada in its totality, I am not yet in a position to verify them, but do not try to make me believe that the English and the French of New Brunswick are not made to get along. They do not know one another, that is the tragedy. No one really knows his neighbour in Canada.

MORE FASCINATING THAN A MOVIE It was clearly an old moving-picture theatre, with its luminous marquee, its multiple glass doors, and its inner lobby. The letters 'Full Gospel Hall', which stood out very clearly on the marquee, seemed to announce a film. A man stood in the entrance hall: he might have been offering tickets. At the end of the foyer, the doors opened upon a lighted hall. People were going in: it was half past eight; the show was no doubt about to resume after the intermission.

In fact, as you have guessed, this large hall came alive only in the evening, when service was held. But it was not a service as we imagine them. I asked permission to mingle with the crowd; it was granted me very willingly. I was handed a leaflet, which bore the title 'What it Means to be Born Again', and offered innumerable extracts from the Gospel to make me understand that I had just been born for the second time. Another leaflet, entitled 'Hello There', informed me that Jesus was seated beside me and that I could tell him my sins, my failures, and all that had stained my soul during the day. I considered my seat-companions carefully; on one side Jesus had borrowed the features of a tender young girl whom my confidences might shock and on the other those of a large woman who seemed not to care that

tears were flowing silently down her cheeks — here was someone to whom too much had already been said. In a box music
was being played, a rather gay tune that I could not identify, by
an electric organ and a violin. A man of about fifty was already
on the stage when I arrived. Back to the crowd, he seemed to be
concentrating. At the last note of the music, he turned towards
us and in an overwhelming voice uttered a series of Amens.

For one not forewarned, an incredible spectacle then commenced. I had seen this only in the cinema. An old gentleman
recounted, at first in a tranquil voice, how he had come to sense
the presence of Jesus in his daily life. Suddenly the voice swelled
and vibrated. He was too far away for me to hear all his words
and for a moment I thought he was becoming angry. But a broad
smile illuminated the face of the prior, who was punctuating the
narrative with Amens. The old gentleman terminated his story
in a sort of frenzy, which made several conquests in this crowd of
about three hundred persons. There were eddies on the right,
the most moved section. This was about to be balanced, for a
girl rose on the left. Her disclosures, delivered in a sort of chant,
promptly raised the whole hall to the same diapason. One would
have had to be of marble not to be physically stirred by this
excitement. I was perhaps the only one at that moment able to
observe the spectacle from the outside. And I owed this to my
ignorance of these rites. I could see the moment approach when
the emotion, stimulated by more and more vibrant and sustained
Amens, would culminate in collective hysteria. Just how far can
one continue in this direction? Would they all roll on the ground
as certain sects of Shakers do in certain circumstances? No. Calm
suddenly returned when the prior judged that the testimonies
had continued long enough.

Behind all this was a great knowledge of human nature. I had
never seen so attentive an audience. After this nervous explosion,
it was clear that these people felt a physiological need for sooth-
ing words. I could feel them partaking of the prior's remarks.
The music resumed and four pretty girls left the hall and appeared on the stage to interpret a polyphonic hymn that an ear

less attentive than mine might have confused with the latest yé-yé creation.

At the door of this cinema-church you can buy a considerable number of brochures, pamphlets, and magazines, which stir up rather neurotic fantasies of the end of the world. Jesus was there, and you did not see him. You were deaf-mute and blind.

I have on my table a copy of *Pentecostal Evangel*; this is a pious weekly magazine with a circulation of 200,000. It is published in the United States but its content varies little from that tide of evangelical literature that has invaded all America; we have known for a long time that our Protestant neighbours are fond of such literature, but each time a magazine of this kind falls into my hands I am struck by the great despair that seems to constitute its basic fabric. We are always on the threshold of the Day of Judgement, and if we knew how to listen we would hear the trumpets of Jericho. Each time I encounter this sort of literature, which includes in its entirety millions of copies in all the Protestant milieus of America, I am surprised that it does not provoke an epidemic of suicides.

A ROMANTIC VALLEY   I had imagined a wilder countryside and more violent landscapes. As I drove up the Saint John River towards Fredericton, the mountains grew rounded from village to village, clung to the riverbanks, and seemed little inclined to climb towards the clouds. And it would be like this until I reached the border of Quebec. Throughout its length the Saint John River cleaves a romantic setting. This is characteristic of the Maritime Provinces, where the highest peaks seldom exceed three thousand feet. The geological formations are of the Cambrian epoch. In places the river possesses a peculiar charm, which it is very wrong to compare with that of the valley of the Rhine. It is less affected, one is less aware of the intervention of man, and I promised myself to drive here again during the summer months.

After the Indians and the first Acadian colonists, the Loyalists made their way up this river. Some Acadian families, scarcely

*At the last note of music, he turned towards us and in an overwhelming
voice uttered a series of Amens.*

returned after the Expulsion, preferred to pack their bags a second time and move farther to the north. So it was that in their quest for readily habitable places the Loyalists were sometimes surprised to find newly built cabins, wells, and outbuildings. On the site of the old French village of Sainte-Anne, they discovered only ruins. But they found the situation so charming that a good number of them decided to settle there. So they came to lay the foundations of what was to become Fredericton, the capital of New Brunswick.

FRENCH LESSON   On the list of the activities of my Fredericton hotel, I suddenly noticed: 'French lesson, little salon, 8.30.' This was not the first time I had had occasion to meditate upon the proliferation of French courses across the greater part of Canada. All the governments have established evening courses for lovers of French and each evening the most varied locations are put at the disposal of equally varied teachers. One makes use of what one has, all becomes grist to one's mill, and I remember many chance encounters with very amiable persons of whom one would believe almost anything except that they were teachers of French. But this was the first time, at least to my knowledge, that a teacher could afford to set himself up in a hotel, in this case the pleasantest hotel in Fredericton.

I was so intrigued that I postponed my evening appointments till next day so that I could have the pleasure of attending his lesson. I asked the receptionist to show me into the presence of the distinguished teacher.

He wasn't there, I was told. He came from Saint John by car and usually arrived half an hour before the lesson. They would tell him of my intentions. He would certainly not have the least objection to receiving a transient pupil. He was dealing tonight only with beginners. One less, one more. But the professor gave right here, at another time, a more advanced course, which prepared you for conversation. I understood my informants' regrets; with his beginners, the teacher would not have a chance to show me his exceptional gifts. The tone of solidarity with which they spoke to me at the reception desk put me in the best possible frame of mind. I was delighted that these French courses had a reputation of such seriousness here.

A SYMPATHETIC ATMOSPHERE My first confrontation with the teacher Ronald McDonald of Saint John was a little staggering, but cheerful. He is immense, his voice is stentorian, he displaces a great deal of air as he walks, and he has a fine gift for irony. It was the separatists that had sent me, he suggested. He would find a bomb in his letterbox. I would have found the allusion annoying if he had not been so far from intending it so. He liked writers, he told me, especially writers that travelled. My name was not unknown to him, but where in the devil had he heard it?

Together we climbed the great staircase that would take us to the little salon. He was speaking to me all this time in English, an excellent English, moreover. What a pity I couldn't sit in on his more advanced course. He had polished up some personal teaching techniques. The French his pupils would finally speak would put the French of Quebec to the blush. Some Frenchmen from France had told him so. So I was warned. At the slightest reservation I would be ranged among the barbarians. But I hoped to make him understand that I had not come here as judge or arbiter, but simply as a writer. I had thought it would be interesting to place the teacher and his courses within their particular atmosphere and describe the whole thing without comment.

Now we were at the top of the staircase. Half a dozen pupils were sitting about. They rose and came towards us, introductions were made, and we exchanged joking remarks as is our way at the beginning of all encounters. This convention of humour at all costs might be only a form of timidity, a way of overcoming the timidity that is natural to us and that we would be wrong to rid ourselves of, I believe, since it gives our social interchange a warmth it might not always possess of itself.

From the outset I was the object of a sympathetic curiosity that in other circumstances I should have had to prove I deserved. I was being offered a gift, in a sense. I still had not had time to utter a word and yet already I was considered interesting.

We all went together into the little salon that was to be our classroom. The teacher's long table was already in place and we had only to form a semi-circle. I was beginning to learn a little about my fellow pupils. The teacher left the room for a few minutes, which enabled the group to engage in a sort of general conversation. They were members of the middle class. For some of them the course was a luxury, of no special purpose. They had always wanted to learn French so as to be able to read it and then have the advantage of another culture. To hear them, this sudden desire owed much more to De Gaulle than to recent events in Quebec. In other words it was not a defence reaction but the fulfilment of an old childhood dream. I accepted this version of things like an imbecile. I was not there to reopen the debate but to observe. And I did not miss a word that was said to me. Others wanted to learn French to improve their chances of promotion in their section. They were members of large organizations that were obliged to become increasingly concerned with bilingualism. I had heard the same sort of thing at Moncton, where thirty-six employees of the CNR and two directors of Air Canada had enrolled in the French courses of the Modern Language School of the University of Moncton.

In all the big cities, the CNR and Air Canada lead the way with French courses. These two crown companies are making a considerable effort to arrive some day at complete bilingualism. I am not drawing from the information in the annual reports but from life. I have seen these employees, I have seen them at work almost everywhere. One day when I met a high personage of Air Canada, I believed I was being agreeable to him by pointing this out. He almost had a stroke. Nothing is more disagreeable to Air Canada than to have its interest in bilingualism connected with a recent period. This company, we are to believe, has always been actively interested in bilingualism. But until now perfectly bilingual people were to be found only in Quebec — and should the company recruit all its stewardesses and all its other personnel in Quebec? Now bilingual people are springing up in Ontario and several other provinces. In a very few years all Air Canada personnel will be perfectly bilingual and this by virtue of a principle in force since its creation.

I am willing to believe this. Those that often take Air Canada's great carriers notice from one time to the next the progress that has been made in this direction. But they can also measure the length still to go, especially as regards short flights above provinces considered to be English. But let us acknowledge that the problem is not slight and that it is very obviously bound up with Canada's recent awareness of itself. It is clear that French courses owe their popularity to the convulsions of Quebec — no more so in Air Canada than in the other crown companies or in the big industries interested in the Quebec market, but just as much. And a good thing too!

M-N-Â-P . . . The group was now complete. Ten pupils waited, textbook in hand, for the return of the teacher. I was shown the textbook. It is a hefty volume, published by the Institute of Modern Languages of Saint John and with the expected enough title of *Cours de conversation française*. Price five dollars. The course is distributed over thirty-five weeks.

I was happy to have succeeded in introducing myself into the group without causing the slightest embarrassment. Once the first moment had passed, I was sure no one took me for a judge or an inquisitor. As well as the several employees of important organizations of whom I spoke, there was a member of the provincial legislature, a doctor, and a few young women of no profession who were delighted to exchange opinions with me, not only about Quebec but about France, Japan, and the world. The age of my companions for an evening varied between twenty-five and sixty-five. Some of them had travelled widely. The conversation was going so well when the teacher returned that we would have liked to pursue it. But a thunderous, 'Well, *la classe,'* had just been heard, serious things were about to begin, the lesson went hell bent for leather from the beginning.

A teacher cannot be judged by a single lesson, especially when it is addressed to beginners, but Ronald McDonald's vigorous humour burst out at every point. And this I am sure is one of his secrets. He turns each lesson into a show and, even if he appears to be doing it all with a flick of the wrist, he takes pains over the fixing of details that leave you a little thoughtful. For instance, I remember the technique he has perfected for the pronunciation of the letter 'u', that bête noire of all the English in the study of French. He has his pupils whistle — yes indeed, whistle like a boy, to assure the correct position of the lips and the tongue — and then pronounce the sound 'ee'. Perhaps this is the technique used everywhere, I would not know, but for one that is witnessing it for the first time it is a delightful spectacle. I watched the member of the legislature whistle conscientiously a hundred times, emitting 'u's of all sorts before he hit upon the correct one, at which the teacher announced in a voice that would have carried to Saint John without the help of telephone lines, 'Well, *la classe,* there is hope for everyone since even our MLA's can do it.'

The alphabet included all the letters as we know them, with the addition of the sounds 'é' and 'è'. The problem of accents is thus settled once for all. I was also surprised not to encounter the sound 'o' in this alphabet that everyone was reciting in turn, with splendid seriousness, including I myself when my turn came. Everyone had said 'i-j-k-l-m-n-â-p', so I thought it very intelligent of myself to say, as I had learned in my childhood, 'n-o-p'.

'Well, *la classe,'* our teacher interrupted, 'that is precisely what you must never do, otherwise you will always have trouble with the letter "o". In French the sound "o" is very rarely kept in the body of a word. For instance, one says, "robe-monopole-farandole". . . . So it is better to learn from the beginning the sound "â" as in robe, monopole, farandole. . . . You understand? . . . Continue, Monsieur Cloutier.'

I continued, while thinking of something else. I thought of how great the responsibilities of Quebec are at this precise moment in the history of our country — great as is the need for goodwill, such as that of these pupils and this teacher and all the others like them. They are not tricksters, they do their work as seriously as can be imagined, but they are simply doing what they can with the means at their disposal. There . . . *dont ils disposent* . . . the sound 'o' as I was taught in my old outmoded alphabet. I haven't completely wasted my childhood. There are still a few of them left, dear Mr McDonald.

Quebec

DAVID AND GOLIATH   A slight shock on the threshold of Quebec
— I saw big signs on all sides bearing the inscription: 'Quebec
border'. For a split second I wondered if I had missed an important news bulletin. Then I remembered that the transition
from one province to another is always indicated in this way. If
separation took place, all the apparatus would be in place: only
the customs shed need be added. Such ideas send a shiver down
your back.

I had often heard about winter work. Governments join in
these projects to help small municipalities reduce their seasonal
unemployment. I had never encountered any of them before, but
on almost the entire coast of the Baie des Chaleurs, practically to
Percé, all the little towns seemed to be taking advantage of winter
work to install water pipes, sewers, and a thousand luxuries of
the sort. The road unreeled infinitely varied perspectives. The
last leaves clung to the trees of forests ready to receive their
first snow, but I would not often be able to lose myself in contemplation. I would have to thwart trucks, cranes, and machinery
of all sorts, spitting out cement, tar, smoke and fire — I who

had dreamed for so long of making the complete tour of the Gaspé and had wakened very early this morning, to be among the first to make certain that the sun, the sun that was indispensable to this part of my journey, would be at the rendezvous. And the sun shone as it had never shone before, it seemed to me, and I was assured that it would hold for several days, and I had a thousand happy plans. I had not dreamed of winter work. The industrial era is always spoken of as the promised land. And this I do not doubt for an instant. Far from me is the thought that it will always look like a building-yard. But what machinery is needed to plough the promised land!

There was one machine I had never seen before. I abandon all attempts to describe it, and I have never understood what it could be used for, though workmen bustled about it by the dozen like docile termites. Perhaps they were simply building a bit of road upon the debris from the last storm.

I had stopped in front of the bearer of the red flag when I suddenly noticed some enormous metal hooks descending towards me like the claws of a giant eagle. And I remember nothing more. There were shouts. I pressed the accelerator, stopped, got out, and found everyone laughing. They had wanted to give me a fright, it seemed. They had succeeded. By this single little incident I could have understood that I was in the Gaspé now. But I was too angry for such thoughts.

I do not say that such incidents await travellers on the Baie des Chaleurs, even during winter work. But looking back on it later, I see what must have happened. Tourist cars are rare at the beginning of the winter. They have even begun to seem exotic. I had chanced by when the workmen, comrades, all from the region, had wished to give themselves a few seconds of entertainment. To everyone his little comedy. Just the same, they had placed a lot of confidence in the machinery. And if I hadn't pressed the accelerator? Or done it a little too late? Or if they hadn't been able to halt the immense metal hooks? I believe these are much the protests I uttered, along with others in the same style. Some rages put strokes of genius in your mouth, others inanities. It seems that today my words weren't entirely appropriate to the occasion. Louder and louder bellows of laughter punctuated my observations.

I got back into my car and resumed my journey, despair in my heart at having been so amusing. Without knowing it, I had just passed my initiation into one of the very particular facets of Gaspé humour. I don't know all of them but I do know that, for the people of the Gaspé, life, the sober and serious life of others, unwinds like an endless Chaplin film.

OUR MEDITERRANEAN   One searches in vain for the Gaspé of the films. I mean desolation tucked into the crannies of a grandiose landscape. The cross of death on the forehead of an austere beauty. The solitary little cabin surrounded by snow-covered mountains and an icy sea. I was to find these images, especially inland from the coasts, deep inland in little dying villages. But one feels, going from Paspébiac to Anse-aux-Gascons, or from Newport to Grande-Rivière, that one has been tricked. After what I had seen elsewhere, notably in Newfoundland, all this seemed smooth, solid, vital, and almost middle class. Unlike so many of the coastal regions of the Maritimes, where one might believe many of the villages are living on their initial impetus while awaiting some unnamed cataclysm, each settlement here possesses its own reasons for pride and a certain dynamic quality that appears quite justified. But this comfortable impression holds true only in comparison with what exists elsewhere. The moment you project it towards the rest of Quebec, it breaks into a thousand pieces.

The situation of the region is still infinitely precarious and, as an old man in Gaspé expressed it later, 'It has a chance of recovery with ARDA. Will it meet the challenge?' If it does not, it will have no real share in the rapid transformation of all Quebec.

Honoré Mercier, the famous member of parliament for Bonaventure, said of the Baie des Chaleurs, 'It is our Mediterranean.'

He was scarcely exaggerating. Here is a sheet of water that is a good two hundred miles in circumference and twenty-five miles wide from Cap d'Espoir to the island of Miscou. The climate here is very much milder than elsewhere on the Gulf, the tide never rises higher than five feet, thick fogs and strong ocean winds seldom occur. The temperature does not generally go below zero in the winter, which is quite a feat in this part of the country. As well, the bay is protected from north winds by the great Appalachian Range, which changes its name three times during its journey from Vermont to the Gaspé. Here it is called by its Micmac name of Shickshocks. With very few exceptions the summits are hardly more than two thousand feet. Lakes are scarce and of very little extent. The rivers are powerful and of heavy volume.

MEN OF THE SEA Port-Daniel is one of the most picturesque villages on this part of the coast and an important centre of fishing to boot. It was here perhaps that Cartier first set foot on the soil of New France. According to the researches of a certain Mrs Ada O'Sullivan, the great navigator entered this harbour in July of 1534 with two small vessels. He even read Mass here before his officers and crew. There is no mention of the presence of Indians but they used to spend the summer months on the bay and knew it as Epsegeneg, 'the place where one warms oneself'. They camped on a strip of sand between the natural harbour and the sea and drew drinking water from a small stream that still flows. They did a little fishing, while the women occupied themselves with various agricultural tasks. Mrs O'Sullivan even found a few blades of Indian corn near the harbour and wondered, not unpoetically, whether they did not spring from a few seeds that slipped years ago from the hand of a young Indian girl.

Cartier was explicit, these Indians had already known 'pale faces'. We no longer need be astonished. Since Newfoundland I had heard the same refrain everywhere I went. The entire eastern part of the country, and particularly the Gaspé peninsula, had been visited by the Norsemen from Greenland or Iceland many centuries before the appearance of the first discoverers. There were even considerable fishing centres here in the eleventh or twelfth centuries. Cartier met Indians that already had some notion of navigation and had heard of our God.

Port-Daniel today has a population of twenty-five hundred. Its pioneers were of varied origins, as in most of these coastal settlements. But Mrs O'Sullivan points out that in spite of big cars, television aerials, and the rhythm of modern life, only an hour of sudden peace is needed for a certain permanence with the past to reawaken, 'in the silent snow, the sparkling of the stars, the return of the birds in spring, the autumnal forest and the squealing of the gulls'. This is a schoolgirl's poetry but very moving and I have found it to be true on many occasions. It may be a question of a very ancient awareness of one's roots, a matter perhaps of the composition of the chromosomes. We who have sprung from concrete and live amidst stone, smoke, and noise, have lost this faculty, this power of suddenly vibrating to the mere passage of a flight of birds.

They have too, of course. One cannot be in a state of emotion every second of the day. But you will be speaking to them, and then for a moment you have lost them. They are elsewhere. They will return to you but, without being aware of it themselves, they have entered another dimension — that of the wave, of a bird's cry, a gust of wind, the trees, of this rocky beach to which they have taken you. Or perhaps they are only listening to the silence, that silence you believe comes from the sea and that wells up from the inner self. You take up the conversation again at the moment where you left it. They are quite different now. Their laugh has no longer the same spontaneity. They have forgotten what they had to say to you. But unwittingly they have told you the essential thing about themselves, that they have remained men of the sea.

PERCÉ Curiously, whether you come by the road or from the sea, it is not the famous Percé Rock that first attracts your attention but Mont Sainte-Anne. This is a mass that rises to more than fourteen hundred feet and whose abrupt cliffs give a dizzying rhythm to the entire landscape. We know today that it is of the same geological formation as the rock, which became detached from it in prehistoric times. It was Breton fishermen who gave it the name it bears today and made it a place of pilgrimage, in acknowledgement of the numerous services to mariners in peril of this natural landmark, which is visible in clear weather for eighty miles. The mountain is still a place of pilgrimage. The whole rear side as far as Montagne Blanche is full of curiosities — crevices, grottos, waterfalls, caverns, and paths where botanists will find Gaspé antemaria, dryas, hairy willows, and all that could invite the summer walker to excursions of a sort and an interest almost unknown elsewhere. Two capes rising from a promontory balance the backdrop dominated by Mont Sainte-Anne. The more rounded and graceful of the two is Mont-Joli, the more severe one Cap-Canon.

It was all this I saw coming towards me when suddenly at a turning in the road Percé Rock appeared, like a phantom ship stranded on the village reef, tiny first but rising as I approached until I could no longer see anything but its reflections bronzed by this crude winter light. And I understood why the poets, filmmakers, and painters have adopted it. It is living matter. As the hours passed, I never saw it in the same tones.

OUR YOUNG PEOPLE ARE HUNGRY   I made my tour of the Gaspé in the contrary or clockwise direction, and I hold the beauties of Percé responsible for my lack of emotion when I made contact with Gaspé. A real town at last and in a setting of mountains and sea, but I ought to have seen it first.

Though I could only glimpse and sound them out a little, I thought the young people particularly interesting. One feels that they live with the ceiling pressing on their heads, as do all young people of our day who live to one side of the great urban centres. The time has ended when they could be kept at home with lies. They are well-informed on all subjects and dream of going to breathe a free air and build themselves great careers. Gaspé will find it harder than ever to keep its young at home. The town is an industrial and commercial centre, a rail terminus, it is not far from the great mining developments, it has boat-building and an active fishing industry, it is the see of an expanding diocese, possesses numerous educational institutions, it is developing its hospital centre, it possesses a very rich history symbolized by the enormous stone cross overlooking the town that commemorates Jacques Cartier's first landing on Canadian soil, it will probably be the first to benefit from the redevelopment of the entire territory, it has a prosperous tourist industry and accommodation that could easily be made adequate . . . and yet something essential must be lacking, since it is soon clear that the young people are living with their eyes turned towards the world outside. A climate of intellectual liberty is perhaps what is missing.

Some young people put on conspiratorial airs to speak to me of separatism. Yet this is a question that is openly debated in the big daily newspapers. What they said to me on the subject did not really capture my attention. It was too sentimental, abstract, and empirical. They were talking about a country of which they knew nothing. Some were better documented about the question, for at Matane I was offered remarks that were assured, clear, and very logical. But what struck me here was the taboo character of these conversations, the mystery with which they were surrounded. I had the feeling suddenly that I was in Spain. It was very disagreeable.

How could one know? Perhaps it was a climate of moral freedom that was lacking. The young people might imagine they could find this more easily elsewhere. Yet might they not be victims of an illusion? It is true that Quebec suddenly felt its windows swinging in the wind and a sensation of euphoria invaded it. It was drunk to the point of exaltation. And then it became apparent that certain windows had been piously closed, and great tempests had changed into a tiny breeze. In the expressions of some Gaspé young people I saw hopes that were destined to disillusionment. Intellectual and moral freedom still seemed to me a luxury and not widely available. I note just the same, for further reference, a great disproportion between the dreams of some of the young people of Gaspé and the place that will be made for them in our big cities, if they ever manage to become part of them.

SEXUAL SEGREGATON   Through the window I could see the Gaspé bridge and, on the heights, the hospital buildings, so magnificently situated that you would like to indulge in a small illness. I would ask to be entrusted to the care of Sister Denis. Here was a person of astonishing patience and courage. She worked for years at not only gathering together but analysing all the works about the Gaspé. Books, periodicals, films, unpublished manuscripts. It was truly prodigious. My companion had a complete list of them; it contained three hundred and seventy-five titles. I allowed him to tell me the dozens of works I absolutely must read before I wrote my first line about the Gaspé, for I had become the attentive observer of a little drama.

One of the protagonists was a young man of perhaps twenty. He was alone at his table and he never took his eyes from the entrance door except for the time needed to spoon up a generous load of chocolate ice cream surmounted with whipped cream. It was enormous. I have never seen its like. It must be the specialty of the house. It is clearly the privilege of only the non-wine-drinking countries to advertise such sound and healthy livers. The spoon was suddenly immobilized, half immersed in that species of flower-vase that enclosed the precious nectar: three girls had just appeared. One of them was visibly the young lady awaited at that table of chocolate solitude. But she had seen nothing and seemed delighted to be quickly intercepted and carried off. No normal mind could doubt that girls come here to be carried off as rapidly as possible. It is the land of fusion. These are very inoffensive abductions, of course, and the fee is a blushing conversation on a bench, or an invitation to the movies or next Saturday's dance.

The spoon was suddenly immobilized . . . three girls had just appeared.

The spoon got furiously back into action and I saw two blazing eyes fixed upon the new couple while tons of chocolate mounted towards the mouth at a precipitate rate. One might have believed this young lion was about to leave his bench, skirt the groups of boys and girls, and spring upon his rival. Not at all. The girl had seen him at last, and it was she who took the initiative. She signalled him to join them. Docilely the young man betook himself to her table, seated himself beside the one he had just shot down a hundred times with his eyes, and the conversation resumed — but it had become a monologue. The pretty little girl, apparently very sure of her charms, had decided to reconcile them. They were too far away for me to hear what she was saying, but her words must have been persuasive, for I saw the young men begin to exchange remarks and then to clap one another on the back and even to laugh heartily. The girl no longer existed. She grew bored. A little later her companions came to join her, and I saw segregation re-establish itself — on one side of the table three young girls talking animatedly together and on the other two reconciled boys who no longer took the least notice of their presence.

The group finally separated, boys and girls departing in opposite directions.

A HEAVY PAST   I know that such little scenes have no particular significance, but when they are repeated they become traits of behaviour. And they were repeated in one manner or another an incalculable number of times. Not so long ago the girls in small Quebec towns were not able to go out in their leisure time, even in twos or threes, so the social games of the café-restaurants represent an image of emancipation to them — as does permission to go to the movies with a boy or to dance on Saturday nights. But at the doors of the movie theatres too you will see girls together, or boys. And sometimes at the community centres you will see a few girls dancing with one another while the boys revel at the soft drink counter — truly a curious picture.

What do I deduce from all this? Simply that our male-female relations are not yet on the track. A heavy past of puritanism weighs upon our shoulders. Even in the biggest cities the social liberation of our women is a sham. It is for specialists to find the reason for this. The traveller only looks and poses the questions. But this particular one touches upon history, education, the family atmosphere, the industrial era, and finally a civilization.

I envy those that find their bearings in it with facility. My companion was not aware of any particular problem. The woman of America, he said, is the freest in the world, even in our smallest towns, compared to the situation in other countries. And he was not entirely wrong. He cited conclusive arguments, which he drew from France and elsewhere and that I was able to check. He almost convinced me. I could only extricate myself with a sally: 'I will believe in the real emancipation of women, when our newspapers and magazines no longer have "women's pages" and "women's sections" and when television and radio give up their "women's programs".'

Just a sally, yes, but with distance I wonder whether it wasn't justified. Has legal and political emancipation been accompanied by intellectual and moral emancipation? I received some confidences from a young woman of Gaspé. She is fighting for her rights. What are they? Today she can drive the car, smoke a cigarette, have a drink in company, despite what gossips may say. She has not entirely gained her point, but she will win, and this makes her happy. Such victories are distressing.

THE MAJESTIC ST LAWRENCE After Rimouski, the metropolis of the lower St Lawrence, the river would give up its ocean or lake airs and openly assume its river face, which it would not lose again and which would grow ever more precise throughout its twelve-hundred-mile course to the interior. In the distance, snow picked out the mountainous côtes of Saint-Siméon and La Malbaie, like a theatre flat that an invisible director was drawing ever closer to us as we journeyed towards Quebec. This is one of the most beautiful scenes in the world and it is a great pity that our eyes can become so used to it that it no longer stirs the excitement the stranger knows. We are curious animals. A wit from Rivière-du-Loup said to me, 'You're not going to pull a "majestic St Lawrence" on us?'

Well, yes, I am. Travel all over the world and you will not find a river that is able to stand comparison with it. It is a single flow between banks that industrial civilization has not yet had time to spoil. God grant that our city planners will hide the factory chimneys of the future and that for a long time to come the water, the mountain, and the forest will keep their leading roles in the tragedy that pits nature against society all over the world. Here nature triumphs with the greatest ease until the boundary of the Great Lakes, and industry leaves the wings only long enough to utter a few bleak lines that have nothing to do finally with the principal action.

IN THE BRITISH TRADITION   Today the whole neighbourhood is adorned with old houses, remodelled inside, their façades re-surfaced but not tampered with — such a happy formula one wonders why the city took so long to adopt it. How many houses might have been saved from demolition, not only in this privileged neighbourhood but throughout most of the city. Let us not quibble, this part of Quebec is still the pleasantest and most harmonious in the city. Even in rush hours the stroller can trace out an itinerary of beauty and calm.

But it was afternoon. I was walking past buildings overrun by civil servants. All was calm. In a few minutes I would reach parliament hill. It has a proud look, our parliament, and I am glad that its architecture is not vaguely Greco-something-or-other. The parliamentary system is an English invention, and I cannot understand all these false temples that have flowered in our land. If one is anxious to evoke at all costs the Greco-Roman civilization that gave birth to ours, it is a pity to be content simply to set an arrangement of columns and a triangular pediment upon an utterly styleless stone cube. One should go the whole way and justify the pious heresy by a masterpiece of harmony. Here everything is appropriate. I am not immediately certain that I am in a French-language capital but it is obvious that I am on a parliament hill.

I had my small place in the press gallery here for two years and heard debates that in the period of lucidity we know today would stir the population to disgust if not to revolt. It must be believed that we perform our trade badly or that the population is slow to get heated. There were certain individuals that used to put an end to the most important debates with wretched witticisms. I lost my small place in the press gallery for reporting some of them too freely. Radio had made a timid entry, it was dislodged without stir. I shiver when I think of that not-so-distant time. Only two or three young members, enthusiasts for justice and reform, preserved some tradition of dignity in the assembly.

I attended a session of the chamber. What a different atmosphere. That day the opposition had decided to discourage the government by a systematic obstruction. Speakers followed one another. The marathon had lasted since the previous evening, but the undertaking was conducted with intelligence and a good deal of humour — a certain elegance as well. The evolution of a milieu makes itself felt in small things as in large. This climate was unimaginable in former days. Debates were most often at street level. Our members sometimes used the language of horse-traders, and our laws showed it. They reflected the electoral bargaining. Generally speaking our debates are of a higher level now. It is a sign of the times.

TO EACH HIS TRUTH   I had encountered separatism almost everywhere in the country, in one form or another. Everyone offered his own little version of it. At Quebec chance, several conversations, and a certain number of experiences made it seem that the moment had come to give my own. This will still be just one more and I have no illusions about its significance. The situation is changing and the smallest inquiry is a form of vivisection. All the versions seem wrong and no one of them is entirely true. Different interests send them off in a thousand different directions. A certain magazine mobilized a research crew to show that the matter finally involved only a small number of people. Many English Canadians are attached to the notion of what they call an 'epiphenomenon', lacking any real significance. At Quebec certain groups demonstrated to me that separatism had taken the way to the tomb, with a first-class funeral, by entering the political arena. In London and Paris, where I had occasion to travel after the Queen's visit, I was asked more than once, 'Well, have your separatists collapsed yet?'

In retrospect no one could possibly doubt the importance of this venture — in the first place, because it led some extremist elements to violence. I don't believe that there have been enough questions asked about the causes of this violence. Everyone hastened to lay the responsibility on the shoulders of certain young madmen, visionaries, and hotheads . . . and this is not in doubt. But history tells us that the act of violence is always bound up with real suffering and that this suffering should be taken seriously. In the perspective of history these sufferings are always of two orders — hunger and humiliation. I believe that we must eliminate hunger. Moreover, it has been found that entire populations have accepted hunger provided they were not humiliated. There is a trail there that our experts have not yet followed. They might find 'speak white' and all sorts of vexations deeply rooted in the consciousness and never forgiven. Humiliate your friend and you have lost him forever.

The movement is of importance because it depends upon fascinating ideas: ultimately such movements do not need funds to carry out their campaign. Who does not dream of total independence? The success of operations of this sort depends only upon the vitality and constancy of its leaders.

It is of importance, also, because from the start it carried with it all the already existing nationalistic structures, the strength of which must not be underestimated.

Another point is that the thirteen or fifteen per cent that scientific inquiries grant to the separatists is recruited from social strata in a position to influence a milieu. Among those concerned are university professors, teachers in secondary schools, and politicians. I myself have encountered separatists at all crossroads. Openly socialist magazines such as *Parti Pris* are not road accidents. I have bought a few copies. A salesgirl burned me with her eyes. 'Everyone's buying that trash,' she said furiously. I understood her but this is a false and even dangerous reaction. I know *Parti Pris* readers well; they are of high quality, as is the magazine itself. It is the best edited of any of our magazines and is marked by as much lucidity as courage.

Finally it must be remembered that those that inspired the movement and its leaders are not tricksters. They may be mistaken, and in my private view they are mistaken, but they are not tricksters. I have just read tons of Bourgault, d'Allemagne, and Léger. I have seen programs on the French television in which all the philosophers of all shades of opinion were planted on stage uttering historic statements, which had, even so, their instructive value. I shall content myself with recalling a conversation with the vice-president of the RIN — Guy Pouliot — a friend from Collège Garnier, whom I was very happy to meet again.

PORTRAIT OF A SEPARATIST LEADER We were together for twenty years, we were bound for life. But our paths separated. Rediscoveries are not easy. One must circle around, seek a meeting point. We finally found it. Our definition of engagement differs considerably but it was in this direction we must search.

He was athletic, of a comfortable family; he launched himself brilliantly into a legal career, became Belgian consul, and suddenly I found him at the head of a separatist movement. He has the face of an aesthete and deepset, sorrowful eyes. A few details relieved me a little. He rides a bicycle two hours a day, he drinks wine at meals, he has five children and an adorable wife. But the rest? How to explain to one that knew him at twenty, how to recognize in him the man who signed the celebrated telegram, the man of the overcharged demonstrations and the impassioned public meetings.

I would soon possess all the elements necessary to understand him. And I was not searching for anything else. I did not set any trap for him. I had not come to betray his confidence. He knew this well and we spoke openly for hours. However, because he has become a public man and because knowledge of the way he has travelled sheds a certain light upon the way travelled by separatists as a whole, I feel under obligation to note down a few of his principal steps.

First came what might be called romantic engagement. The affair always begins this way. The idea of liberation and independence underlies all the most fascinating proposals that can be made to human beings. He was touched at the beginning by an article by André d'Allemagne, the first high priest and the theoretician of the RIN. Came an exchange of letters, then meetings. For months he shared a fascinating adventure, whose interest owed a great deal to the mystery with which it was surrounded.

Then followed the phenomenon of the snowball. He must go farther or withdraw. Guy went farther, for he had had time to taste human solidarity, one of the most refined pleasures of existence. As well, he had delved into the question, he had encountered men whose minds compelled his admiration, he felt ready to play his part on the Quebec front, where arms and direction were lacking. The romantic period was over, and now action commenced, with all the sacrifices this demands. There were difficulties with his consular status in Belgium; he left the consulate. His clients stayed away . . . he would get along without them. We know what happened. He became president of the RIN on 22 October 1961. Today he is Bourgault's lieutenant. Present membership: eight thousand in the Montreal and Quebec regions. Annual dues twelve dollars. A weekly newspaper: L'Indépendance. Ten per cent of the members are under twenty, twenty-five per cent from twenty to thirty, forty per cent between thirty and forty. Lake St John is developing rapidly. The structures correspond to counties, but regrouped into eight regions. Since March 1963 the RIN has been a political party.

I met Bourgault almost everywhere: for several months he had been conducting his electoral campaign on a province-wide scale. He did not expect a tidal wave in 1966 but he was working on a long-term basis. I pointed out to Pouliot, figures in hand, that it might well take the RIN centuries to achieve power. He would have to gather all the separatist movements under his banner. This of course was the objective they had set, he told me.

'Isn't it just a lovely dream?' I asked him.

He smiled a little sadly, and we talked about other things.

ON THE SAME SIDE OF THE WALL   What emerges from all this, at least to me as a traveller? First that separatism is a considerable fact that it seems to me illusory to minimize. At worst this denial would even be a carrier of violence. It would be a constant provocation to those that know. Secondly, as long as the movement is able to contain its extremist elements, and seemingly it will be able to henceforth, it includes several positive factors. Above all, it will have forced our society to take inventory of its resources and its aspirations, and it continues to be a haunting presence to the other provinces, which have also acquired a taste for having their own way with the central government. Finally it has unleashed a process of identification, which I was able to catch on the wing throughout the country and which will result in its little discoveries, one of which might well become of decisive importance. I have seen and I know that the English are wondering in their turn whether they are not themselves a colonial people of our generous, irreplaceable, boundless, and encroaching neighbour. All the assumptions will then be changed. And the good French Canadians and the nasty English Canadians will be surprised to find themselves on the same side of the fence and to discover that they are neither good nor nasty but all equally poor and depleted and dependent. It is little discoveries of this sort that suddenly make great countries.

THE CHAUDIÈRE   I knew this valley when visitors from Maine had not yet found their way there. The few hotels served only the stable but not very numerous clientele of commercial travellers. Today tourist accommodation is considerably developed all along the road that links Boston with the city of Quebec. The general atmosphere of the valley has changed, at least during the summer months. But it has kept an unusual charm, which perhaps comes from the permanent confrontation of farming and lively little towns that consider themselves up to date, modern, and without complexes.

I know some farmers in the back concessions of Sainte-Marie-de-Beauce who still live almost as our ancestors did, going to the pigpen or the stable through a shed that is the only space between the family living quarters and those of the animals, while only a few miles away modern suburban houses spring up like mushrooms and a bakery has expanded to serve the whole province. By chance I got to know one of these old farmers rather well. A real brute, completely illiterate and insensitive, lost to civilization and fit only to rank with his animals. I often tried to find some characteristic about him that could hold the interest, but it was wasted time. We have failed with some of our farmers, despite the general progress. Such failures take on a frightening dimension, and you will not find them in the fishing communities. I have very often met illiterate fishermen, but you are drawn to them from the outset by a certain quality of the spirit. And there is admiration mingled with the pity they arouse in you. But when we set ourselves to fail with a farmer, the resulting spectacle is an enormity, almost awe-inspiring. I have never encountered this type of man elsewhere; perhaps I would have to go to the jungles of New Guinea. Fortunately these are exceptional cases. How many other farmers surprise you with a supreme accord with their fields, their animals, their sugar bushes, their lives as free men — the life that has been so often sung about. But it isn't the only life and I am still suffering the shock.

THE GOOD INDIANS AND THE BAD INDIANS Near Quebec was the Huron village and, right beside Montreal, an Iroquois reserve. By chance I knew the Huron village quite well. I had a full-blood Huron in my class at Collège Garnier, a lad of remarkable intelligence that a stupid death took from us at the age of the most marvellous plans. Some of us were inconsolable.

The young Huron girls of the village were known for their beauty, although I made their acquaintance at an age when I was scarcely qualified to judge. But all this part of my life is still permeated with happy visions. True, our textbooks and our teachers prepare us to see in the Hurons the good Indians and in the Iroquois the bad Indians.

Later, equally fortuitous circumstances allowed me to know the Iroquois reserve of Caughnawaga. And I was drawn to certain comparisons. At Caughnawaga there was never the gentleness I had known in the Huron village. All our childhood experiences finally sink into another dimension in which there is more sentiment than lucidity. And yet there were those remarks of the village barber. Between two amusing stories, not always suitable to our age, he would manage, all the while shaving our scalps with a generosity that was remarkable considering the ten cents he took from us, to set forth at some length the grievance of his people and all the Indians in general against the seizure of his country by the whites. All this without the slightest passion. He was simply trying to convince and to persuade, and the least contradiction struck him in the raw.

I found this barber later on the front pages of all the newspapers. He had started a hunger strike, which he intended to continue to the death. He was demanding the return of Canada. He did not consider anyone qualified to deal with him except the prime minister, and strictly the King of England. I am no longer very clear about how the affair came out. I know only that Canada was not given back to him and that he probably took up his barber's scissors again. But I cannot forget the absence of anger or bitterness in this man whom I knew at the moment he was preparing to lay claim to a whole country. To him no one was guilty. He was simply obeying a fundamental necessity, and his folly seemed to us the very image of wisdom. Although illiterate, he spoke good French. If he sometimes permitted himself linguistic audacities, there was never the slightest vulgarity about them.

I afterwards knew a great many Hurons, several of whom have prospered in various industries. Today most of them are integrated into the surrounding society, from which they can no longer be distinguished except by some rather incidental traits. Their tribal institutions are purely symbolic and they have always lived in comfortable houses, similar in all cases to the others in the region. But today if I happen to come across a particular sort of black eyes, lit with a little flame, I know where they come from. And I know I shall find that gentleness of manner and behaviour that so struck me when I was a child. Indian blood flows freely in Quebec veins.

The problem of the Indian is not of the same nature here as in the less peopled provinces. In Quebec, as in Ontario, the young Indians have burst out of the reserves and become integrated. The marriage game has done the rest. They had great merit, we had still greater luck. They have brought us much more than we had given them, and we have restored to them only a tiny portion of all we took away.

Although the Huron village neglected to play its tourist card — all I ever saw there was a little moccasin factory — Caughnawaga, near Montreal, has made this its chief modern vocation. Some of these Iroquois have acquired a world-wide reputation for their skill at working on the highest and most dizzying bridges and skyscrapers without the slightest vertigo. But this has never involved more than a small number of them. Most of their effort is directed towards tourist attractions. And they are of excellent quality. Many of us have witnessed the war dance in the peaceful village of carefully reconstructed wigwams and made an inventory of the Iroquois pharmacology — a gamut of concoctions sufficient to put all Dr Knock's patients on the road to health.

I like the atmosphere of Caughnawaga very much, simply because it is so artificial. It partakes of the theatre — living theatre that summons up for us, in continuous performance, certain images, very true images, that spring from our most distant past. Faces, however peaceful and amiable they may be today, will make you understand the old terror of the first colonists more easily than the reading of the most learned tomes. True, their blood is so mixed now it is impossible to say what race they are, but some of them have at times, for the space of a second, the Iroquois eye. And they would be very surprised to learn that they have kept the power to stir us on occasion, between two bursts of laughter.

A FASCINATING CITY   No one ever means the same thing when he says, 'Montreal is a beautiful city.' One compares it mentally to other cities one has known. And very often those that consider it ugly are thinking of Paris or Rome, which is not only unjust but a sort of intellectual perversion. For how can a city that has not yet had its four centuries of life bear comparison with two of the most marvellous cities of the world steeped in the greatest civilization of the West? To judge Montreal, one must be able to forget everything one has known outside America. And then certain signs of its personality will sketch themselves.

What struck me first was the number of shady streets. And I am not thinking only of sumptuous Westmount, where one does not quite know whether the houses have been built in a park or the forest has invaded the streets. In most parts of the city there are streets edged with oaks or maples. They are not edged, actually, and it is regrettable that they are not. The trees are most often pressed against the houses when they would have created such beautiful perspectives if they had been aligned along the sidewalks, next to the road. But still they are there and they are invaluable to the city, some sections of which would be indescribably broken-down and scabby without them.

Old Montreal has character, but one must not give way to lyricism. Except at the Séminaire de Saint-Sulpice and the Chapel of Notre-Dame-de-Bonsecours, few strong emotions await us. On Place d'Armes rises the most interesting church on the island — and there are more than four hundred — but its interest lies in its long history rather than in its aesthetic value. Let us not speak of the Basilica of Marie-Reine-du-Monde, the Cathedral of Montreal. To copy St Peter's of Rome has always seemed to me childish. Today it does penance as the prisoner of radiant skyscrapers. Several of our old monuments are of an aggressive ugliness. The Nelson Column, erected shortly after Trafalgar, has at least the merit of provoking us a little. Monuments are obliged to be beautiful, otherwise they are very vulnerable. They have no significance except the one we give them, and this varies from one individual to another. A French peasant complained on his return from England, 'We erect our monuments to celebrate victories — the Arc de Triomphe, the Vendôme Column — but in England they insist upon celebrating defeats — Trafalgar, Waterloo.'

Modern Montreal shows a fine aggressiveness. Our skyscrapers seem higher than they are. They rise up without warning. They might come from almost anywhere. There is an irresistible vitality in all this. And I got great pleasure from rediscovering Dorchester Boulevard, which was only a little sordid street when I left. I grant without discussion my partiality for the cruciform building which makes concrete and stone sing, gives a sense of movement to the entire Dorchester complex and adorns the silhouette of the town from every angle of vision. I like to lose myself in its subterranean galleries, which at certain hours are filled with the animation of a Spanish town. Many of us have learned how to stroll again here.

The explosion of modern architecture in Montreal is so appealing to me that I wanted — at least for some time — to install myself in its centre of gravity. I am living in one of those big apartment blocks that have sprung like mushrooms right up to the flanks of the mountain. The building rises on the height of

Pine Avenue and offers an exceptional view from all its windows. The entrance hall, for no special reason, is decorated in a curious Moorish style.

It was from my apartment that I fully realized Montreal's two great strokes of luck, for I consort with them daily, and I know that our city planners should do everything to make the most of them lest our metropolis become just another American city — the river and the mountain. In my childhood I could not hear the slightest allusion to the majestic St Lawrence without smiling. Now that I see it every day, and at every hour of the day, I realize that it is not only majestic but alive, capricious in its moods. One would think that a mad painter were amusing himself by constantly correcting his colours. It goes from steel grey to mediterranean blue in a few hours and never melts into the landscape. Its colours are mobile, subject to constant vibrations. It sinks into the surroundings only with the falling of night, when the festival of light arises from all sides.

The mountain — well who could deny that it is a real jewel? What other city has its forest of five hundred acres right in the middle of its built-up area? I have learned to take long walks there. I have always been surprised to find only New Canadians there during the week. It fulfils its function only on Sunday and on the evenings of open-air concerts. And one can live for years in Montreal without suspecting that the city holds in the hollow of its hand escape, fresh air, silence, and beauty. Such care has been taken to protect it that it has been made to disappear from the map. A concerted effort will make it escape from its quarantine. Some day it must be opened to the whole city, incorporated into our lives. The mountain is Montreal's great wealth. Its character and beauty can be saved while letting it break out of its isolation.

Living in Montreal, I want to profit every day from a wild nature that extends right to my doorsill. It is a challenge to our city planners. A walk on the mountain should not be an expedition. The little squirrels meet us there each day. They have already learned not to flee at sight of us. They come to eat from our hands. The trees are also tame. Yet the picture has not lost any of its exoticism. The Montrealer has the unique good fortune to possess trees, squirrels, plants, underbrush, and birdsongs as part of his daily existence. He is the citizen of one of the great cities of the world, and yet he has this unique opportunity, without till now making much use of it. At adult age he can scarcely distinguish a linden from an oak or a nighthawk from a lark.

A CITY ON ITS FEET I returned to Montreal one day with a high civil servant, whom I saw in a state of shock. Yet his last stay in the metropolis did not date back to the flood . . . scarcely a few months. He could not stop devouring the city with his eyes, turning his head, raising it, making it pivot in all directions as if it were on ball-bearings. Three or four new skyscrapers had made their appearance, and in the distance on Sherbrooke Street, yet another big apartment block was beginning to prick up its ears above the roofs. Montreal has unashamedly chosen the silhouette of the great American cities and it will never cease raising long arms towards the sky. From an aircraft it is like an assembly voting with upraised hands. From the new Champlain Bridge, it is Céline's upright city. Behind this phenomenon there is Expo 67 of course, but above all the expression of a great capitalist confidence in the future of our metropolis, and in the background the stubborness of a mayor who has fallen violently in love with his city and wages his war on all fronts at once.

My companion could not stop looking. The formless metropolis of yesterday is in process of making its own rhythms. It is the song of concrete and glass. Our film-makers are mad with joy and their cameras eat up skyscrapers hungrily. The time is past for 'should have' and 'could have', the population has been drawn into the game. In its entirety it is the most dynamic symbol of Quebec just to see the great city grow *par en-haut et par en-dessous, de tous les côtés,* as in the song.

Try to distract yourself from it and you will always be brought back to it in one way or another. You have a simple business appointment which you count on disposing of quickly; there you are perched with your companion in a sort of eagle's nest where the meal will unfold in a festival of light, silence, and panoramic views. More than once your most serious conversations are drowned in the St Lawrence or hang themselves on scaffolds, are crushed among the cars of Dorchester St, or play truant on the side of the mountain. You have a city of two million under your eyes, in your conversation, almost on your plate. When you raise your cheese-knife, you might decapitate a skyscraper, just as it appears on the end of your blade. All the small pleasures of the great American cities are now in the crook of your hand, it will take us years to tire of them. Montreal is essentially committed to this explosion towards the vertical. All the conditions that gave rise to it elsewhere are joined together here. And the city's physical metamorphosis symbolizes in its own way the other profound metamorphosis, which has made a whole province rise suddenly to its feet.

CHERISHED FREEDOM   Freedom . . . not only a climate of freedom but a wind, a gust, a storm of freedom covers Quebec at this moment. Not so many years ago Roger Martin du Gard's *Thibault* was burned on the public square, and Barrès's works were kept in the bowels of the provincial library. Today I have the impression that you could obtain Sartre in the parish library.

There is freedom of speech; above all our problems are brought into the light, discussed, and dissected. Big newspapers, formerly celebrated for their immobility because of their commercial ties, now publish open analyses of the most explosive questions every day.

I knew the day in television — and I am not precisely an old man — when the pressure of a readily shocked public opinion forced all who were engaged in it to an obsessive self-censorship. Every day, in that unusual public forum, *Aujourd'hui*, the whole province unwinds in an atmosphere of total freedom that places the program far in advance of all productions of the kind in the world.

It seems that one can write everything and say everything today. I mean the young man quietly explaining on television the circumstances under which he lost his faith and the others who offered figures — about two-thirds — of the students at the secondary school level who no longer go to Sunday Mass. There are the two little nuns who want to succeed Soeur Sourire on the hit parade and the group of Redemptorists who render Halle-lujahs to yé-yé rhythms. There was the program about homo-sexuality on which a young woman asked a frail little priest enormous medical, if not Freudian, questions as if to settle the matter once for all. There is the film censor who has laid aside his scissors and put us henceforth in the first rank of free coun-tries, after we had held the next-to-last place among puritan countries immediately before Spain. . . . It is incredible — Quebec the land of freedom, of all the freedoms. They should reclassify the novels published in the fifties. Along with Langevin, I was one of those whose work was classed as 'D' for danger, which did not surprise me at the time but which becomes quite ridicu-lous in the present context. Today our books should be distri-buted as prizes in the primary schools.

THE POINT OF VIEW OF AN EXTREMIST I look at the young people, and I wonder if they know how lucky they are to be young pre-cisely in 1966 . . . in the Canada of 1966 — in the Quebec of 1966. Of course, and this is quite in the order of things, they feel that it is all their work.

I had a fairly long talk with an admitted extremist — a serious and convinced boy, whose knowledge of Canadian history is at his fingertips, who knows exactly what he is engaged in and the risks of his actions, but despite this keeps a certain detachment about his group and a keen sense of humour . . . a sense not over-exerted in his circle. If he published a revolutionary maga-zine, he would distribute it without charge and force his staff to work at Vickers or Canadair to pay the expenses. He would accept no compromise and would certainly not have a booth at the *Salon du Livre*. You see the type. A great deal of fantasy on a basis of seriousness.

He had no trouble explaining the engagement of the young. To him it is all very clear. They had to define themselves against their elders, or against the clergy, or against the English. Their elders — well, they made only a mouthful. With a few exceptions, they were of no account. Send all that to the incinerator. The clergy? In his opinion, no one is more supple than our clergy. Rather than be left behind, they were running along with their guitars and their yé-yé Masses. There was no one else but the English. If the English decided once for all to understand the irreversible nature of the independence of Quebec, he declared, our extremists would be all washed up and their bombs good only for the trash-can. He said this very sadly.

MADE IN THE USA   Julien is fourteen. He belongs to an intellectual family and is what one would call a serious and brilliant adolescent. He is not afraid of study, and he can spend whole evenings at his desk. He sleeps little, drinks a great deal of coffee, does not refuse an apéritif, and often takes a glass of wine with his meals. He draws up his own program of reading, and Sartre is next to Balzac on the shelves of his personal library. He has a hi-fi set, and I see that Beatles records mix in friendly fashion with Mozart sonatas. Julien has free access to his parents' living room, willingly joins adult conversations, and his remarks are marked by intelligence and humour.

I could add a thousand details to his portrait, which till this point could be considered healthy in the American context. And why should our social existence, which borrows less and less from Europe, be required to take Europe as a guide in child-adult relations? The only problem with Julien is his habit of Saturday parties — parties that sometimes last until four o'clock in the morning. Average age of the boys and girls, fifteen. His parents are upstairs, prisoners in their room. If they appeared, Julien would be the laughing-stock of his group. It is now admitted that young people have a right to entertain themselves as they choose.

Am I shocked? Not in the least. The society we have invented will perhaps revolve very well with adolescents that age quickly. This society offers fewer unsurmountable challenges and perhaps it would not know what to do with well-tempered characters, moral force, or our disciplined minds. I am not shocked or even anxious. I believe in the extraordinary powers of the human mind to adapt itself to the contingencies of a society. Excesses bring their own correctives. I state only that Julien does not exist anywhere else but in America. He is an adolescent of a make unknown in the rest of the world.

Marie-Hélène is twelve. She belongs to a very modest milieu. She is already beautiful. I left an unformed little girl and I found a sort of starlet. She sometimes makes up her eyes, and on certain days she goes to school with a Brigitte Bardot hairdo, reddened lips and nails, silk stockings, and high-heeled shoes. Why not? At ten in the morning, the women and girls of her circle are dressed as for the evening. It is natural that Marie-Hélène, at twelve, should already be seeking to join the game. She has of course access to all the fashion magazines, reads everything she can get hold of, and sees at her convent school the movies our laws forbid her to see at the cinemas. . . . Marie-Hélène really has only one problem: at twelve she already has a steady — a faithful, too faithful, boyfriend of her own age. This came about naturally. She goes to an advanced convent, which organizes dances, expeditions, and sugaring-off parties with the boys from the college nearby. How could her parents oppose these pious activities, which are under the surveillance of the teachers? Marie-Hélène is from a poor family, which is still deeply rooted in its old ways of doing things. That need be no obstacle. Our society is full of resources. Liberty, fraternity, equality, and may they all join together for the greatest glory of Jesus.

Marie-Hélène is a good little girl. She never misses Sunday Mass, she makes her annual retreat, and she never skips her

evening prayers except when she doesn't come home till time
for morning prayers. And she does well at school with never
any trouble at the end of the year. It isn't as in the upper grades.
Till now the balance isn't too disturbing.

'In the whole convent there were only seven or eight girls
pregnant last year,' she confided to me in her birdlike voice.

Well there, frankly, I confess my backwardness. I almost died
of shock. Average age? From fifteen to seventeen. And not in a
middle-class convent, where parental neglect might be blamed,
but in one of the most modest convents in the city. But let us
not be perturbed. Our great educators are undoubtedly equipped
to confront such little problems. And if they are, our society will
perhaps have gained a maturity that all the other countries in the
world might envy. I say only that Marie-Hélène does not exist
elsewhere than in America, nor does that sort of convent. Not
even in Sweden. The Scandinavian countries believe they are very
advanced. Well, pardon. Let them come and see what goes on in
the shadow of our church-steeples. Our present experiments in
sexual education are certainly the most advanced and the most
daring. If they succeed, hats off to you, dear Sisters and Brothers.

I do not believe that Julien and Marie-Hélène are isolated
cases. I have received too many confidences from parents. They
have no means of action. It is too late. If they insist upon
prohibitions, these prohibitions will not change the behaviour
of the adolescents but will only make them withdraw their confidences. For, strangely, there has been no interruption of dialogue between children and their parents, who had reconciled
themselves to total resignation. And it is an adult dialogue. I
have been present at some rather odd conversations. A fifteen-
year-old child was consulted about the establishment of a family
budget, about the decoration of the living room, about the pur-
chase of a car, and what not. Still, this is a positive aspect of the
phenomenon. As the child demands the adult's freedom of behaviour, he adds to his responsibilities. At this rate, he may
quickly grow tired of it and he will dream of the archaic up-
bringing he casts off today without passion, without needing to

put the least passion into casting it off, since he does not encounter any real opposition to the freedoms he gives himself.

Another positive aspect is that adolescents do not acknowledge
the ready-made truths by which some of us have more or less
lived. They wish to go to the bottom of problems. They do not
possess the truth, they seek it — not only in religious matters
but in politics. This questioning, already observed in other demographic layers, can only enrich the collective consciousness of
the young.

They are interested in the newspapers too. And they pass over
the wave-lengths designed for their parents. They have quickly
learned to turn off the most futile television programs. Television
will have to raise the level of the programs destined for them
or it will lose their support.

Are our adolescents working? How can we know? It is clear,
however, that this is the ground on which the fate of their generation will be settled. Competition will be much keener in our
society of the future, and university degrees, until now the
achievement of a few favoured people, will be common change.
They will have wasted the privileges of their precocious maturity
if they do not forge at the same time discipline and passion for
work. This is the only real challenge that their immediate future
imposes upon them. Those that content themselves with a mediocre education will be completely out of the running. But there
again, it seems to me, their behaviour inspires confidence. A
change has occurred. Though it is very difficult to acquire definite information on this subject and studies would be of little
use, the adolescents of today seem more fitted than those of
preceding generations to force themselves to long periods of
concentration and study. Perhaps because those around them do
not impose the same constraints. Perhaps because they have the
sense of freedom of choice. Perhaps because they are better able
to handle their leisure time.

I should have liked to grow up among these adolescents of
today. Whatever we are, they will make us better. We can no

longer thrust their judgements of us aside. Their lucidity is a guarantee. They will be well able to turn it upon themselves.

PITY FOR THE GODS I have just spent the afternoon with a gravely wounded man. How sorrowful are men over fifty when they no longer advance in the world. When they have not managed to free themselves from their sensitivity. When they have the so-called artistic temperament. And how many of these flayed persons I encounter, I am dazed by them. What is amiss with our society that the souls of artists — one must give them a name — should be in tatters on the threshold of old age? The bull of the *corrida*, covered with blood and *banderillas*, at the moment of the *faena*. We saw him come vigorously into the ring. This one could not be overtaken. He would always be able to ward off little conspiracies. And then you find him suffering, wounded, bleeding. I am not dramatizing. One must know that certain men of over fifty, who are among the finest specimens of our society, are reduced to suffering in the shadow beyond anything that should be asked of human endurance. How did this happen in this case? I wished to ask him the question. We spoke of literature, travel, and music.

I understand everything that has taken place within this man, but he forbade me to speak of it. Modesty prevents him from making a confession. He is a powerful oak, I am only a twig. A gust of wind brought us together, another will no doubt separate us forever. There is no dialogue possible between twigs and oaks. And yet I understand the inner tragedy of this man. He is of a species that has moved me many times among old actors. There is not so much of the fear of death about them as one might believe or even of the approach of old age. It is the look they turn towards their youth that gives you the signs of their distress. They had seen their lives otherwise. They felt that they were armed, powerfully armed, to face all sorts of struggles. And in their battle they gave the best of themselves without hesitating. When you look at their existence from outside, you judge it a complete success. They have not only marked their society: they have been in a position to transform it, and they have not shirked. But in the final count, their rendezvous was with themselves. And this confrontation is unbearable to them. They could have considered their career unique, exceptional, irreplaceable. They abruptly drew back when to us they seemed in full flight.

What was lacking then? By what virus are we attacked that the best among us suddenly collapse when to us they seem to be engaged in the struggles that do them the greatest honour? I have not yet found the answer. The reply touches upon too many tiny details perhaps, those details that weave the net stitch by stitch. The terrible solitude of our gravely wounded at the end of their careers. To the refuse-bin with them, and let us not mention them again. At this rate we will send the best of us to the refuse-bin. I have the feeling that this has just happened, and that no one has either the time or the wish or the leisure to notice it.

GHOSTS FOR SALE   In the aircraft that took me to Val d'Or I was surrounded by ghosts. My friends and my family had often spoken to me of Abitibi and Témiscamingue. It was the first time I had travelled in that direction. I could not believe I would be there in under an hour. It all dated back so far, to the time of my childhood. I saw people I loved board a crowded train in the middle of the depression and go off to Val d'Or. My friends also saw such things and were haunted by them for a long time. Letters seemed to come to us from across the ocean. And they told us extraordinary things, that the house would soon be finished, that now only the roof was needed, that they would work like beavers to be finished before winter. How had they lived meanwhile? Their letters were full of trees, of the building of roads, of stumps that must be pulled out of the ground. People were at once beadle and schoolteacher. They sang Mass, dried moose and deer before the cold. City-dwellers like ourselves had engaged in a colonization experiment with makeshift means with which only the toughest would be able to endure.

I quickly learned that I must no longer see Abitibi in that light, as a distant land of colonization. Today the railway, an excellent road, and the aircraft have drawn it considerably closer to Montreal, so close that Val d'Or hockey fans can drive down for the Saturday evening game at the Forum and back again the same night. So I had to begin by killing my ghosts and try to look at this western part of Quebec with new eyes.

GUYENNE FORMS A SCHOOL   With very rare exceptions the colonization efforts of the thirties could be considered a complete failure. Aside from the mining cities of the Abitibi, and particularly Amos, there is little real prosperity. The most fortunate townships are still economically feeble. There is room for a complete reconversion of crops and for large-scale cultivation as practised in the Canadian West. But whatever it is, something must be decided: the back country of Abitibi is slipping rapidly towards ghost-colonization. Only an overall plan can restore this soon-to-be deserted territory to life. Local attempts have borne fruit and shown the despairing that they often give up the fight just when they might win.

The most interesting experiment of this nature is at Guyenne. It is called 'little Russia' to show its socialist trend. But it is a natural socialism: the people there have created socialism as Monsieur Jourdain spoke prose. This sort of socialism is within the capacity of all the townships and, far from leading them into an impasse, it could lead them out of one. It has been imitated. Here and there townships have taken up the Guyenne formula. But more timidly. And the results of it are felt.

At Guyenne the matter is frank, open, conducted in the round, and this is the result. At first sight it is a concession as desolate as the others. But already you notice television aerials on the roofs and big cars beside the clapboard houses, which are sometimes merely covered with tarpaper. Most of the houses are large and comfortable. Olric Lebreux has a ribbon saw among his accessories. Léopold Villeneuve has a good middle-class house, with a wooden swing behind. Everywhere around are cleared fields. The forest has been pushed back. In the meadows there are sheep. The stock seems considerable.

Opposite the church there is a small modern building in which is situated *Le Centre Syndical* of Guyenne. It comprises the syndicate, a *caisse populaire*, and a work syndicate. The formula is simple, as was explained to me by Guyenne's longtime legal representative: 'The syndicate gives you a lot, builds your house and gives you complete work security. In return, it pays for its expenses by the imposition of an obligatory savings.'

There is still a great deal to be done, but the matter is in gear. The syndicate operates on a communal base of farm products, forest concessions, and pasturage. The work of each individual is part of the overall plan, for there is an overall plan and this is the great novelty. The analyses that preceded the plan showed that seventy-five families could live at Guyenne and that its occupation should be more agricultural than lumbering. Agriculture is chiefly dairy-farming, and the raising of beef cattle and sheep. If you prefer cattle-raising to dairy production, no one will forbid you. But it will be pointed out that only twenty farms can live by cattle and attempts will be made to guide you in another direction if all these places are taken. Criticisms are numerous; they are not all stupid. It is clear that in an experiment of this sort you will not have the same freedom as you would on your own little patch of land. Above all you will be obliged to work, for there is total work security. There is hope. For whoever really wishes to work, the Guyenne formula offers not the slightest inconvenience and an incalculable number of advantages. Socialism? Little Russia? At least vest-pocket social planning. Very intelligent, well run, and the sort of thing one hopes will spread. In the magnificent country that awaits you sometimes in the interior roads between Amos and Rouyn, I have seen too many facets of loneliness and poverty.

On the shores of Macamic Lake, an image of sudden peace. You will learn that this is a former sanitorium, more or less converted into an ordinary hospital for lack of patients. The last cases of tuberculosis are among the Indians. Against a background of the Laurentians, you continue to Rouyn through pastures and great fields of wheat and oats. It is there that you discover some of the most harmonious landscapes in Abitibi.

ROUYN-NORANDA Noranda, the city of the bosses, Rouyn, the city of the employees. On the boundary the brand new law court, of which it is impossible to tell whether it is in Rouyn or Noranda. Present everywhere the enormous plants of the Noranda mine, which spits black and white smoke upon the two towns, having long polluted with its refuse the magnificent lake that is its nervous centre. But here lakes are not the object of a cult; there are dozens of them, and many people have built summer cottages on the shores of a lake no one else knows of.

Noranda has become one of the most important mining corporations of Canada, the only one in a position to convert copper into products ready for the market. Its largest refineries are in Montreal East, and it operates three gold mines near Timmins, in Ontario, an iron mine on Vancouver Island, foundries at Murdochville, sawmills in British Columbia, while increasing its mining interests throughout America. Noranda and its affiliates provide work for twelve thousand Canadians for a production on the order of a hundred and twenty-five million dollars. Though it was originally controlled by American capital, ninety-one per cent of its twenty-four thousand shareholders today are Canadians.

I walked in Rouyn-Noranda. The bustle of the one contrasts with the peaceful residential character of the other. Noranda, the town of bosses, but not necessarily English-speaking. All those who have succeeded in Rouyn dream of their stucco, stone, or brick house in Noranda.

THE KINGDOM OF THE SAGUENAY A hundred and fifty thousand square miles, seven times the area of New Brunswick, sixty-seven times the area of Prince Edward Island. Total population

around 320,000, ninety-seven per cent of French culture. A
high birth rate, average age lower than in the rest of Quebec.
An immense lake, the reservoir of the Laurentians, a spectacular
river that becomes transformed into a fjord eight hundred feet
deep for the greater part of its journey towards the St Lawrence.
Low lands around the lake, 200,000 acres under cultivation.
Several fair-sized towns, an infinite number of little industrial
centres, the highest urban concentration after Montreal and Quebec. A particularly colourful accent, an open and dynamic
mentality, a history.

One could go on forever about the Kingdom of the Saguenay
— a land as fascinating as the Gaspé, for very different reasons.
And the people of Quebec have a sort of predilection for it. In
the old days it was a far-off and inaccessible country. Today the
road through Laurentian Park transforms the former expedition
into a happy and easy journey, full of seductions. The train or
the aircraft is preferred by Montrealers. In the old days the land
of Maria Chapdelaine, today that of Frère Untel and the dynamic
priest, Villeneuve. The eternal 'we're on the move' used to define
the climate of evolution of a province is here a daily practice, a
way of life.

Nothing is less asleep than this Quebec, which heavy forests
hide from our eyes.

It is not astonishing that the young people should be the most
drawn to all that concerns the separatist movements. I do not
know that this attraction is always founded upon an ideology
or a system; people here are simply ready to buy everything that
is new and announces change. The success of the Créditistes can
have had no other explanation. It must be understood that the
people here were on the move before the rest of us were, and on
an infinity of subjects, and that this was a spontaneous phenomenon revealing very diverse characteristics.

One day I decided to make one of those gratuitous experiments, which fail nine times out of ten, but for which I have a

certain bent. I spotted a taxi-driver and asked him point-blank to drive me to whatever in Chicoutimi inspired him with the greatest pride. Not to thirty-six places. Just to one. He reflected for a moment, then took me like an arrow to the other side of the bridge where I saw, in an island of greenery, a modern church, of a revolutionary style. You will find dozens like it in the Kingdom of the Saguenay, and they are for the most part of an inspiration and a quality you would not expect.

The hospitals of Chicoutimi have become a sort of medical empire, through the work of a single nun. It is one of the most modern complexes in Quebec, and all surgical operations of interest were broadcast by closed circuit in colour when television cameras had still made only timid appearances in the biggest hospitals of Quebec. Its administration is different, and I could name several other institutions of the same sort. They all have one characteristic in common. They are the work of a single man or woman.

In a part of the province where few structures exist except parishes, there is always some giant to seize the society in his arms and set it on new ways. These giants are all of the race of the first among them: John Murdock. He not only built a financial empire, he was the Announcing Angel. We are approaching the end of the era of giants. The age of structure has come, as in all Quebec, as in the world. The Kingdom of the Saguenay must turn the corner. There will be grindings and gratings. Beside an impoverished, primitive society, such as one finds in the back country, an advance guard has been built up gradually on this cult of personalities. It will be hard to get rid of this worship of personality, which spreads from the man to his region, his town, or his township. The challenge by which the Kingdom of the Saguenay finds itself confronted, at least as I was allowed to get an inkling of it, depends for its response entirely upon the ability to regroup the energies and resources of the region to form a common front in the industrial reconversion of the province. There is danger that fragmentation of the attention and regional interests might make it miss its real entry upon the stage. But

these are only the remarks of a free traveller, which ultimately
concern no one. I did not hear anything of the sort in any of the
circles I entered. Perhaps I am wrong to place a sign 'Attention,
danger' on the personality cult as it is practised here.

Two steps from my hotel was an immense establishment, part
bar, part dance-hall, part club. A good many of the young people,
and the less young, betook themselves there each evening, sometimes just for a few minutes, to see their friends, take a turn on
the dance floor, and have a drink — or ten. I mention it for a
single reason: I had not encountered this sort of thing along my
route except in our large cities. Personally I am not complaining.
The journalist who had arranged to meet me there was a cheerful companion; he knew everyone and introduced me to several
groups of young people who, even apprehended on the wing,
were worthy of attention and sometimes interest.

In certain cases and at certain hours the place took on a
sophisticated character. On the right you would have tables of
quieter and slightly older people, who sat amidst the thunderings
of the orchestra, conversing as one would in one's own living
room. Most of them were assiduous readers of *L'Express* and
Match, and similar magazines that make their appearance here
only a few days after their publication in Paris. The Quebec
newspaper, *Le Soleil,* is solidly implanted here in its regional
edition. They read the current books and follow the important
television programs, some of them have studied in Quebec,
Montreal, or Paris . . . many things that Louis Hémon did not
foresee. It is enough to know that they exist, beside a traditional
universe that forms a continuing watermark and that no one
need any longer describe, now that its genius has granted it
immortality. For I encountered young Marias, and Father Chap-
delaines, and more than one François. Outside the towns they
are everywhere, but you will not find them here. They have the
same inner dimension as the poets sang of, the same flavourful
lumberman's vocabulary; they have kept the dignity of a race
that is not close to extinction.

DYING VILLAGES   As soon as you arrive at Baie Comeau, various indications give you to understand that you have just fallen into some quiet little backwater. Notices are attached here and there to the walls of the airport: 'It is forbidden to drink alcoholic beverages.' 'Quarrelling forbidden.' 'No blaspheming.' But as you examine the faces of those coming and going in the tiny airport, you decide that the notices are perhaps not excessive. These, it seems, are not choirboys.

But this is only a first impression, which will not last. The hide is rough but it often covers the heart of a lamb. Later I had occasion to talk with several lumbermen of the district. Their status has been transformed: they have become industrial employees. The last real lumber-camps as we imagine them are in the Gaspé. Here cutting and transport are expedited by machines of every sort. The men work by the hour, by the day, by the week, and are protected by their union. They travel from town to town a great deal, even to Quebec and Montreal. There is always a great deal of travelling when the men outnumber the women.

Baie Comeau is the natural entry to an immense network of new towns, created by great industries, mining developments, and immense hydro-electric works in a part of the province where there used to be only little fishing villages. These little villages are the forgotten, the sacrificed. Even so they are not going to commence to fish for the giants of the sea — beluga, porpoises, sharks, seal, or even the whales that have begun to appear again. Their isolation and the poverty of their equipment does not permit them to concern themselves seriously with cod or mackerel; and the volume of the catch would not justify setting up air transport. Here people lived chiefly by salmon, which abounds in several rivers. All the salmon rivers have been leased to fishing clubs. They also lived by trout. All the trout rivers have been leased to fishing clubs.

The solution is clear and easy. Block off along the coast north from Baie Comeau a band of territory inviolable by the fishing

clubs to a depth of about twenty miles. Instead of barely existing, the villages will be restored to life. They are dying by inches,
and no one is paying any attention. Very often poverty in Quebec is not inevitable. A re-examination of the agreements with
the fishing clubs would be enough to put an end to it here. And
no one can make me believe that the proprietors of fishing clubs
are murderers. They are within their legal rights and do not ask
questions about epiphenomena. But if they were suddenly aware
of the seriousness of the epiphenomenon, they would not hesitate to move their camps farther inland. Their aircraft would be
none the worse for it. Human lives are at stake. One has the
feeling that they do not even suspect it. Otherwise their splendid
salmon and their fine trout would gag in their throats.

A man, an old lumberjack, wept on my shoulder at the fine
prospects for the future of the region. He had come too late, or
too soon. Some day, no doubt, the unions will take care of
wretches like him. He had only one trade, lumberjack, with an
axe. This is no longer done. He is a physical wreck at fifty-seven.
He could not be salvaged by new techniques. One phrase returned to him like a leitmotif: 'Excuse me. I'm discouraged.' A
young chief cook, who works on an engineer's crew at Outarde
55 — a project tied to those of the Manicouagan — was showing
around his pay envelope: $174.75 for eleven days. A specialized
worker earns on the average eighteen dollars a day. My old
lumberjack burst into tears again. He was more 'discouraged'
than ever.

No one had time to listen to him. For the time being everyone
was busy. And so much the worse for those caught in the gear-
shafts.

THE GREAT NORTH   Indians and Eskimos have always been more
or less a federal concern, but there can be no doubt that they
will some day depend exclusively upon the provinces, at least in
the matter of education. For other aspects of the problem, it will
be necessary to readapt the treaties, encourage the climate of

self-determination, and find legal and political means to make them citizens in every respect.

I am looking as I write at an official map of New Quebec. I note in passing that the boundaries of Labrador are not even marked by a dotted line and that its territory is of the same shade as the rest of Ungava. I do not see any particular intention in this, but the matter seems to promise vigorous and lengthy debates. If I dare attempt prophecy I shall suggest that it seems to me inscribed in history that Labrador will some day be an integral part of Quebec. But what most draws my attention as I look at this map is the limitless resources of New Quebec and its immensity compared with the thin inhabited fringe on the edge of the American border.

I know, I know, it becomes irritating to be always talking about immensity and riches, especially at the moment in our evolution when we are examining ourselves with the intention of becoming our own masters. Rich as we are, we have had only the crumbs from the table of a feast to which we were not even invited. The new phenomenon here is that the matter is being initiated in a new climate in which the state will be free to play its role as leavening in the development of innumerable mineral veins, which extend like a sort of dorsal fin of several miles' width from the extreme north to Abitibi. We have made a great commotion about the hydro-electric developments at Manicouagan, but one could draw a circle hundreds of miles in radius from the Saguenay to Havre Sainte-Geneviève and construct enough dams to provide the whole continent with electricity. The same is true north of Abitibi, where the circle this time would break on the shores of Hudson Bay, from Mouette Bay in the south to a few dozen miles north of Fort George. If the prophets go to it to their hearts' content, they will never have enough imagination to explore all the facets of the long-range future.

One thing is certain: our twenty-seven hundred Eskimos will be turned away little by little from their traditional existence to become miners or industrial workers. Besides, they wish to do so. Go almost anywhere to visit them and you will see that igloos belong to the past, or to fishing or hunting expeditions. They live in houses of all sorts, often in conditions of comfort not always known in certain villages in the south of France or Italy. The Eskimo village has its council, composed of a chief and three or four councillors, depending upon the size of the settlement, which may have a population anywhere from fifty to five hundred. They correspond frequently, but several village chiefs met for the first time in their lives on the occasion of a study conference arranged by the government.

In about 1936, Oblate missionaries began to work among the Eskimos. Some ten missionaries made in all only about fifty conversions. The others are Anglicans — but let us be honest, this does not mean a great deal. The Eskimo does not offer the slightest resistance to imported religions but remains in deep communion with a mythology that has been forged during the course of several millenia.

IVUJIVIK   He appeared younger than he was, and he wasn't yet thirty. This very young man had lived for an entire year in the little Eskimo village of Ivujivik. This means a year at the most northerly point in Quebec. He didn't make an exceptional adventure out of it. The provincial government has formed the habit of maintaining such agents on mission throughout the far North. They must first learn the Eskimo language but above all act as intermediaries between the village councils and the ministry.

This particular young man was now preparing a bilingual teaching curriculum: Eskimo-French. His research would take account of the studies of Dr Penfield, the Montreal experiment of Notre-Dame-de-Sion, and the Danish experiments in Greenland.

He spoke excellent French, though he was born in Windsor of Irish and Scottish parentage and educated at Toronto. On his table I saw a letter he had just drafted in Eskimo. He was explaining to the village council why the government had recalled him. They had asked him to come back. They could not understand his departure after a year of friendship. It is perhaps the chief characteristic of the Eskimo temperament to wish to understand things of this sort. And the explanation must take care not to lay hands, even distantly, on his pride. The Eskimo cannot bear ridicule. He never needs to slap his child, it is enough to humiliate him. Above all, you must never lose face.

No one can live for a year in the most northerly village in Quebec without having a great many adventures, even though the aircraft has broken the vicious circle of the old isolation. This young man of twenty-seven, who was received by an English school teacher — on the primary level all our Eskimos have had their schooling in English till the present — and by an Oblate missionary from France, suddenly found himself for two months the only non-Eskimo in Ivujivik. One can imagine the panic he felt. All that can happen in two months. All the advice he must give, the decisions to make, the difficulties to overcome, the judgements to hand down. And at just that moment a case of suicide was tossed into his hands, of rather obscure nature, a love-story perhaps.

I do not believe the suicide rate is very high among our twenty-seven hundred Eskimos. I remember only that this young man had fallen in love with Ivujivik and that the next day he would once more board the monoplane that had taken off from Fort Chimo a year ago at a temperature of 38 below to carry him towards what might well remain the crucial experience of his life. It was all rather confusing. I might have passed him on the street and seen only a young middle-class intellectual.

QUEBEC IN ORBIT   Quebec is not living its political adventure in the eyes of the whole world, as is often believed, but it has made its appearance on the Canadian stage in a starring role. The rest of the country is following its movements with the keenest attention, even when it appears to be thinking of something else. I felt this everywhere.

There is not yet any real political thought, as far as I know, and reactions depend most often upon factors of an order that had better not be too deeply explored. There is too much of what I would call 'cinema' about them. But opinion exists, can be affected, and this is a giant's pace, I think, that we have accomplished. Men are censured, and measured. And interest, much more than passion, marks the comments, which means that we have required only half a dozen years to come out of the Middle Ages.

Politicians are as we make them. Good politics cannot be carried out in the shadow, unknown to the public. At this moment we are experiencing the most vital period of our political life, because the voter has come out of his torpor. If he puts his head back on the pillow and falls asleep again, our politics will become what they became before, a La Fontaine fable, the one that begins, 'An evil that spread terror . . .'

Ontario

Through the fault of a friend I arrived at Toronto in tears. He had decided to meet my flight from Montreal. But it turned out that I had to walk up and down awaiting the pleasure of seeing him again. He then drove me all over the city in a car whose heating system had broken down. Outside temperature, ten below. He turned towards me from time to time to swear with conviction that I was in no danger of catching cold. I agreed readily between chattering teeth. He himself was wrapped up like four Eskimos. He had never had even a minor accident and yet he drove in a highly personal way, sometimes pressing the accelerator when circumstances seemed to me to warrant applying the brakes.

You would spend years guessing his real nature. You might know already that he is a great lover of music, reading, art galleries, good food, and fine wine, and you will not have time to wonder where he has been able to cultivate those rare passions in a milieu based upon the useful, the practical, and the profitable. You then go from discovery to discovery. You learn that he is considered an expert skier and that horses are the great passion of his life. But don't then imagine that he rides to obey the fashion horsemanship has become just when the noble beasts have disappeared from our streets. No, for him it is part of the long cavalier tradition that comes to us from France.

I found him particularly happy because he had just bought a magnificent horse. Everyone knows that horses are not very intelligent, but the real horseman can make his mount an extension of himself. The horse finally has the caprices, the reflexes, and the moods of his master. I would have liked to be able to discuss this with him at length and know why he had suddenly got rid of a horse he had always spoken of in the highest terms. But is it from modesty? This is a subject about which he does not willingly unburden himself. He never unburdens himself willingly, even if you have been able to win his confidence. And this is a slight change from all those chatterers who proliferate in our living rooms, offering their own psycho-analysis about total unknowns. I believe that it is because of this instinctive restraint that I am so fond of this man, even though I am not sure whether he is capable of real friendship for anyone but his horse.

THE JOURNALISM OF THE YEAR 2000   So I arrived in Toronto weeping and the amiable people waiting for me had found nothing better than to catapult me forthwith towards Niagara Falls. It was with the celebrated peninsula, then, that I would begin my exploration of Ontario. I had seen the falls more than once and lacked only the sight of the improbable ice sculptures that frame the falling water throughout the winter. Summer tourists will never have a precise idea of this spectacle. It is a carnival setting. Yet there was no one in the streets except the first honeymoon couples of March. They would become more numerous every week and hotels would soon declare themselves 'full up'. For these Niagara honeymooners are still the darlings of the tide of tourists that invades this part of Ontario each year. They are given certificates of honour, they sign the guest book, they are the object of minute attentions. There were almost forty thousand couples last year, a figure that gives you confidence in the future of the race.

Chance had it that I should make my first exploration of the vicinity in the company of a young German journalist. He is employed by the largest newspaper in Hamburg, an enormous publication in the American style. In the space of about ten days he had visited innumerable Latin American countries and was now spending four days in Canada, one of them at Niagara, a second in Toronto, and two in Montreal. He showed me his travel schedule, set out in detail to the last second. The instant he arrives in a place, machinery is set in motion to enable him to see the most things possible in a minimum of time.

How fine it is to see a German journalist of the new school from close at hand. He was not the first of the species I had encountered; they all have the same inner assurance. His paper had given him the status of offical guest wherever he went. And as he went by like the wind he was no trouble to anyone. He would write long articles when he returned about all he had seen. The purpose of his Montreal stay was to gather all necessary information about the separatist crisis in Quebec. He would then wrap the whole thing up for his readers. Others might tremble at putting so little time into informing oneself about so many countries and such various crises — a mere ten days. This young man of less than thirty was of admirable serenity. I believe the young people of all countries have learned not to tremble, no matter in what situation you dare to place them. It is a fine picture. A fine picture that makes you do a little trembling of your own. When I informed him that I would soon have spent five and a half months travelling across my own country, he replied spontaneously, half serious, 'Did you cross it on foot?'

I do not know what he wrote later about Niagara, but his visit was split into two parts: contemplating the falls and downing a yard of beer at a celebrated local tavern. A yard, yes, a glass of beer three feet high, a skilful bit of borrowing from old

English folklore. After that I lost sight of him. He was whisked off to Toronto, via Kitchener and probably Stratford. Back to Hamburg in three days . . . And now I shall settle down at my typewriter and tell you about all those countries across the seas. It is the new way. It is not the exclusive property of any one country. I have noticed that it is practised in all latitudes. I think it has its minor disadvantages. At the very moment when we possess all the means needed to know one another better from one end of the earth to the other, we have learned to misunderstand one another with a good conscience.

OF AN UNREAL BEAUTY   Pictures of Niagara. The falls themselves, made for the cinema, which has not failed to display them to us. The American falls, straight, without surprise, 182 feet high and a thousand and seventy-five feet wide. The Canadian falls curved in a semi-circle at a slightly lower level. As I saw them together from the top of the Seagram Tower, they suggested the hammer and sickle much more than a horseshoe.

In the evening the whole is illuminated from a turret equipped with immense projectors, and this is an imposing sight. White for the first twenty minutes, then various colours in alternation, ending with white. These colours are played from a sort of keyboard and I was permitted one evening to create my own scales: I understand why the foreman did not yet seem to have wearied of his work. It gives you a feeling of thrilling power. In this little corner of earth, you have become the night sun — a sun of changing moods, which depend only on your will.

I was told that the region was destined for a great industrial boom, which was already under way. I was given impressive statistics, which left me rather cold. Isn't this the case with all Canada? And wasn't this the language I had been offered everywhere? I preferred to wander at random and make my own discoveries. It was thus that I was drawn towards an institution I found fascinating. There are perhaps others like it across the country, but this was the first time I had encountered a gardeners' school along my route.

It is situated upon a height of land overlooking the Niagara River on the Queenston road. It depends upon the Niagara Parks Commission, an organization that not only does not receive any government subsidy but shows a profit each year. The School of Horticulture is a relatively modest enterprise and the apprentice-gardeners have only about a hundred acres to work with between winter courses. Students come from almost everywhere, but their total number is rigorously kept at twenty-four. It is believed that former facilities trained only amateurs. So, since the creation of the School of Horticulture in 1936, the eight holders of diplomas that graduate each year after a three-year course are assured of a fine career. They become professors of horticulture, as well as park superintendents or industrial or technical advisers. I have a list of all graduates for the thirty years: I can point to very few French Canadian names. Perhaps they do not know that this school is open to them.

As the practical teaching is given in a setting as much park as garden, visitors have learned their way here. In May they come to admire the tulips, lilacs, Japanese cherries, and irises; in June the roses and rhododendrons; and from September to the first frost, the dahlias and the chrysanthemums. And in all seasons there are the numerous hothouses or winter gardens.

UNEXPECTED DISCOVERY   If you travel about Niagara a little, you will find it hard not to hear mention of the millionaire, Sir Harry Oakes. To get some small idea of how rich he was, you need only set foot in the residence of his personal physician, now in use as a private club. It is a sort of manor-house in Tudor style, in the middle of a park and, at that season, when the trees had not yet had time to drape themselves in their leaves, offered an unexpected vision of Niagara Falls.

It was in this privileged place that I discovered a dry — yes, really very dry — Canadian wine. So we do possess one, unknown to ourselves. Unfortunately for me, it is white and I am a great lover of red wine. Later I was offered a Canadian liqueur that the monks of the Abbey of Sénanque would not disown.

It is made of Quebec and Ontario maple syrup but distilled in Alberta.

All this prompted me to spend the next few days making an inquiry in depth into the production of our wines, which is almost entirely concentrated in this same Niagara Peninsula. It is not too common to be able to converse in Canada with real vine-growers, and I decided to try to find out from the producers themselves the reasons for the poor quality of our wine or, better, why our wines have so little appeal for real connoisseurs. It is no longer just a simple matter of using French wine as a criterion though we can rightly do so, on several scores, but wine-lovers of the entire world, and I have discovered them in Australia, all agree upon certain types of dry wines that we cannot manage to produce here, even starting with vine-stocks imported from France. I believed for a long time that our winters had something to do with it. Drive through the vineyards of the Niagara Peninsula and you will see for yourself, without any need to consult an expert, that Darwin's law has been at work: only the strongest have survived. And some of these survivors are as tall as young apple-trees. I saw them when they were stripped of their leaves and covered with snow, and I could not imagine their branches bending in the autumn under the weight of bunches of ripe grapes.

Well, having obtained information at the source, I would have to search for the real reasons in another direction. True, the grape varies each year according to the weather, the degree of exposure to the sun, the number of sunny days and, most of all, the rigour of the winter. But I had proof that we were in the position to produce a dry white wine, at least one, and wanted to understand why there are not two, or three, and why there was not a single really dry red wine.

'DRY ON THE BOTTLE' Results of the inquiry: we would be quite capable of producing a number of very dry red or white wines; but they do not suit 'the Canadian taste'. So sugar is added. Some ten years ago our champagne was still *brut*: it remained in the cellars of the distributors. They began to sweeten it a little, the market picked up. The 'Pinot Chardonnay' that had caught my attention is being gradually withdrawn from circulation; the vendors have torn out their hair and consider it a complete fiasco. Let us stop accusing our soil, the exposure to sun, or the harshness of our winters. Most of the wines of the Niagara Peninsula could be dry at their point of departure; they have gradually come to disguise themselves as bad port through the fault of the public, to the great despair of several vine-growers who make much better wines for themselves than those we are able to buy. As one of them expressed it to me, 'They like "dry" on the bottle, but sugar in the wine.'

THE KITCHENER MARKET   I had expected to see factory chimneys everywhere. Ontario is the most highly industrialized province in Canada. And it is true that wherever you go you will find significant industrial apparatus. But until now I had not seen this aspect, only new facets of Ontario's rural face. And to terminate it, I went to the well-known Kitchener market.

The market is held every Saturday morning, from six o'clock till noon. Each time it is the occasion for a great gathering of shoppers. One could find strictly everything all the year round — and at prices that sometimes justify a round trip of several dozen miles. Most of the farmers that come here are Mennonites. There is the same graciousness here as I had seen among the Mennonites of the West, the same communal instinct, the same traditions. I inquired the price of honey. The beekeeper guessed that I was a stranger and offered me a pot with such spontaneity that I hadn't time to find the slightest excuse to refuse it without offending him. I noticed some 'pigs' tails', which are grilled on the spit here and seem to be a great speciality of the district. My education is incomplete in this matter so I asked for an explanation. The girl kindly gave me a 'course' — it would have been an evening course if it hadn't been given at six-thirty in the morning. I was surrounded, customers began to gather from all directions. But at the risk of losing sales, she didn't cut her exposition short.

After that I did not dare speak another word to any of those eager and gracious vendors . . . for there is no other word but 'graciousness' to describe their behaviour.

'OPEN SEA' A Martian told that Ontario is an inland province would wonder if his informant had lost his senses. For at every turn the highways skirt the sea . . . what could be the sea but is only the Great Lakes. In France and elsewhere, when lakes attain this size, they are called 'inland seas'. And these are actual inland seas. When I drove from Niagara to Hamilton or went up to St Thomas, Chatham, or Windsor by the long way round, I had sudden glimpses of a limitless horizon. It was the same on the shore of Lake Huron, going north from Sarnia, the same at Sault Ste Marie . . . and from Toronto to Trenton. All Ontario is outlined against masses of water, which I am told are fresh and which owe to this peculiarity alone their deceptive name of 'lakes'.

WHAT IS A CANADIAN? Along the navigable waterway that links Lake Erie with Lake Huron, there is a tourist region to which Americans pour by way of Detroit and Windsor, one of the most important points of contact between Canada and the United States. It would be hard to say whether industry, agriculture or tourism holds first position in the counties of Essex, Kent, and Lambton. If there is one province in Canada where all the resources of the economy blend into a harmonious whole it is Ontario. Seen from a certain angle, these elements influence one another and finally obey the same factors. And who can say at what moment agriculture or tourism break free of the old concepts to fall under the heading of industry? Industrial maturity perhaps comes on the day when you have industrialized everything. This is the impression I often had in Ontario.

Whether at the making of our Niagara wines, at the auctions of the tobacco producers at Tilsonburg or the automobile assembly-lines at Windsor, the rules of the game are the same. It is true that the presence of man can still preserve all its warmth as we saw at the Kitchener market. But on the whole I saw few essential differences between the industrial plants of Ontario and those of the large American states. This is the direction that all Quebec is taking at an accelerated rhythm, that Alberta has already taken, the direction the whole country will take in the long run. Our behaviour will be changed by it; it has already changed. I do not say whether this is for our good or our very great harm, I say only that we cannot escape it. Less than a century ago, the Windsor district was eighty per cent agricultural; today the metropolitan area includes two hundred thousand people and is eighty per cent industrial. The same seesaw is operating in all Canada. Ontario is far ahead of the rest of us. And this has resulted in a curious phenomenon.

In this province that I expected to find more English than Prince Edward Island or Newfoundland, at least in its traditions and its external aspects, I constantly met along my route a type that was not of England or of the United States and that might well be Canadian. But just as one is mistaken when one imagines the French of Quebec and the other provinces to be entirely bound up with France, I discovered here English and New Canadians who have developed for their province and their country an authentic sense of belonging, much as the French Canadians have come finally to feel American, and retain only sentimental and cultural bonds with their mother-country, and these so thin as to surprise you more than once.

A fact, a single little fact will suffice. At the time of the flag debate, everyone here believed that the abandonment of the Union Jack or the Red Ensign was a concession to Quebec. I was surprised to see our new flag floating everywhere in Ontario and it was rarely the subject of pleasantries or argument. New as it then was, it seemed to be already the object of a spontaneous cult. On my return to Montreal I saw it still floating timidly here and there, without attracting any attention other than jokes.

We are strange specimens of humanity and not always very

easy to understand. But one certainty shines forth: we are no longer of France or of England or of Holland or of Hungary or of anywhere else. We are of a corner of North America, and in the two key provinces we are already of Canada, more often than not unknown to ourselves. And in the two key provinces, both on the English side and on the French side, we have fashioned ourselves a personality that does not resemble anything that is met with anywhere else, even in the United States.

I remember a certain man. He was born in Ontario and his parents before him, he studied at Toronto, he is deeply rooted in his province, but he considers himself 'American' because he 'does everything in the American way'. To begin with, what does that mean? In the entire western world people 'do everything in the American way'. This began with traits of behaviour, became a particular way of life and might also become a new civilization. At any rate, my man was wrong about himself. In the first place, you will find a great variety of accents in the United States, but not his. He was of the London region. There are people from England there who are not only of more recent importation than any to be found among our neighbours but have developed in a different environment.

I began to make severe judgements about our country. He immediately took up a position of defence. I pushed the experiment further and criticized his province, Ontario. He looked at me furiously. I had finally the courage to attack his region; he flew into a passion of rage that sent me and a witness I had let into the game into gales of laughter. And this was a man who considered himself an American and had demonstrated to me only an hour before that Canada was simply a dim extension of the United States. I had just proved to him that he was of his country, his province, and his region.

A very thin layer covers our chauvinism, from one end of the country to the other. This would be a manifestation of only slight interest if I had not sensed more than once that this chauvinism might in its turn be the precursory form of a real sense of belonging — precursory, that is to say, until the moment when we all become aware of it. And when we do, I shall begin to feel that Canada is becoming a real country.

HURONIA   Each province has found itself a slogan to entice vacationers. We have our 'ocean playground', our '*la belle province*'. Ontario claims to be 'Canada's variety vacationland'. And this is quite fair, and as justified here as everywhere else. Winter and summer alike, one might wonder whether Canada is not above all the paradise of the rich. In this respect, the map of Ontario is a little breathtaking. If I had to choose one place rather than another, I would not know where to turn my eyes.

For relaxation, beauty of landscapes, and calm, I would select the north shore of Lake Superior from Sault Ste Marie to Port Arthur and Fort William. Here we are at the terminus alike of the St Lawrence Seaway and of the rail transport of the entire Canadian West. But I remember above all that this region, besides opening out constantly upon Lake Superior, is abundantly provided with national and provincial parks and that it must be very easy here to guard against the heat of the summer and the noise of our cities.

My preference would be drawn next to a region very well known to the people of Ontario, more and more of whom establish themselves there for the season, but where one can still find oneself a little spot. It is called Huronia. Here you will, of course, find all the summer pleasures — beaches, excursions of the most various kinds. But it is its history that makes the French Canadian already attached to the region. Huronia lies between the southeastern part of Georgian Bay and Lakes Simcoe and Couchiching, immediately north of Toronto. Here Samuel de Champlain intended to establish an advance post of French culture in 1615, at a time when the first English colonists clung, as they would continue to do for a long time still, to the shores of the Atlantic.

This attempt was a complete failure, but Champlain encouraged missionaries to establish themselves there, without losing sight of his long-range political intention. It was the Recollets who first answered Champlain's call, soon followed by the Jesuits, whom we find implicated in so many of humanity's great adventures, colonial as well as intellectual. At first the missionaries did not possess a roof of their own; they lived with the Hurons, sharing their meals, their work, and their various occupations — it was the formula of the worker-priest, three centuries before ours. This lasted until 1639. It was then decided to unite the missionaries in a central residence, which was called Sainte-Marie.

Recent excavations have brought to light the remains of two chapels, a cemetery, a hospital, a forge, stables, and several other buildings that are sufficient to show that Sainte-Marie was not only a residence for missionaries but a centre of social services for the Indians. At one time there were about forty Frenchmen employed at Sainte-Marie — millers, blacksmiths, masons and other artisans, who taught their techniques to the Indians while the missionaries performed their work of religious education. The one reason for anxiety was the Iroquois attacks. They continued to make plans for the future, but the Iroquois vice grew steadily tighter.

Disaster came in 1649. All the Huron villages were razed, the Huron nation was completely destroyed, and the few survivors had to flee to Quebec. Eight missionaries were put to death with the atrocious sufferings that overwhelmed our childhood — at least for those of us whose history teachers were inclined to sadism. I still remember certain horrible details that I have never managed to find in the chronicles of the period. Three missionaries were martyred near Auriesville, in New York State, and five in the region of Sainte-Marie, where a national shrine has been erected to their memory. They were all canonized. We shall never forget their names: Jean de Brébeuf, Isaac Jogues, Gabriel Lalemant, Antoine Daniel, Charles Garnier, Noël Chabanel, René Goupil, Jean de la Lande.

TORONTO IN SEARCH OF A FACE   Here is a city that must be contemplated first from the window of an aircraft if one is absolutely bent upon finding it beautiful. The arrangements of great autoroutes give it a certain rhythm, especially the arteries that follow what is called the river, which appears from high in the air as a zone of greenness, several miles long and in the very heart of the city. Here and there are patches of green — these are parks. What I like about the parks of Toronto are the signs one sometimes finds: 'Please walk on the grass.'

Once you are back on the ground, well, you must study the city in detached pieces. Beauty has taken refuge in the new residential sections, but the centre of the city often presents the aspect of a building-yard. Scaffoldings thrust themselves right into the middle of the few perspectives that might hold your interest. Here, as elsewhere, city planning is of recent import, and the splendid semi-circular city hall will have a great deal of trouble integrating with a rather nondescript general silhouette, of which the Royal York is no longer the point of convergence.

Montreal has openly decided in favour of a silhouette in the American style and has thereby already found a triumphant personality. Here hesitation makes itself felt. Toronto is seeking originality of line. The anxiety to be different tempers audacity. I met several of those that have taken it upon themselves to give Toronto its face of the future. Steel and concrete are still powerless to deliver to us their ultimate intentions, as I believed I understood them. Toronto wishes to be a great metropolis that will be different from the great American metropolises. It is studying each of its problems in terms of its particular and specific nature. The planners are giving the matter all the time it needs. But on the level of intentions, there can be no doubt of the wish to make Toronto the first original big city — that is to say, modern but in a personal, hence Canadian, style.

Precisely what does this mean? We still have not enough elements in hand to judge. It seems only that the curved line will play an important role, as at the airport, or the city hall, or in the design of the new residential areas, some of which revolve around an arch of triumph, for the moment invisible.

Although there are pedestrian ways and automobile through-ways on Lake Ontario, sometimes offering lovely perspectives, Toronto will have to decide to make a very little place for pedestrians, in its centre, where the island can now be seen between the buildings of the harbour and only if you are able to look at it from the upper storeys of the offices downtown.

I sensed other, much more personal preoccupations. I sensed essentially that Toronto was trying to adjust to the new situation created by the 'American' explosion of Montreal. It is evident that the Queen City is in a state of rivalry with the metropolis. Such rivalry, which is a widespread phenomenon in Canada — and I even found it in the most remote corners of our provinces, often between two minuscule farming centres that might better have united their energies — is nevertheless a sign of good health, rather in the nature of athletic competition.

When it is learned that you come from Montreal, comparisons are first made between Toronto and the American cities recognized for the rapidity of their growth. But if it is made clear that you do not suffer from chauvinism, cards are laid openly on the table and comparisons offered between Toronto and Montreal. And this gives you a keen satisfaction. There is room in Canada for twenty Montreals or Torontos. The first two in the ring are only heralding the future Calgarys, Edmontons, and Vancouvers, and all the many others waiting in the wings.

TORONTO ADMITS ITS PURITANISM Puritanism is America's portion, even in the West. But generally speaking, the big cities have cast it overboard. Only Toronto seems to be having a little trouble ridding itself of its own. And now that it has formed a taste for emancipation in all domains, its citizens suffer more openly than ever from the complexity of its liquor regulations, the precariousness of its night life, the boredom of its Sundays. Plots are being woven in the shadows to be done with these habits of a bygone age.

Meanwhile private clubs have multiplied. Behind the dozen big ones, which have always existed as in London, several others have been born and lead an occult and hermetic existence. A few rather innocent nightclubs recall the restaurant-show formula that prevails throughout the West as far as Vancouver — the proliferation of a style commenced at New York, probably by Playboy, that adorns certain of the better restaurants with an army of scantily clad waitresses. This fashion has spread to Montreal; we are in danger of finding it everywhere. I say 'in danger' because it offers the customer no protection from the ridiculous. I wager that it will find its promised land in Toronto. Nothing prevents you from undressing your waitresses if you are the proprietor of a big restaurant. Everyone tries to go furthest, without appearing to and without frightening away the customers, who are usually highly respectable couples.

One such restaurant has had the idea of a mediaeval cellar with chevaliers in red tights; another offers a western atmosphere with cowgirls or blue angels; but what must be recognized is that Toronto has departed this way, by the side door, from a long tradition of poor eating. Today the food offered is good and fresh. Getting customers is easy. Toronto is a young city, seven out of ten of its inhabitants are under thirty. So good restaurants spring up as new ideas are found to justify the presence of scantily clad waitresses. We will not linger over this any longer; it is enough to know that one of the two great cities of Canada is setting up a network of restaurants of the first class, which were lacking only yesterday.

Some have gone so far as to toss bouquets at the old puritanism, though it has failed to muzzle this immense city. I read the statement of a 'leading person' on this question. I quote it verbatim: 'I believe that Toronto's dynamism is based on a solid rock of puritanism. Our blue laws and the famous Toronto Sunday have gained the city a certain notoriety, especially in Montreal and other effervescent societies, but all this is only a trivial manifestation of its foundations. For', adds the distinguished person, 'puritanism goes far beyond public behaviour or domestic habits. It shows itself on all levels of the intelligence like a gift of God.' Perhaps he is right. In his opinion, 'Puritanism is a source of energy, when it is allied with social and democratic discipline.'

No one will object to my using the word after this very distinguished individual. I do not know whether puritanism is profitable to a big city, I only know that Toronto is in process of losing hers. Yesterday's straitjacket has split. Now it is open to the thigh. And we are surprised to discover what a beautiful, very gay girl was wearing it. She is full of repressed desires. She still keeps a profound silence all day Sunday, but you cannot meet her eyes for very long. They are full of envy. This girl will make her way in the world.

A PREJUDICE DIES HARD   Each of the four colleges of the University of Toronto has its French department, under the jurisdiction of a joint committee, whose members are elected each year. The program is common to the four colleges. In all, about three thousand students take the various French courses, for which about a hundred professors share the responsibility. Most of them were trained at Paris, in the United States, or at summer courses held at Saint-Pierre and Miquelon. It is a great deal of effort for still rather scanty results. Nothing authorizes me to believe that students leave the University of Toronto's French department with a very profound knowledge of the language of Molière or for that matter of French culture.

The apparatus is in place and it is only necessary to know that it has existed for almost a century, if not in its present form, at least in spirit. The paths of the future, if it is intended to give them substance, seem to me traced out in advance and they all go by way of Quebec.

I spoke of this openly with Professor Flynn, who is still a young man and quite prepared to consider the situation with new eyes. I asked him a number of questions. Why do the professors go to train themselves hastily at the University of Paris by courses of the 'French made easy' sort, conceived for foreigners eager to win a diploma that will open the doors of teaching even if not those of real culture? Why Saint-Pierre and Miquelon? Why the United States, and just how does it come about that the strongest part of the contingent go to learn their French in American universities? Is not all this an open flight from the only province that is able to offer on American soil a French instruction that goes beyond utility to a real knowledge of a culture?

These questions did not trouble my companion. He had analysed them. And with Professor Rouillard, he has established a program that will more and more openly canvass the resources of Quebec. But our resources are very slim. We still do not possess a surplus of teachers. This is the source of the whole difficulty. There remained a confused point, which was not cleared up. Why have the Universities of Laval and Montreal not become the most sought-after training grounds for all the apprentice-professors of the French department? It was sworn to me that they would be, that they were already. But the tendency is so recent that it makes one shiver a little. What is back of all this? Yes indeed, the old prejudice about our patois. A prejudice that is failing but dies hard. Thanks to university exchanges, the spread of our publications and our literature, the creation of CJBC, and everything that allows Quebec to show itself in its true light, we have a fascinating challenge to meet. We are at last allowed a language, a real language; we are allowed a culture, an actual culture. Oh, not in all milieus, of course, and the recognition will take many years to reach the popular levels.

A 'YOUNG' OLD LADY   The most delicate memories do not easily let themselves be captured in words. I recall that French lady, a trifle lost in her big Rosedale house. She settled in Toronto with her husband and her two daughters in 1939. She symbolizes for me those thousands of Europeans that have had the courage to begin their life over again with us, often at an age when many of us are thinking about retiring. Death came, her daughters married, she lives alone, but do you believe she is lonely? She has learned to love so many things.

Mrs Straus is certainly among the privileged. She seems not to have to worry too much about material problems. But it is precisely among the privileged that boredom strikes with most force. She loves, truly loves painting, literature, and music — music above all. She is admitted into what is called 'society', but she does not accept the rules of the game except to the extent that they agree with her program of life.

'After a certain age,' she said, 'you drop everything that is false, empty, or artificial.'

Her preferences in painting include Riopelle, Borduas, and Harold Town among what she calls 'the young'. In music, if one forgets the great classics, she has a predilection for Weinzweig and Barbara Pentland. In literature few of the young have found favour. She is attached to Proust, Henry James, Chekhov, and Faulkner. She usually tears up her invitations to cocktail parties but I saw her set out one evening at nine o'clock to go to an exhibition of painting in a gallery in the centre of town. She drives her own car. But her best moments include the most refined pleasure of our civilization: a dinner with friends. Not at a restaurant but at home.

I asked her, 'You have never wanted to leave this very, very English city?'

The reply sprang forth, almost naïvely. 'Yes, once . . . and then I went to a concert, and the wish passed.'

I have often met in Toronto people who were really addicts of music. They are undoubtedly to be found everywhere, above all in Montreal, where, as is well known, it was their fidelity and their demands that helped make our symphony orchestra one of the best in America. But I did not expect to find the same passion in Toronto.

FABRICATORS OF BEAUTY   Our big cities have suddenly become provided with excellent schools for the training of models. In French until now painters reserved the word 'modèle' to designate the subject of their inspiration. But as they now do not paint from models, or so little, the term has come to agree with the sense given to it in English, and usage outstrips the dictionary to group under the word all the products of these specialized schools, who make a career in haute couture, in art photography, in publicity, even in television, films and allied arts. There is an increasing demand for them and, in general, they can expect to earn fairly high incomes. Because of our old background of puritanism, the modelling profession has not yet been altogether freed from certain suspicions. Beauty in a woman frightens us. Feminine seductiveness has long fallen under the vengeful thunder of the seventh and tenth commandments in which our collective morality is bogged down. The sin of the flesh is still the champion of the deadly sins.

Every day 'professional models' are still spoken of with a sidelong look and a small meaningful smile. This smile used to be used for 'airline stewardesses'. We got over that. In several foreign capitals the model has not only won her title to nobility but a new function has been added to those we already know: she has entrée to great premières, sophisticated parties, and the most exclusive receptions. They are considered living flowers. And our century needs to put beauty back on her pedestal, which should be the highest of all. We are far from this still but perhaps we will come to it some day.

These are a few of the ideas I was turning over as I presented myself at the most important school of models in Toronto. I wasn't too sure what I should expect. Chance had put the vice-president in my way and I had accepted his invitation to visit his empire without any illusions about the profit I might obtain from it. I was mistaken. I found it a fascinating experience.

Fascinating first of all because of the constant coming and going of beautiful girls. Let us be clear. 'Beautiful' is an excessive word. If you look at them attentively, one after the other — especially since some of them have just enrolled and will gradually be transformed by techniques of makeup, hairdressing, carriage and so on — you will discover a number of annoying but minor structural flaws. But on the whole they provided an impression of beauty of a sort of which our streets are often niggardly. It is clear that there is a prior weeding-out. All are not models who would be. And the girls I saw had successfully passed their first exam, which consists much more of a lengthy interview than of photographs.

The premises were small and compact, the narrow tortuous corridor opened at every instant into tiny rooms, and the stairs to the upper floors were steep as ladders. But each time the vice-president opened a door I was rewarded by a vision of beauty. Here the girls were learning to walk with books on their heads. There they were performing ballet steps. Elsewhere they were reciting speeches from poor Shakespeare. Now we were on the floor of the makeup room, fashion modelling, and magazine photography, and I noticed that the vice-president prudently waited to see whether or not the door would be opened, so as not to expose the models to indiscretions . . . though this might have left them rather indifferent. To each his trade, and modelling must of necessity be founded on a rather broad notion of modesty. In fact, I understood that certain courses will release a student from her inhibitions. One cannot imagine a Miss Toronto or a Miss Montreal who refused to appear on the stage in a bikini.

I had the opportunity to talk to a girl of eighteen who was preparing for her admission exams. She had enrolled in preliminary courses so as not to miss this first step in her career. What then were the basic qualifications that seemed to her so formidable? First, a pleasant physical appearance, whether conventional or not. One hundred per cent in her case. An average intelligence so that she could assimilate the courses. Six out of ten. Self-discipline: the courses are difficult and the diet severe. She would be given a very long questionnaire on this subject. Lastly, she was asked to turn a deaf ear to the remarks of her friends: 'You won't make a go of it. I can't see you as a model.' 'Who cares? I want to be a secretary,' she must say.

And here was the real revelation, at least for me. Information from the source: 75 per cent of the candidates have no dreams of being professional models, but intend to take up secretarial

Here the girls were learning to walk with books on their heads.

work, administration, hotel work, dancing, singing, the stage, commercial aviation . . . or simply family life. The number of married women attending these courses, in Montreal as well as in Toronto, sometimes even equals that of single girls. Considered at this angle, these big commercial factories might be considered houses of charity. Personally, I should gladly enrol them on the list of a Federation of Good Works.

AN ENCEPHALOGRAM? Before I commenced my journey across Canada, I remember, a Quebec intellectual said to me, with humour but against a background of seriousness, 'In your place I would begin with Ottawa. If you wait a year, you may find only dust.'

I am not of a particularly optimistic nature and I had to struggle many times against the obsession that our country was breaking into a thousand pieces. And how many overdue accounts await us several years from now. How many scandals, how many resounding inquiries, how much agitation in the political circles of the capital! There are innocents who have plunged back into their middle-class habits with utmost serenity, without any more concern for what is taking place in their city and in their country. Yet it is immediately apparent that this peaceful provincial town has become an immense kettle. The entire problem is to know whether the fabric will hold against the formidable pressure exercised not only from within but from without. For it is no longer just the work of a single province. The ten provinces have undertaken to define themselves against, or in relation to, a constitution that will soon be a hundred years old. The experts started the debate and it is from them that new directions or total impasse will come. But the problem concerns us all, and I cannot understand the debate of experts being conducted in an empty hall. From now on, we will have to account to future generations if we leave our seats, even if only for a few seconds. The play that is being acted on the stage, we have written.

When Queen Victoria decided to install the wandering capital of a country already in the works in the little town of Bytown, everyone knew she was simply playing safe. The city then had only to forge little by little the face we know today — among the most harmonious in Canada. Is this because of its situation at the juncture of three rivers, the abundance of green spaces, the apportioning of the residential districts, the profusion of shady streets? Several of our cities are amply provided with such charms. I think it is Parliament Hill that gives Ottawa its particular rhythms and harmonizes them in some way. It would have been very possible to spoil our parliament, as we spoiled so many others; we made a success of it, and in a remarkable fashion. Without setting myself to describe the group of buildings that adorn the hill and that we have all frequented, at least in films, I shall note in passing some details I think are less known. I saw the model of the first parliament that was built in 1866. I don't believe we have any reason to complain of the fire that ravaged it during the First World War. We did much better afterwards. Especially if it is remembered that the fire spared the jewel of those first buildings, the library of parliament, which is in the Gothic tradition.

So . . . only a few details, which will be grafted on our already acquired knowledge. In the senate chamber, the red chamber, gold and purple dominate the decoration. The ceiling is covered with gold leaf and pierced with small circular windows, on whose glass are painted the national emblems of the various ethnic groups of the country. I was pleased to find on its walls more of the fossiled Tyndall stone. The commons chamber, the green chamber, is particularly fine. If it were of smaller dimensions, the profusion of ornaments, painted arabesques, Tyndall stones, and oak panels would crush us slightly. But it is very vast, and the whole is impregnated with an atmosphere of sumptuousness, of which our members are not always aware. Here the slightest fault of French or English should take on the character of a sacrilege. It is more like a church than a parliamentary arena;

some day we will find a frame more appropriate to our shirt-sleeve debates.

This contradiction between the premises and their content is ultimately a sign of good health. It demonstrates, in any case, that we are of America and that our parliamentary traditions do not bind us to the old civilizations except with architectural motifs.

WE ARE ALL OF CANADA   Truly a whimsical journey. First stage, from Victoria to the gateway of Ontario; a flea-jump to Newfoundland and a slow return to the nation's capital. What has remained with me? A story of love. I had wished to see others live without being seen. As if this were another country than mine. And little by little I had felt myself personally drawn in. I began to walk openly. In Quebec and Ontario I walked as if I were at home. And I felt in accord, profoundly in accord, with the evolution of our society, its behaviour and its spirit. For this is what I recall particularly: *The French of Quebec are no longer of France but of America. The English of Ontario are no longer of the British Isles but of America. When they have become aware of it, they will all be of Canada.* We will all be Canadian. This is not a prophecy but the conclusion drawn from a considerable number of experiences. Canada is not yet a real country but is in the course of making itself. We are all united, unknown to ourselves, by what we have borrowed from American behaviour. More than behaviour, a way of living and thinking, a concept of the individual and of society, what the historians already hold, rightly or wrongly, to be a new civilization.

Quebec believes that it is at this moment living an exclusive adventure. It is obvious that since its awakening it has become the most essentially Canadian of the ten provinces. Try to make it ride pillion with the United States or France. This rage for definition that suddenly seized it might well be the first awareness of Canadian realities. The others will follow, they are already following. When all the elements have been purified, as in chemistry, the phenomenon of crystallization will take place. This will not happen tomorrow.

But who can really say? On the economic plane Canada already exists. It is a very little country. About seven hundred miles long and one hundred miles wide, from Windsor to Quebec, along the seaway. This narrow band is the reservoir of population, factories, and money upon which the rest of the country more or less depends. Here are still concentrated the most important training schools for our leaders. This country does not belong to itself but it has a chair at the conference table. The experts are explicit: the economic frontiers between Canada and the United States could break without putting our political independence in greater peril than it is at present. The European Common Market does not broach national identity. Present generations will perhaps see the creation of the same dollar from Mexico to the Yukon.

Are these prophecies? They are not even forecasts. They are simply working hypotheses, and I do not know that the present situation allows us to go beyond hypotheses. What are three centuries in the life of a people as scattered as ours? We are not yet of age. We are still playing with our pocket money. Our parents are very rich, but we have too many of them. Our unity will come from our need to make a common front against the demands of all the countries on which we still depend, not only economically but in all cultural domains. Let us have no doubt of this. We will be obliged to make a common front.

The only cloud, but it has consistency: from one province to another we have all developed the 'little saint' complex. Each one of us is beyond reproach, and the evil always comes from elsewhere. There is no longer any place for 'little saints', especially between Quebec and Ontario, the two giants, the two oldest. They will collide if they are not able to sharpen their sense of self-criticism.

This is the trait that seems to me to attach us to our childhood still — narcissism. It is dangerous.

between the experience of reading Lawrence in adolescence and reading him later in life. The extent to which Lawrence has engaged such different emotional levels of experience goes some way towards explaining his undoubted popularity as a novelist. Graham Hough, for example, suggested that Lawrence is influential in a shift away from novels about the experiences leading up to marriage towards novels about the on-going conflicts of marriage and what have become known, symptomatically, as 'relationships'.[6] Lawrence's use of his own experience for so much of his writing is inevitably partial. His experience of living as a writer involved an increasing distance from other experiences of work, and this is reflected in his emphasis on the detachment of personal relationships from economic structures of interaction. It is not just that Lawrence did not experience what it is to be a worker, a woman or a father, though his blindness to other modes of experience is often remarkable, nor that his conception of maleness was limited and ideological. More importantly, Lawrence's considerable fictional ingenuity reveals the limits of individual experience as the ground for political resistance to existing society.

Put differently, Lawrence provokes his readers into exploring the authority of his experience in relation to their own. In *Studies in Classic American Literature* Lawrence asserted: 'Never trust the artist. Trust the tale. The proper function of a critic is to save the tale from the artist who created it' (*SCAL*, 8). The moral conflicts of writing cannot then be resolved by reference back to the authority of the author. In the extended explorations of Lawrence's novels, the insistent moralising of the authorial voice is subjected to narrative analysis. Lawrence's technical innovations project sustained fictions of self-analysis so as to make moral conflicts between narrative and narration into socially intelligible crises of existential experience. Read critically, then, Lawrence's writing suspends the authority of individual experience within the social conditions of fiction. Anaïs Nin, for example, claimed that Lawrence 'had a complete realization of the feelings of women. In fact, very often he wrote *as a woman* would write.'[7] While many other women, especially feminists, have rejected such claims, Lawrence's writing evidently provokes discussion about the truth of experiences of gender and sex, experiences which can perhaps be shared socially only through fiction. The history of Lawrence's controversial reception can be understood, then, as reflections of the conflict of interpretation regarding the authority of experience.

Lawrence developed his fictions through literary critical reflection on the historical possibilities of the novel, perhaps most notably through his study of Thomas Hardy. His fiction is both personal and a negotiation of the representative qualities of the novel. This suggests why it is not sufficient to read

Lawrence's fictions as symptoms of his personal psychology, as if his writing could be psychoanalysed. Nevertheless, Lawrence can be seen as sharing concerns with the no less fictional investigations of Freud. While both Lawrence and Freud have shaped the discourse of sexual politics, what needs analysis is the way these challenges to the fictional and moral authority of experience reject conventional politics through the focus on sexuality. If this involves the construction of sex as a new form of religion, analysis needs to consider the politics Lawrence sought to displace.

Representation and the politics of recognition

There are powerful moral and legal forces determining the freedom of individuals, but even if sex and sexuality represent social struggles for the pursuit of happiness, the sexual conduct of individuals is only one part of the politics of recognition within the reproduction of society. Sex, however, can be understood not just as a representation but as a metonymic part of politics as experience. Sex can also be understood as a metaphorical substitution for politics through which conflict is naturalised as bodily experience. This awkward combination of metonym and metaphor makes it difficult not to wish to separate sex from its social and political mediations, as though sex could be returned to a natural expression which might in turn be the basis of a new politics. An opposing temptation is to dismiss the embodied particularity of sexual activity, as though sex could be experienced solely as a representation or discourse. The union of sex as physical immediacy and a more symbolic act is clearest in the religious and legal organisation of marriage. One way of understanding the so-called 'battle of the sexes', then, is to see sex as one of a number of embodied pleasures and forms of knowledge through which individuals struggle for different kinds of recognition. These struggles often involve challenges to the social and political structures which mediate experience. Someone who is emotionally or economically oppressed may understand their situation politically or they may try to escape such conflicts in more immediate forms of physical recognition and pleasure. Either way, it is difficult to see the causes of oppression: struggles against oppression often produce new kinds of frustration and domination.[8]

Throughout the period in which Lawrence was writing, the right to vote was an important site of struggles for recognition, both for women and for the working class as a whole. Suffrage, however, is only one form of the politics of recognition mediated by the state. In 1912 Lawrence wrote in a letter that his work for women would be 'better than the suffrage' (i. 490). As early as *Sons and Lovers*, Clara Dawes is characterised as the first of what becomes a characteristic Lawrencean woman, a 'lost girl' whose interest in the women's movement is made representative of her incompletion as a woman.[9] As Paul Morel puts it, 'she lives separate from her husband, and talks on platforms' (*SL*, 383). Clara is described as acquiring education through ten years of belonging to the women's movement, and although the novel focuses on her identity as a woman, the narrator tells us that: 'She considered herself as a woman apart, and particularly apart, from her class' (*SL*, 306). This echoes Lawrence's own sense of class separation. Moreover, the narrator tells us that 'Paul had more or less got into connection with the socialist, suffragette, unitarian people in Nottingham, owing to his acquaintance with Clara' (*SL*, 301). Although reference to such political movements is not developed, it is significant that such connections are possible. Within the novel, recognition between Clara and Paul is one-sided and momentary: 'she radiated with joy and pride again. It was her restoration, and her recognition' (*SL*, 383). Lawrence's novels dramatise individuals struggling to sustain such moments but renewal more often remains physical, emotional and individual.

Lawrence focuses on such moments of individual recognition, then, within conflicts of love and family rather than in relation to contemporary political movements. The struggle for sustained recognition nevertheless persists through the ebb and flow of interrupted and incomplete interactions. Sceptical of democracy, Lawrence's own struggles for recognition involved a sustained refusal to recognise the validity of modern industrial capitalism and its class relations. Beyond the formal structures of democratic recognition, most individuals experience the family and the labour market as decisive conditions of misrecognition. Lawrence's more immediate struggle, however, was with individual women, notably his mother and his lovers, within a generalised refusal to recognise the emancipation of women. Thus while Lawrence could suggest that the emancipation of women is 'perhaps the greatest revolution of modern times' ('The Real Thing', *P*, 196), his accounts of how this might relate to modern industrial society were often sketchy, if not incoherent: 'Say what we will, the world is swayed by feminine emotion today, and the triumph of the productive and domestic activities of man over all his previous military or flaunting activities is a triumph of the woman in the home' (*P*, 196). The confusion of gender categories with social and economic forces is characteristic of the confused politics of sexual politics.

It could be argued that Lawrence sought to escape such confusions of class consciousness through sex and writing, but he remained painfully aware of class contradictions in his life and work. In his 'Autobiographical Sketch' (1929), he wrote that:

I cannot make the transfer from my own class into the middle class. I cannot, not for anything in the world, forfeit my passional consciousness and my old blood-affinity with my fellow-men and the animals and the land, for that other thin, spurious mental conceit which is all that is left of the mental consciousness once it has made itself exclusive. (*PII*, 596)

The educated mind of the isolated intellectual is revealed as a split consciousness, while animals and land are suggestive metonyms for a mystified desire to reconcile human nature through physical solidarity with nature. Lawrence lived through his writing but rejected the forms of middle-class recognition available to writers. His semi-autobiographical writings bear witness to persistent desires to be loved and known beyond the limits of personal acquaintance. Proudly resistant to existing modes of recognition and yet a passionate explorer of new personal and public recognitions, his writing is divided between passional and mental consciousness, between private, physical modes of being and more social forms of language. This suggests why so-called 'swear words' and dialect language are so significant in his writing as markers of the conflicting class registers of spoken and literary language. Amid these divisions, the search for recognition through love and sex becomes a key form of the difficulty of class consciousness, combining both a sense of the physical needs understood as sexuality and the more mental forms of mutual recognition associated with love.

Lawrence, then, asks his readers to take sides in the battle of the sexes to find new codes of personal and moral conduct, but does so within the more public codes of writing. As a prophet of individuality he offers an aesthetics of life which displaces the politics of recognition within the representation of existential conflicts. The difficulty, then, is to read Lawrence against the authority of his own terms of representation. Recognition of political subtexts does not mean that his work can simply be read off against a menu of ideological positions. Lawrence's fictional techniques highlight the flow of emotional life rather than the schematic positions of gendered identity which critics have been quick to wrest from the text. His representations of experience need to be read, then, as reflections of the politics of misrecognition within individualism, including the misrecognitions which shaped Lawrence's life and reputation.

Natural communism: the politics of Lawrence's reception

From the banning of *The Rainbow* to the trial of *Lady Chatterley's Lover* the most overtly political debates regarding Lawrence's writing have been about censorship and the legitimacy of explicit sexuality. Whether denounced as a patriarchal bigot and pornographer or defended as a moralist and